# Pro PHP Application Performance

## Tuning PHP Web Projects for Maximum Performance

**Armando Padilla
and Tim Hawkins**

Apress®

**Pro PHP Application Performance: Tuning PHP Web Projects for Maximum Performance**

ISBN-13 (pbk): 978-1-4302-2898-1

ISBN-13 (electronic): 978-1-4302-2899-8

9 8 7 6 5 4 3 2 1

President and Publisher: Paul Manning
Lead Editor: Frank Pohlmann
Development Editors: Jim Markham and Michelle Lowman
Technical Reviewer: Aaron Saray
Editorial Board: Steve Anglin, Mark Beckner, Ewan Buckingham, Gary Cornell, Jonathan Gennick, Jonathan Hassell, Michelle Lowman, Matthew Moodie, Duncan Parkes, Jeffrey Pepper, Frank Pohlmann, Douglas Pundick, Ben Renow-Clarke, Dominic Shakeshaft, Matt Wade, Tom Welsh
Coordinating Editor: Jennifer L. Blackwell
Copy Editor: Mary Ann Fugate
Compositor: MacPS, LLC
Indexer: Becky Hornyak
Artist: April Milne
Cover Designer: Anna Ishchenko

Distributed to the book trade worldwide by Springer Science+Business Media, LLC., 233 Spring Street, 6th Floor, New York, NY 10013. Phone 1-800-SPRINGER, fax (201) 348-4505, e-mail orders-ny@springer-sbm.com, or visit www.springeronline.com.

For information on translations, please e-mail rights@apress.com, or visit www.apress.com.

Apress and friends of ED books may be purchased in bulk for academic, corporate, or promotional use. eBook versions and licenses are also available for most titles. For more information, reference our Special Bulk Sales–eBook Licensing web page at www.apress.com/info/bulksales.

*I dedicate this book to*
*my family, friends, and my dog, Snoopy.*

*—Armando Padilla*


*To my partner, Ester, who always gets the raw end of my endeavors, and puts up with the single-word*
*answers and stunted conversation while I concentrate on the writing.*

*—Tim Hawkins*

# Contents at a Glance

# Contents

# About the Authors

 **Armando Padilla** has worked within the web technology industry for 13 years, participating and leading every aspect of a LAMP-based web application. His PHP experience began in 1998, when he created a small PHP web page for Thomas Jefferson High School (Los Angeles). Armando's most recent work has been for Yahoo! as a senior engineer working on high-profile and high-traffic applications, such as the Winter 2010 Olympics, 2010 FIFA World Cup, and Yahoo News mobile applications. Armando now spends much of his time dabbling with new web technologies, reading PHP/Zend–related books, and being with his family.

 **Tim Hawkins** produced one of the world's first online classifieds portals in 1993, loot.com, before moving on to run engineering for many of Yahoo EU's non-media-based properties, such as Search, Local Search, Mail, Messenger, and its social networking products. He is currently managing a large offshore team for a major US e-tailer, developing and deploying next-generation e-commerce applications. He loves hats and hates complexity.

# About the Technical Reviewer

 **Aaron Saray** has been madly in love with PHP since 2001. As a Zend Certified Engineer, Milwaukee PHP users group organizer, author, and technical editor, Aaron continues to remain active in the PHP community. He continues to push out new open source software as well as keep a web development blog on http://aaronsaray.com.

# Acknowledgments

It's without saying that I want to thank the Apress staff, Jennifer Blackwell as well as Michelle Lowman, for giving me the opportunity to write this book. I also want to thank the countless developers and system admins who assisted in answering my many, many late-night questions about the subject matter. Thank you.

—Armando Padilla

I would like to acknowledge Rasmus Lerdorf, who started this whole PHP thing, and who taught me some neat tricks with APC, as well as my ex-colleagues at Yahoo Europe, who taught me to think big.

—Tim Hawkins

# Introduction

If you're like me, you're picking up this book at your local bookstore or reading this introduction online, trying to get a "feel" for the book. You're either a PHP engineer curious to dive headfirst into the nuances of building a large application, or someone who has just been tasked to support a high-traffic PHP application. This book is for you, the PHP developer who has a good understanding of PHP and is not a newcomer to the language—the PHP developer who wants to understand the "whys" and the tool sets to trace and "look under the hood" of your PHP script.

The goal of the book is to give you the complete picture of all the components that need to be identified when optimizing your PHP application. From the JavaScript to the web server software the application is running, this book covers each of these topics.

The book is separated into two general sections, the front end and back end of a web application. The first part of the book covers the front end, helping you identify bottlenecks the browser encounters during rendering and how to remove these bottlenecks. This initial section also covers the use of PHP best coding practices and how to apply caching using the many tools available. The second part of the book covers the back end, teaching you about the many types of web server software, how to optimize the software, and tips on optimizing your database.

## Overview

The following is a detailed chapter breakdown.

## Chapter 1 – Benchmarking Techniques

We begin by establishing the tools that are required to measure our application's performance. The tools you will learn to install, read results, and apply are Apache Benchmark (ab) as well as Siege, two of the most popular benchmarking tools in the industry. You will learn how to run simulated load tests using concurrency as well as simulated loads for a specific length of time.

## Chapter 2 – Improving Client Download and Rendering Performance

Application performance is not only about your PHP code. In this chapter, we focus on how browsers render content. You will learn the tools available to benchmark JavaScript, measure the amount of data the browser is attempting to load, as well as view how efficiently the browser is loading the content. You will learn to do this by using and installing Firebug, Page Speed, and Yahoo!'s YSlow. Using these tools, we optimize a simple web page by identifying performance improvements for JavaScript, Image. You are not required to be an expert at JavaScript while reading this chapter.

## Chapter 3 – PHP Code Optimization

We begin to jump into the PHP code within this chapter. You will learn about PHP best coding practices when it comes to performance. You will learn about constructing a faster-running for loop, how to include files using the optimal PHP function, and, most importantly, how to use and install VLD, strace, and Xdebug. Once VLD and strace are installed, you will analyze Opcode, as well as the Apache C-level processes that your PHP script requires to run. Using Xdebug on the other, we will identify bottlenecks within the PHP code itself.

## Chapter 4 – Opcode Caching

Knowing the PHP life cycle is important to optimizing, so you will learn about the life cycle within this chapter. You will learn the steps PHP takes during a user request and identify areas where we can optimize using Opcode cachers. You will learn how to install and configure Opcode cachers such as APC, XCache, and eAccelerator, all the while benchmarking our before and after scripts to see the gains from caching our Opcode.

## Chapter 5 – Variable Caching

Building on the information about aching covered in Chapter 4, you will be introduced to variable caching tools, such as Memcached, as well as using APC to store information. You will learn to install, configure, and implement a simple example to get you familiar with the software, as well as a real-world example using a database result set.

## Chapter 6 - Choosing the Right Web Server.

Until recently there was only one game in town, anybody considering a large-scale deployment would use the defacto standard, Apache. Recently however some new and exciting alternatives have come to the fore. In this chapter we will look at Apache in detail, and stack it up against newcomers Lighttpd and Nginx.

## Chapter 7 - Apache Web Server Optimization

Out of the box Apache is a very capable web server package, but with a little tuning and some tricks of the trade we can increase its performance and durability and really make it sing. In this chapter we will also look at some of the secrets of scaling out to support higher traffic and user loads.

## Chapter 8 - Database Optimization.

In most web applications, the database server plays a major role. In this chapter we will look at optimizing the mysql database server, providing methods and tools that will allow you to keep your system in tip top shape.

# CHAPTER 1

■■■

# Benchmarking Techniques

The phone rings and a voice on the other end yells, "Hey! Why can't this application support 200 concurrent users?" You take a deep breath, and in your most senior PHP tone you mutter, "Odd, I'll take a look at what's happening and provide a solution." Flash back to a few weeks prior to this conversation. You were tasked to build a database-driven PHP application, and by all accounts the requirements outlined a simple PHP application. As a seasoned PHP developer, you began to write code, creating the basic architectural layers, the PHP back end, the CSS, the JavaScript, and because you're well-versed in Photoshop, you also created the graphical layout, and released the application to production.

As your application became popular and more users visited your web site, an increased number of complaints arrived. All the messages shared a similar issue—the site is either unresponsive or too slow. Now, you look at your code and wonder how you can squeeze the last ounce of bottlenecks and slow code out of it, and whether the code is even the culprit. You finally arrive at the question, how well is the web application performing when 50, 100, 200, or 300 concurrent users request a web document you host? And, how can you even test your application under such traffic load?

In this chapter, we'll review in depth two benchmarking open source tools that will not only help answer those questions but will also help measure the change in performance while applying performance enhancements to an application throughout the book. The tools we'll use are Apache Benchmark (ab) and Siege.

You will learn how to install both tools, learn how to read their results, and use the tools to request different types of content, from simple HTML to large images. Finally, you will also come away with a foundation on how the HTTP request/response lifecycle is processed and what a request does behind the scenes, and learn the primary areas of concern that cause latency (a.k.a lag) during a request for hosted resources.

But first, let's explore the PHP application stack and the approach I will take throughout the book.

# The PHP Application Stack

Each PHP application has a stack, which, when visualized, resembles Figure 1–1.

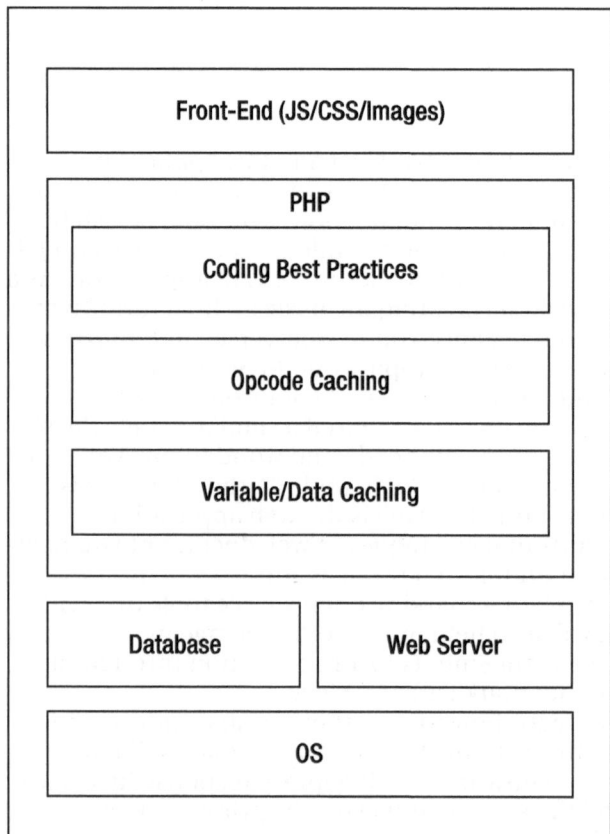

**Figure 1–1.** *PHP application stack and breakdown of the book's chapters*

Most PHP applications are shown to the user within a browser, using front-end code in the form of JavaScript (JS), Cascading Style Sheets (CSS), Flash, other front-end technologies, and resources such as images. The front end, shown in the topmost block of our PHP application stack, helps users navigate through the web application and trigger the PHP layer. The PHP layer contains business logic specific to the application and will typically interact with either a database or a web service to fetch dynamic data, if it uses an external storage system. Finally, all web-based PHP applications share something in common: they must be installed on a web server—such as Apache, or Nginx—that is installed on an operating system.

What Figure 1–1 also depicts is the breakdown of what is covered in the book. Each layer within the PHP application can be optimized and is the basis of all subsequent chapters. From the front end to the web server, this book will touch on each layer shown in the figure, but we need a tool to measure not only how well our current, unmodified application is performing, but also how well it's performing once we apply the performance enhancements to it. Apache Benchmark, as well as Siege, provides that.

## Benchmarking Utilities

ab and siege belong to a group of web server benchmarking tools that provide statistics on how well a web server responds during varied simulated user requests. They allow us to simulate any arbitrary number of users requesting a specific web document on a web server and, most importantly, allow us to simulate a simultaneous visit by any number of users (concurrent requests) to a hosted document on a web server.

For example, each tool provides information about the following:

- Total time a single request took to respond

- Total response size from the server

- Total number of requests a web server can handle per second

What these tools do not do is test functionality. These tools only test requests for a single web document running on a specific web server.

ab and siege were chosen for the following reasons:

- Easy to use: Both ab and siege have only one line to type with a small number of options to use. This means there's a low learning curve in getting started.

- Easy installation: Both are extremely easy to install, and require minimum setup time.

- Command-line based: Most developers use a command line on either a Unix or Windows server.

## Defining the Request/Response Lifecycle

Let's take a quick dive into what a HTTP request/response does by examining its lifecycle. First, we need to understand what an HTTP request is and what an HTTP request does, since it is the request's lifecycle that these tools use to help measure the performance of your application.

HTTP requests are the actions a user or a tool takes when attempting to fetch content from a web server. A typical HTTP request contains information about the Host the request is trying to reach, browser information, and other information useful to the web server. Figure 1–2 illustrates the process of a HTTP request/response from a user's personal computer.

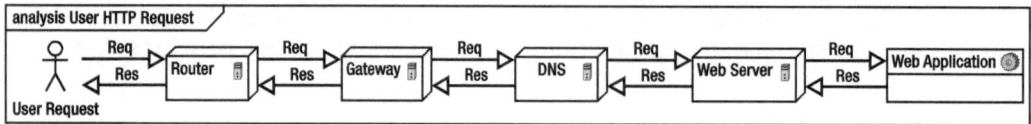

*Figure 1–2. HTTP request lifecycle*

This figure follows a simple user HTTP request for content from a web server. The request originates from the user's machine, encounters the user's home router (if any), ISP Gateway, and DNS, where it looks up the IP associated with the requested domain name, reaches the web server with the designated IP, and finally requests that the web application generate the specific content.

The second portion of the lifecycle is the HTTP response. Once the request reaches a web server, the web server prepares the response by fetching and formatting the data the user requested; the web server then packages up the data into multiple packets, and sends the packets to the user along the same path the user's request followed, but in reverse order. If the data is large enough, the packet is sent in multiple packets, checked for errors during transit, and reconstructed by the browser before the browser can begin its rendering process. All these steps must happen before the browser renders your web page.

Each of these steps incurs a cost to your end user in the form of a slow performing web page. The tools we will cover next will allow us to test our application's response time and thereby test its optimized state.

## Apache Benchmark

The Apache Benchmark (or ab) tool, one of the most widely known benchmarking tools, is part of the default Apache installation and provides the ability to load-test a web server by simulating any number of requests to a specific URL. The ab tool provides the following information:

- Total data size transferred (bytes)

- Total requests per second the web server can support under the simulated traffic

- Maximum time a request took to complete (milliseconds)

- Minimum time a request took to complete (milliseconds)

ab also allows you to run many different load simulations, such as the following:

- Simultaneous requests to a web document

- Requests over a specific amount of time

- Requests with Keep-Alive turned on

Most importantly, Apache Benchmark works independently of the Apache web server, allowing you to run ab while having the web server inactive on the machine you are running the tool from.

## Installing Apache Benchmark

In the next two sections, we'll go over how to install the required files to run the ab tool on both Windows as well as Unix-based systems.

### Unix and Mac Installation

If you're on a *nix OS, you have many options to install Apache. You can install from ports, yum, apt-get, or simply download the source and install. The complete list of installation commands is shown in Table 1–1.

*Table 1–1. Installing Apache Web Server Using Repository*

| Repository | Command |
| --- | --- |
| yum | yum install apache2 |
| ports | sudo port install apache2 |
| apt-get | apt-get install apache2 |

Mac users can use MacPorts and execute the ports-based command shown in Table 1–1 within a terminal.

### Windows Installation

Windows users can open a browser and load the URL, http://httpd.apache.org/. Once the page loads, click the "Download from a mirror" link on the left-hand side of the page, locate the appropriate download package for your system, the Windows 32 Binary version, and download. At the time of writing, the most current version of Apache is 2.2.X.

Once the package downloads, go ahead and install the software anywhere on your system by running the installation wizard. I installed Apache in the default location, C:\Program Files\Apache Software Foundation, but you can install anywhere on your system. The location you choose here will be the `APACHE_HOME` reference going forward. Now, open the directory `<APACHE_HOME>\Apache2.2\bin`. You should see a collection of files and directories similar to Figure 1–3.

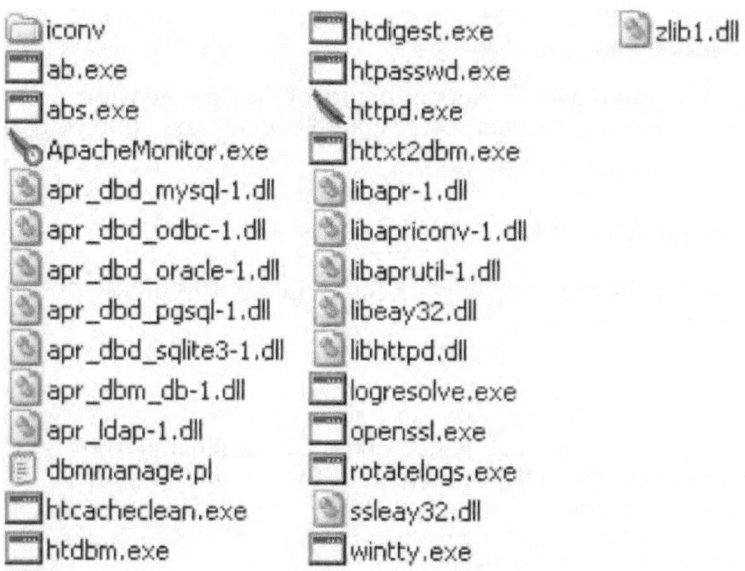

*Figure 1–3. Windows Apache installed bin directories*

You have successfully installed the ab tool—now let's use it.

## Running Apache Benchmark

The first benchmark test we're going to run is a simple test on the domain `www.example.com`. The main purpose of the initial test is to get you familiar with the syntax of the tool, review all the available options, and review a complete response.

The makeup of all ab commands follows this structure:

```
ab [options] [full path to web document]
```

Using the ab syntax, we are going to simulate a single request. Open a command/shell terminal and type the following:

```
ab -n 1 http://www.example.com/
```

The command shown utilizes a single option within the `options` section, the number of requests to perform on the URL specified using the flag n. In this example, the total number of requests allows ab to request the web document once, though the value of n can be any arbitrary number lower than 50,000. By default, n is set to 1.

The next section of the command is the URL section. Referencing the ab command you just executed, the URL is http://www.example.com/. If we had chosen to test a document such as test.php (does not exist) within the domain, the URL to test would have been http://www.example.com/test.php instead.

Let's return to the command/shell terminal used to execute the ab command. By now you have executed the command, and your screen is full of numbers and general data returned by the ab tool. You should have an output similar to Figure 1–4.

```
$ ./ab -n 1 http://www.example.com/
This is ApacheBench, Version 2.3 <$Revision: 655654 $>
Copyright 1996 Adam Twiss, Zeus Technology Ltd, http://www.zeustech.net/
Licensed to The Apache Software Foundation, http://www.apache.org/

Benchmarking www.example.com (be patient).....done


Server Software:        Apache/2.2.3
Server Hostname:        www.example.com
Server Port:            80

Document Path:          /
Document Length:        574 bytes

Concurrency Level:      1
Time taken for tests:   0.094 seconds
Complete requests:      1
Failed requests:        0
Write errors:           0
Total transferred:      860 bytes
HTML transferred:       574 bytes
Requests per second:    10.67 [#/sec] (mean)
Time per request:       93.750 [ms] (mean)
Time per request:       93.750 [ms] (mean, across all concurrent requests)
Transfer rate:          8.96 [Kbytes/sec] received

Connection Times (ms)
              min  mean[+/-sd] median   max
Connect:       47    47   0.0     47      47
Processing:    47    47   0.0     47      47
Waiting:       47    47   0.0     47      47
Total:         94    94   0.0     94      94
```

*Figure 1–4. ab response for the URL http://www.example.com*

■ **Caution** When testing other machines, please be courteous and limit both the amount of requests made to the web server and your testing. You don't want to harm any unsuspecting servers and get into real trouble.

## Making Sense of the Response

If you've never seen the response in the output just shown, or even if you have, the response can be a bit overwhelming. We're going to point out the important items for us and the items that will let us know how well we are doing while optimizing our code throughout the book.

Referring back to Figure 1–4, the data is broken into four major sections, shown in Figure 1–5.

```
Server Software:        Apache/2.2.3
Server Hostname:        www.example.com
Server Port:            80
```

*Server Information*

```
Document Path:          /
Document Length:        574 bytes
```

*Document Information*

```
Concurrency Level:      1
Time taken for tests:   0.094 seconds
Complete requests:      1
Failed requests:        0
Write errors:           0
Total transferred:      860 bytes
HTML transferred:       574 bytes
Requests per second:    10.67 [#/sec] (mean)
Time per request:       93.750 [ms] (mean)
Time per request:       93.750 [ms] (mean, across all concurrent requests)
Transfer rate:          8.96 [Kbytes/sec] received
```

*Connection Information*

```
Concurrency Level:      1
Time taken for tests:   0.094 seconds
Complete requests:      1
Failed requests:        0
Write errors:           0
Total transferred:      860 bytes
HTML transferred:       574 bytes
Requests per second:    10.67 [#/sec] (mean)
Time per request:       93.750 [ms] (mean)
Time per request:       93.750 [ms] (mean, across all concurrent requests)
Transfer rate:          8.96 [Kbytes/sec] received
```

*Connection Metrics Breakdown*

***Figure 1–5.*** *Sections of an ab result*

## Server Information

The server information section contains the software the web server is running. In our example, it's the software Apache version 2.2.3. The data is contained in the first field, Server Software. The value for this field can change depending on the web server software the web site is using. The value for this field might also return something you're unfamiliar with, due to security practices web administrators use.

The next two fields, Server Hostname and Server Port, contain the hostname we ran our simulation on and the port number the web server is listening on.

## Script Information

The second section of an ab response contains information concerning the web document the simulation ran against. Document Path contains the document that was requested, while Document Length contains the sum of all HTML, images, CSS, JS, and anything within the response in bytes.

## Connection Information

The Connection Information section contains the bulk of the information. It answers questions such as, "How long did a request take to receive a response?", "How much data was returned?", and most importantly, "How many users can the web server support when processing the document?"

Table 1–2 provides a complete list and description of data for this section. For now, let's focus on the highlighted rows, which contain the fields that matter most to us throughout the book.

*Table 1–2. ab Response Description*

| Field | Description | Example Value |
|---|---|---|
| Concurrency Level | Total number of concurrent requests made | 1,2,3,...,n, where n is any arbitrary number |
| Time taken for tests | Total time taken to run | 000.000 seconds |
| Complete requests | Total number of requests completed out of the total requests simulated | 1,2,3,...,n, where n is any arbitrary number |
| Failed requests | Total number of requests that failed out of the total requests simulated | 1,2,3,...,n, where n is any arbitrary number |
| Write errors | Total number of errors encountered while using writing data. | 1,2,3,...,n, where n is any arbitrary number |
| Non-2xx responses | Total number of requests that did not receive a HTTP Success response (200) | 1,2,3,...,n, where n is any arbitrary number |
| Total transferred | Total data transferred in response for entire simulation—size includes Header data. | 725 bytes |
| **HTML transferred** | **Total size of the content body transferred for the entire simulation** | **137199 bytes** |
| **Requests per second** | **Total number of requests supported per second** | **5.68 [#/sec] (mean)** |
| **Time per request** | **Total time taken to satisfy a single request** | **176.179 milliseconds** |
| Time per request | Total time taken to satisfy a single request across all concurrent requests | 176.179 milliseconds |
| Transfer rate | Total number of Kbytes received per second | 766.27 [Kbytes/sec] |

The HTML transferred, Requests per second, and Time per request are the key fields for us. These fields give us a glimpse into the amount of data the web server has sent back for a single request, the total number of requests the web server can handle in a single second, and the total elapsed time in which a single request successfully requested data and received a response from the web server.

Our goal is to successfully lower the HTML transferred, increase the Requests per second, and lower the Time per request values throughout this book.

## Connection Metrics Breakdown

The final section contains a table with Connect, Processing, Waiting, and Total fields. These fields tell us how much time the requests took within each of these process statuses. We are mostly interested in the Total field and its min and max columns. These two columns provide data on the minimum and maximum length of time a request took to respond. Let's now look at the optional flags ab provides us.

# AB Option Flags

ab has a number of useful optional flags, which allow you to format the response into HTML tables, set cookies, set basic authentication information, and set the content type, among other options. A complete list of optional flags is shown in Table 1–3.

*Table 1–3. Optional Flags*

| Flag | Description |
|------|-------------|
| -A <username>:<password> | Used to supply server authentication information. Username and password are separated by ":". String sent as base64 encoded. |
| -c <concurrency number> | Number of requests to simulate at a time. 1 is set by default. Number cannot be greater than n value. |
| -C cookie-name=value | Repeatable flag containing cookie information |
| -d | Hides "percentage served within XX[ms] table" |
| -e | Path to .csv file to create. The file contains the results of the benchmark run broken down into two columns, Percentage and Time in ms. Recommended over "gnuplot" file. |
| -g | Path to "gnuplot" or TSV file to create. Output of benchmark will be saved into this file. |
| -h | Displays list of options to use with ab |

| Flag | Description |
|------|-------------|
| -H custom-header | Sends customized valid headers along with the request in the form of a field-value pair |
| -i | Performs a HEAD request instead of the default GET request |
| -k | Turns on Keep-Alive feature. Allows multiple requests to be satisfied with a single HTTP session. This feature is off by default. |
| -n requests | Total number of requests to perform |
| -p POST-file | Path to file containing data used for an HTTP POST request. Content should contains key=value pairs separated by &. |
| -P username:password | Base64 encoded string. String contains basic authentication, username, and password separated by ":". |
| -q | Hides progress output when performing more than 100 requests |
| -s | Uses an https protocol instead of the default http protocol—not recommended |
| -S | Hides the median and standard deviation values |
| -t timelimit | When specified, the benchmark test will not last longer than the specified value. By default there is no time limit. |
| -v verbosity-level | Numerical value: 2 and above will print warnings and info; 3 will print HTTP response codes; 4 and above will print header information. |
| -V | Displays the version number of the ab tool |
| -w | Prints the results within a HTML table |
| -x \<table-attributes\> | String representing HTML attributes that will be placed inside the \<table\> tag when –w is used |
| -X proxy[:port] | Specifies a Proxy server to use. Proxy port is optional. |
| -y \<tr-attributes\> | String representing HTML attributes that will be placed inside the \<tr\> tag when –w is used |
| -z \<td-attributes\> | String representing HTML attributes that will be placed inside the \<td\> tag when –w is used |

For our goal of optimizing our PHP scripts, we need to zero in on only a handful of options. These are the following:

- n: Number of requests to simulate

- c: Number of concurrent requests to simulate

- t: Length of time to conduct simulation

We've run a simulation using the n flag after initially installing ab. Now let's use the other flags and see how our initial benchmarking figures of the www.example.com site hold up.

## Concurrency Tests

Depending on your web application, a user's time on the application can range anywhere from a few seconds to a few minutes. The flow of incoming users can fluctuate drastically from small amounts of traffic to high traffic volumes, due to the awesomeness (if that's even a word) of your site or some malicious user conducting a DOS attack. You need to simulate a real-world traffic volume to answer the question, how will your site hold up to such traffic?

We're going to simulate a concurrent test, where ten concurrent requests are made to the web server at the same time, until 100 requests are made. A caveat when using the c flag is to have the value used be smaller than the total number of requests to make, n. A value equal to n will simply request all n requests concurrently. To do so, we execute this command.

```
ab -n 100 -c 10 http://www.example.com/
```

After running the command, you should have a response that looks similar to Figure 1–6.

```
$ ./ab -n 100 -c 10 http://www.example.com/
This is ApacheBench, Version 2.3 <$Revision: 655654 $>
Copyright 1996 Adam Twiss, Zeus Technology Ltd, http://www.zeustech.net/
Licensed to The Apache Software Foundation, http://www.apache.org/

Benchmarking www.example.com (be patient).....done


Server Software:        Apache/2.2.3
Server Hostname:        www.example.com
Server Port:            80

Document Path:          /
Document Length:        438 bytes

Concurrency Level:      10
Time taken for tests:   4.469 seconds
Complete requests:      100
Failed requests:        0
Write errors:           0
Total transferred:      72500 bytes
HTML transferred:       43800 bytes
Requests per second:    22.38 [#/sec] (mean)
Time per request:       446.875 [ms] (mean)
Time per request:       44.688 [ms] (mean, across all concurrent requests)
Transfer rate:          15.84 [Kbytes/sec] received

Connection Times (ms)
              min  mean[+/-sd] median   max
Connect:       31    44  14.4     47      94
Processing:    47   379  72.1    391     500
Waiting:       31   215 122.7    219     500
Total:         94   423  69.5    438     547

Percentage of the requests served within a certain time (ms)
  50%    438
$ _
  75%    453
  80%    469
  90%    469
  95%    500
  98%    531
  99%    547
 100%    547 (longest request)
```

*Figure 1–6. Concurrent simulation results for* www.example.com

With a simulated concurrent request, we can look at the Request per second field and notice that the web server can support 22.38 requests (users) per second. Analyzing the Connection Metrics' Total min and max columns, we notice that the quickest response was 94 milliseconds, while the slowest satisfied request was 547 milliseconds under the specified traffic load of ten concurrent requests.

But we know that traffic doesn't simply last one, two, or three seconds—high volume traffic can last for minutes, hours, and even days. Let's run a simulation to test this.

## Timed Tests

You're noticing that each day, close to noon, your web site experiences a spike in traffic that lasts for ten minutes. How well is your web server performing in this situation? The next flag you're going to use is the t flag. The t flag allows you to check how well your web server performs for any length of time.

Let's simulate ten simultaneous user visits to the site over a 20-second interval using the following command:

```
ab -c 10 -t 20 http://www.example.com/
```

The command does not contain the n flag but by default is included and set by ab to a value of 50,000 when using the t option. In some cases, when using the t option, the max request of 50,000 can be reached, in which case the simulation will finish.

Once the ab command has completed its simulation, you will have data similar to that shown in Figure 1–7.

```
$ ./ab -c 10 -t 20 http://www.example.com/
This is ApacheBench, Version 2.3 <$Revision: 655654 $>
Copyright 1996 Adam Twiss, Zeus Technology Ltd, http://www.zeustech.net/
Licensed to The Apache Software Foundation, http://www.apache.org/

Benchmarking www.example.com (be patient)
Finished 427 requests


Server Software:        Apache/2.2.3
Server Hostname:        www.example.com
Server Port:            80

Document Path:          /
Document Length:        438 bytes

Concurrency Level:      10
Time taken for tests:   20.125 seconds
Complete requests:      427
Failed requests:        0
Write errors:           0
Total transferred:      311025 bytes
HTML transferred:       187902 bytes
Requests per second:    21.22 [#/sec] (mean)
Time per request:       471.311 [ms] (mean)
Time per request:       47.131 [ms] (mean, across all concurrent requests)
Transfer rate:          15.09 [Kbytes/sec] received

Connection Times (ms)
              min  mean[+/-sd] median   max
Connect:       31    45   14.7     47    141
Processing:   281   412   88.8    391   1828
Waiting:       31   278  113.0    297    656
Total:        328   457   90.8    438   1859

Percentage of the requests served within a certain time (ms)
  50%    438
  66%    453
  75%    469
  80%    484
  90%    531
  95%    594
  98%    641
  99%    688
 100%   1859 (longest request)
```

*Figure 1–7. Benchmark results for www.example.com/ with ten concurrent users for 20 seconds*

The results in this simulation point to a decrease in performance when ten concurrent users request the web document over a period of 20 seconds. The fastest satisfied request took 328 milliseconds, while the longest was 1859 milliseconds (1.8 seconds).

## AB Gotchas

There are a few caveats when using ab. If you look back at the command you just executed, you'll notice a backward slash at the end of the domain name. The backslash is required if you are not requesting a specific document within the domain. ab can also be blocked by some web servers due to the user-agent value it passes to the web server, so you might receive no data in some cases. As a workaround for the latter, use one of the available option flags, -H, to supply custom browser headers information within your request.

To simulate a request by a Chrome browser, you could use the following ab command:

```
ab -n 100 -c 5 -H "Mozilla/5.0 (Windows; U; Windows NT 5.1; en-US) AppleWeb
Kit/534.2 (KHTML, like Gecko) Chrome/6.0.447.0 Safari/534.2" http://www.example.com
```

# Siege

The second benchmarking tool we'll use is Siege. Like ab, Siege allows you to simulate user traffic to your web-hosted document, but unlike ab, Siege provides you the ability to run load simulations on a list of URLs you specify within a text file. It also allows you to have a request sleep before conducting another request, giving the feeling of a user reading the document before moving onto another document on your web application.

## Installing Siege

Installing Siege can be done by either downloading the source code from the official web site, www.joedog.org/index/siege-home or http://freshmeat.net/projects/siege, or using a repository such as port or aptitude using one of the commands shown:

```
sudo port install siege
```

or

```
sudo aptitude install siege
```

By using one of the commands, Siege will automatically install all necessary packages to run successfully. As of this writing, the latest stable version of Siege is 2.69.

Unfortunately, Windows users will not be able to use Siege without the help of Cygwin. If you are using Windows, download Cygwin and install the software before attempting to install and run Siege. Once Cygwin has been installed, use the steps outlined within this section to install Siege.

If you decided to install using the source, you might have had trouble downloading the packages. If you're having trouble downloading the package, open a terminal window and type in the following.

```
wget ftp://ftp.joedog.org/pub/siege/siege-latest.tar.gz
```

The command will download the package onto your system. Once the package has been completely downloaded, execute the following commands:

- tar xvfz siege-latest.tar.gz

- cd siege-2.69/

- ./configure

- make

- sudo make install

The commands shown will configure the source, create the `install` package, and finally install the package on your system. Once installed, change your directory location to `/usr/local/bin/`. You should see the Siege script within this directory.

Now, let's go ahead and run a simple test on the domain `www.example.com` to see a sample result.

## Running Siege

Our first example will be a simple load test on `www.example.com`. Like ab, Siege follows a specific syntax format.

```
siege [options] [URL]
```

Using the Siege format, we will simulate a load test with five concurrent users for ten seconds on the web site `www.example.com`. As a quick note, the concept of concurrency while using Siege is called transactions. So the test we will simulate is having the web server satisfy five simultaneous transactions at a time for a period of ten seconds using the Siege command:

```
siege -c 5 -t10S http://www.example.com/
```

The command utilizes two option flags: the concurrent flag c as well as the time flag t. The concurrent flag allows us to test a request by X (in this example, 5) users simultaneously visiting the site. The number can be any arbitrary number as long as the system running the test can support such a task. The t flag specifies the time in either seconds (S), minutes (M), or hours (H), and should not have any spaces between the number and the letter.

Once the command runs, you should see output similar to Figure 1–8.

```
Lifting the server siege...      done.
Transactions:                102 hits
Availability:             100.00 %
Elapsed time:               9.71 secs
Data transferred:           0.04 MB
Response time:              0.02 secs
Transaction rate:          10.50 trans/sec
Throughput:                 0.00 MB/sec
Concurrency:                0.24
Successful transactions:     102
Failed transactions:           0
Longest transaction:        0.03
Shortest transaction:       0.02
```

*Figure 1–8.* *Siege response on www.example.com with five concurrent requests for ten seconds*

## Examining the Results

Like the ab results, the results for the Siege tool are broken down into sections; specifically, the result set has two sections to work with:

- Individual request details
- Test metrics

### Individual Request Details

The individual request details section displays all the requests that the tool created and ran. Each line represents a unique request and contains three columns, as shown in Figure 1–9.

```
** SIEGE 2.69
** Preparing 5 concurrent users for battle.
The server is now under siege...
HTTP/1.1 200   0.03 secs:      438 bytes ==> /
HTTP/1.1 200   0.03 secs:      438 bytes ==> /
HTTP/1.1 200   0.02 secs:      438 bytes ==> /
HTTP/1.1 200   0.03 secs:      438 bytes ==> /
```

*Figure 1–9.* *Siege request data*

This output contains a sample of requests from the initial Siege command you ran. The columns represent the following:

- HTTP response status code
- Total time the request took to complete
- Total amount of data received as a response (excluding header data)

## Test Metrics

The test metrics section contains information on the overall load test. Table 1–4 lists and describes all the fields, which you can look over. We are interested only in Data transferred, Transaction rate, Longest transaction, and Shortest transaction. We will focus on these specific attributes of the results because they are the indicators that outline how well our optimization has helped our application.

*Table 1–4. Siege Test Metrics Section Description*

| Field Name | Description | Example Value |
| --- | --- | --- |
| Transactions | Total number of transactions completed | 102 hits |
| Availability | Amount of time the web document was able to be requested | 100.00% |
| Elapsed Time | Total time test took to complete | 9.71 secs |
| Data transferred | Total size of data in response—does not include header data | 0.0.4M |
| Response time | Average response time encountered through the entire test | 0.02 secs |
| Transaction rate | Total number of transactions to satisfy per second | 10.50 trans/sec |
| Throughput | Total time taken to process data and respond | 0.00 MB/sec |
| Concurrency | Concurrency is average number of simultaneous connections, a number that rises as server performance decreases. | 5 |
| Successful transactions | Total number of successful transactions performed throughout the test | 102 |
| Failed transactions | Total number of failed transactions encountered throughout the test | 0 |
| Longest transaction | Longest period of time taken to satisfy a request | 0.03 |
| Shortest transaction | Shortest period of time taken to satisfy a request | 0.02 |

The Data transferred section contains the total size of the response each request received in megabytes. The Transaction rate helps us understand how many concurrent transactions (simultaneous requests) can be satisfied when the web server is under the load specified by the command we ran. In this case, the web server can satisfy 10.50 transactions per second when a load of five concurrent requests for a length of ten seconds is being placed on the web server.

The Shortest transaction and Longest transaction fields tell us the shortest period of time (in seconds) taken to satisfy a request and the longest period of time (also in seconds) taken to satisfy a request.

## Siege Option Flags

Siege also contains a wide range of optional flags, which can be accessed by using the following command if you are ever interested:

```
siege -h
```

## Testing Many URLs

Let's focus on two new flags: the "internet" flag (i) and the "file" flag (f).

When using the t and i flags, we allow Siege to randomly select a URL within a text file and request the web document. Though it does not guarantee that all the URLs within the text file will be visited, it does guarantee you a realistic test, simulating a user's movements through your web site.

To specify the file to use, we use the flag f. By default, the file used by Siege is located within SIEGE_HOME/etc/urls.txt, but you are allowed to change the path by setting the flag equal to the location of the text file.

## URL Format and File

You're now going to use the two commands to perform the next test. Create a test file anywhere on your system. I placed my file under HOME_DIR/urls.txt and placed the three URLs into the file, following the Siege URL format shown in Listing 1–1. The complete sample urls.txt file is shown in Listing 1–2.

*Listing 1–1. Siege URL Format Structure*

```
[protocol://] [servername.domain.xxx] [:portnumber] [/directory/file]
```

*Listing 1–2. urls.txt File*

```
http://www.example.com/
http://www.example.org/
http://www.example.net/
```

The three URLs are in three different domains. You normally would not have it in this fashion but, rather, would have a list of web documents to request within the same domain.

Now let's run the test with the following command:

```
siege -c 5 -t10S -i -f HOME_DIR/urls.txt
```

As you can see, the output looks very similar to that shown in Figure 1–8, with the only difference being that the URLs to test were randomly selected from the urls.txt file.

Now that you've run both ab as well as Siege, you might be wondering what affects these numbers. Let's now look into that.

# Affecting Your Benchmark Figures

There are five major layers that ultimately affect your response times and affect the benchmarking figures:

- Geographical location and network issues
- Response size
- Code processing
- Browser behavior
- Web server configuration

## Geographical Location

The geographical location of your web server is important to the response time the user experiences. If your web server is located in the United States, yet your users are located in China, Europe, or Latin America, the distance the request is required to travel to reach its destination, wait for the web server to fetch the document, and then travel back to the user located in one of these countries will affect the perceived speed of your web application.

The issue is about the total number of routers, servers, and in some cases oceans the request must travel through in order to reach its destination—in this case, your web site. The more routers/servers your users must go through, the longer the request will take to reach the web application and the longer the web application's response will take to reach the user.

## The Traveling Packets

Packets also incur cost in some instances. As stated earlier, when a web server's response is sent back to the user in packets, small chunks of manageable data, the user's system must check for errors before reconstructing the message. If any of the packets contain errors, an automatic request is made to the web server requesting all the packets, starting with the packet the error was found in—which forces you to think about the size of your data. The smaller the data, the lower the number of packets the server needs to create and send back to the user.

# Response Size

Let's examine how the size of the data affects the time it takes for the data to reach its destination. If our web site renders 1MB of content to the page, that means that the web server needs to respond to the request by sending 1MB of data to the user—that's quite a few packets! Depending on the connection rate of the user, making the request would take much longer than responding with a much smaller content size.

To illustrate this point, we are going to benchmark a request for a large image and a request for a small image and compare the response times.

The ab command to fetch a large image is the following:

```
ab -n 1 http://farm5.static.flickr.com/4011/4225950442_864042b26a_s.jpg
```

The ab command to fetch a small image is:

```
ab -n 1 http://farm5.static.flickr.com/4011/4225950442_864042b26a_b.jpg
```

When we analyze the response information shown in Figures 1–10 and 1–11, three items stand out: the Document Length, the Total min, and Total max times. A request for the smaller image took less time to satisfy compared to a request for the larger image, as shown in both the Total max and Total min values. In other words, the smaller the data size requested by the user, the faster the response.

```
Document Path:          /4011/4225950442_864042b26a_s.jpg
Document Length:        3407 bytes

Concurrency Level:      1
Time taken for tests:   0.188 seconds
Complete requests:      1
Failed requests:        0
Write errors:           0
Total transferred:      3906 bytes
HTML transferred:       3407 bytes
Requests per second:    5.33 [#/sec] (mean)
Time per request:       187.500 [ms] (mean)
Time per request:       187.500 [ms] (mean, across all concurrent requests)
Transfer rate:          20.34 [Kbytes/sec] received

Connection Times (ms)
              min  mean[+/-sd] median   max
Connect:       78    78   0.0     78     78
Processing:    94    94   0.0     94     94
Waiting:       94    94   0.0     94     94
Total:        172   172   0.0    172    172
```

*Figure 1–10. Response to request for small image*

```
Document Path:             /4011/4225950442_864042b26a_b.jpg
Document Length:           308235 bytes

Concurrency Level:         1
Time taken for tests:      1.109 seconds
Complete requests:         1
Failed requests:           0
Write errors:              0
Total transferred:         308731 bytes
HTML transferred:          308235 bytes
Requests per second:       0.90 [#/sec] (mean)
Time per request:          1109.375 [ms] (mean)
Time per request:          1109.375 [ms] (mean, across all concurrent requests)
Transfer rate:             271.77 [Kbytes/sec] received

Connection Times (ms)
              min  mean[+/-sd] median   max
Connect:       63   63    0.0      63    63
Processing:  1047 1047    0.0    1047  1047
Waiting:       94   94    0.0      94    94
Total:       1109 1109    0.0    1109  1109
```

**Figure 1-11.** *Response to request for large image*

In later chapters, you will learn how to reduce the response size by analyzing the content of your web application to determine what and where you can minimize and optimize, be it images, JavaScript files, or CSS files.

## Code Complexity

The logic a document must execute also affects the response. In our initial testing, this was not an issue because we were testing a very simple, static, HTML page, but as we add PHP, a database to interact with, and/or web services to invoke, we inadvertently increase the time it takes to satisfy a request because each external interaction and PHP process incurs a cost. In later chapters, you will learn how to reduce the cost incurred by these executions.

## Browser Behavior

Browsers also play a role in the way users perceive the responsiveness of a site. Each browser has its own method of rendering JavaScript, CSS, and HTML, which can add milliseconds or even seconds to the total response time the user experiences.

## Web Server Setup

Finally, the web server and its configuration can add to the amount of time the request takes to respond. By default (out of the box), most web servers do not contain the most optimal settings and require skilled engineers to modify the configuration files and kernel settings. To test a simple enhancement to a web server, we need to jump ahead of ourselves a bit and test the web server while the Keep-Alive setting is turned on. We will get to a much more detailed discussion concerning web server configurations in a later chapter.

The Keep-Alive setting, when turned on, allows the web server to open a specific number of connections, which it can then keep open to satisfy additional incoming requests. By removing the overhead of demanding the web server to open a connection for each incoming request and then closing that connection once the request has been satisfied, we speed up our application and decrease the amount of processing the web server must do, thereby increasing the number of users we can support.

Let's capture baseline data we can compare. Run the following command:

```
ab -c 5 -t 10 http://www.example.com/
```

Follow it with this command:

```
ab -c 5 -t 10 -k http://www.example.com/
```

The command contains the Keep-Alive flag k. This flag allows the web server to keep the five concurrent connections open and allow other connections to go through them, thereby reducing the time the web server takes in creating new connections. The side-by-side comparison is shown in Figures 1–12 and 1–13.

```
Concurrency Level:      5
Time taken for tests:   10.063 seconds
Complete requests:      184
Failed requests:        0
Write errors:           0
Total transferred:      133400 bytes
HTML transferred:       80592 bytes
Requests per second:    18.29 [#/sec] (mean)
Time per request:       273.438 [ms] (mean)
Time per request:       54.688 [ms] (mean, across all concurrent requests)
Transfer rate:          12.95 [Kbytes/sec] received

Connection Times (ms)
              min  mean[+/-sd] median   max
Connect:       16   53 220.9     31    3031
Processing:   125  214 437.3    141    3141
Waiting:       31  142 385.6     94    3141
Total:        156  267 487.7    188    3188
```

*Figure 1–12. Results for ab test of five concurrent periods of ten seconds*

```
Concurrency Level:      5
Time taken for tests:   10.000 seconds
Complete requests:      1412
Failed requests:        0
Write errors:           0
Keep-Alive requests:    1412
Total transferred:      1023700 bytes
HTML transferred:       618456 bytes
Requests per second:    141.20 [#/sec] (mean)
Time per request:       35.411 [ms] (mean)
Time per request:       7.082 [ms] (mean, across all concurrent requests)
Transfer rate:          99.97 [Kbytes/sec] received

Connection Times (ms)
              min  mean[+/-sd] median   max
Connect:        0    0   2.5      0      47
Processing:    16   35  56.1     31    1234
Waiting:       16   35  56.1     31    1234
Total:         16   35  56.3     31    1234
```

*Figure 1–13. Results for ab test using Keep-Alive*

Comparing both figures and referencing the Requests per second, Total min, and Total max, we can clearly see that using Keep-Alive drastically increases the number of requests per second the web server can satisfy and also increases the response time.

With a solid foundation of the measuring tools we will use to rate our success in optimizing our code, it's time to start optimizing for performance.

## Summary

In this chapter, the goal was to give you a look at the tools available for conducting benchmarking tests and point out the important features of each tool used for our specific purpose of optimization in the following chapters.

The tools you learned to use, install, and analyze data were the Apache Benchmark and the Siege tools. You also learned about the four major items that affect the benchmarking figures and, in turn, affect the response time of your user's request. Finally, you learned about the HTTP request lifecycle and how knowing what goes on within the HTTP request can also help you optimize.

# CHAPTER 2

■■■

# Improving Client Download and Rendering Performance

In the previous chapter, you learned how to measure response time and determine how a web page would respond during different traffic loads, using the tools Apache Benchmark (ab) and Siege. With these results, you could determine if your web server could serve sufficient amount of pages while under duress and determine how fast (or slow) the response would be. If only life were this easy and everyone used a terminal to view a web page, we could retain these results and skip this chapter. Unfortunately, reality is much more complicated than that, and it comes in the form of a web browser. You will now focus on the initial component, and a key component to any online PHP application, the front-end side of your application. In this chapter, we will focus on the performance of your application from the user's browser.

As shown in Figure 2–1, the front end is the first layer of our PHP application, and the component we will cover in this chapter. We need to optimize this component right away, since it is the first technology the user will encounter when visiting your application.

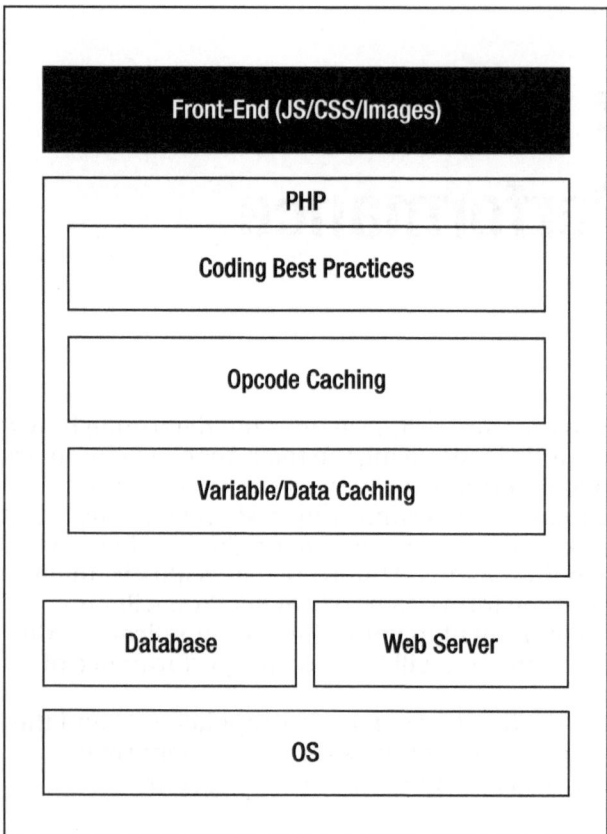

*Figure 2–1. PHP application component stack*

In this chapter, we analyze the response from the web server from the perspective of a web browser. Specifically, we analyze the response a web server sends when a browser requests a web page using the tools available within the browser, Firefox.

There are several tools we will focus on in this chapter. The first set of tools (Firebug, YSlow, and Page Speed) will help us analyze the response by providing the following:

- An in-depth look at the response from a web server

- Profile front-end logic within your JavaScript

- An itemized list of resources that the browser will fetch

- The length of time the browser took to fetch and receive the resource

- Suggestions on how to optimize the response

The second set of tools (YUI Compressor, Closure Compiler, and Smush.it) will help us optimize the response. Briefly, the tools help us compress both JavaScript and CSS files, and compress images required within your web page.

In both cases, you will learn how to install the tools and read the results. Once you have installed the tools, we will apply a few of the suggestions to optimize our response from the server.

## The Importance of Optimizing Responses

Let me start off by saying that this chapter will not require you to know a great deal of JavaScript (JS), Cascading Style Sheet (CSS), or image optimization. There are many great JS and CSS optimization books in the market if you're interested in the topic; you're here to optimize PHP! In the context of this book, we will look at what affects rendering time in the web browser and touch on high-level optimization techniques that you can quickly apply with great success within your web page. What this chapter will require you to know is what each of the technologies offer on a web application, where they are placed within a web page, and to know that a response from a web server may (more than often, it does) contain references to these resources. That's it.

So why dedicate a complete chapter to understanding how to measure and optimize these technologies and the response from a web server? Because without optimizing the response, the user will continue to feel that your web page is not fast enough.

For example, a user loads a web page where the total size of the page is 3MB. The response contains 30 un-cacheable large images, bloated CSS, and numerous JavaScript files that your web page does not require. Regardless of the effort and progress you make in optimizing your PHP code, the user will continue to download 3MB as a response before viewing the web page. On a standard DSL cable modem (1 Mbs), a 3MB file will take one minute. According to a Juniper Research survey, the average length of time a user waits for a web page to load is up to four seconds. At one minute, that's 56 seconds too many and the loss of a user.

# Firebug

As any web developer/designer will tell you, Firebug has saved his or her life more than a handful of times when creating cross browser applications—I know it has for me. Firebug is a plug-in widely used by web developers that provides detailed information about a web page's DOM, CSS, JavaScript, and, most importantly for response optimization, resource request information. The plug-in retrieves information about the specific web page you're currently on and presents the information within its different tabs.

---

■ **Note** Firebug contains many helpful tabs for web designers that are beyond the scope of this book. If you would like to read more about the tool, go to http://getfirebug.com/ for a complete list of features Firebug offers.

---

## Installing Firebug

At the time of this writing, the latest version of Firebug was 1.5.X, which could be installed only on Firefox 3.5–3.6 browsers. Although there is a "light" version (FirebugLite) of the plug-in, which contains a limited subset of the functionality for other browsers, I recommend the full version.

To install the plug-in, open your Firefox browser and load either the Firebug home page or the Mozilla Add-ons Firebug page using the URLs shown here:

- Firebug home page: http://getfirebug.com/

- Mozilla Add-ons Firebug page: https://addons.mozilla.org/en-US/firefox/addon/1843/

Once the web page loads, click the "Install Firebug for Firefox" or "Add to Firefox" button, followed by the "Allow" button when prompted by the install window. Once Firebug is installed, you will need to restart your browser for the plug-in to be used.

## Firebug Performance Tabs

Once Firebug has been successfully installed, open Firebug by clicking the bug icon in the lower right-hand corner of the browser window, as shown in Figure 2–2.

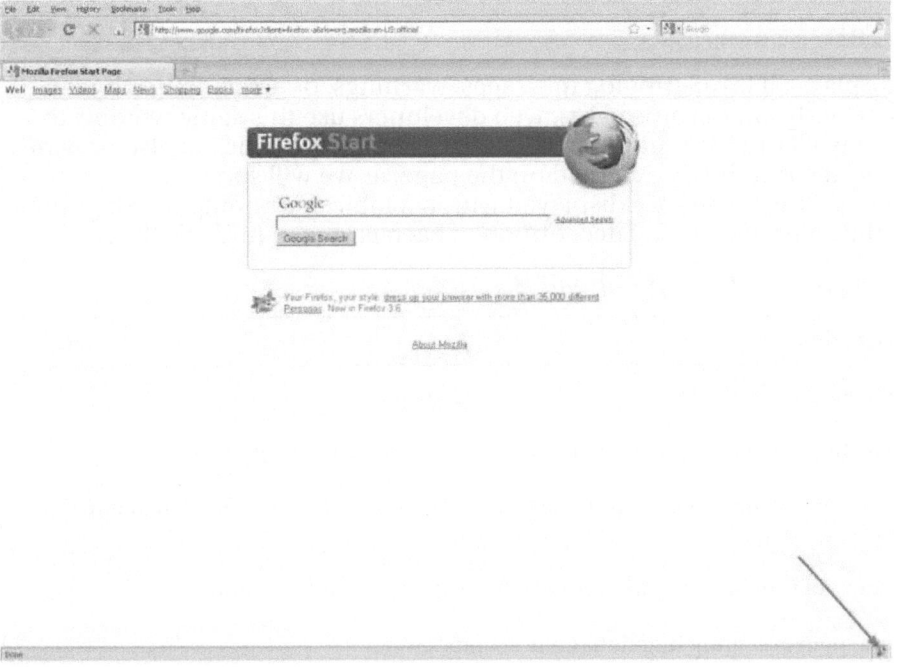

***Figure 2–2.*** *Starting Firebug on Firefox*

This will start Firebug and open the console window. As you'll notice, there are quite a number of tabs you can use that can provide insight into any web page's structure, as well as style. We're going to focus on two tabs: Console and Net, shown in Figure 2–3.

***Figure 2–3.*** *Firebug Console and Net tabs location*

## The Console Tab

The Console tab displays all JavaScript log messages, warnings, or errors issued by the web page you're currently on. In some cases, web developers use this same window to trace through their JavaScript by issuing console.log() JavaScript. This tab also provides a means to profile JavaScript that is executed on the page, as we will soon see.

The JavaScript profiling results are displayed within a table containing nine columns. A complete list of the columns and full description of each is shown in Table 2–1.

*Table 2–1. Firebug JavaScript Profiler Column Descriptions*

| Column Name | Description |
| --- | --- |
| Function | Function that is invoked |
| Calls | Total number of calls made to the specific function on the page |
| Percent | Percentage of time spent within the function in respect to the collection of functions invoked |
| Own Time | Amount of time spent within the specified function, in milliseconds |
| Time | Time spent executing function (milliseconds) |
| Avg | Average time spent executing function (milliseconds)—Calls Column/Time Column |
| Min | Minimum time spent executing the function (milliseconds) |
| Max | Maximum time spent executing the function (milliseconds) |
| File | Static file that contains the function called |

Along with the information presented in the table, the JavaScript profiler also contains the total number of function calls made as well as the overall time spent in the JavaScript, as shown in Figure 2–4.

## Running JavaScript Profiler on a Web Page

Let's profile a simple web page. Load the Google home page, www.google.com, with the Firebug console open. Once the page completely loads, click Console, Profile, and type in a word (I used "php") to invoke the Ajax. Click Profile once more to stop profiling and display the results. You should see something similar to Figure 2–4.

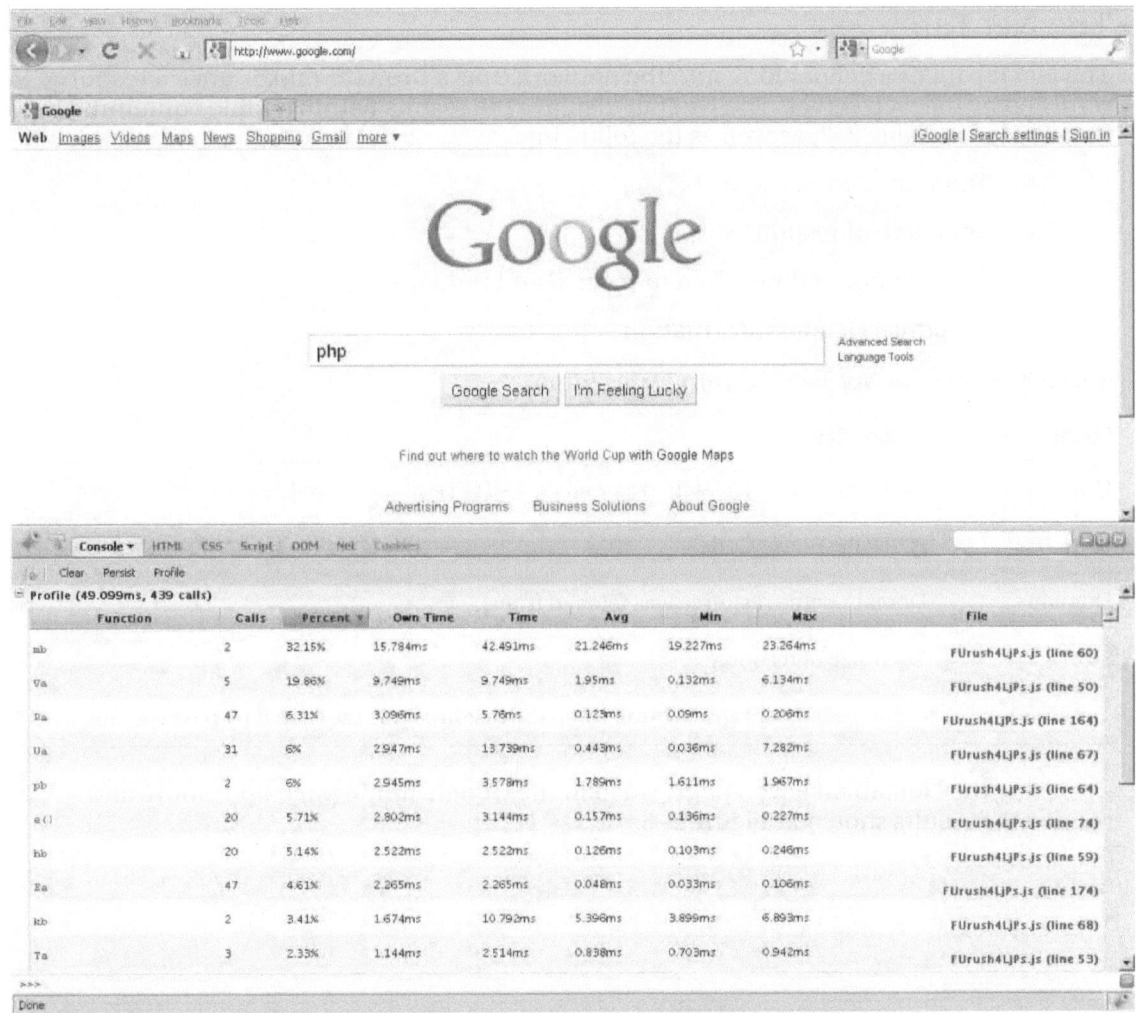

***Figure 2–4.*** *Firebug JavaScript Profiler results for Google.com*

Referencing the Profiler's results table, we can quickly see that there were 439 calls to JavaScript functions and the total time executing the collection of functions was 49.09 ms. We also can see that the function that takes longer to execute is the mb function and 32 percent of the overall time is spent within this function. Since we are not going into detail on how to optimize JavaScript code within this book, we will stop here and let you know that you can now walk up to our JavaScript developer with some useful metrics to both isolate the potential bottleneck and pinpoint where to start optimizing the JavaScript code.

## The Net Tab

The Net tab takes a deeper look into the network calls a browser makes once a response is returned by the web server. The Net tab displays the results within a table containing the items listed in Table 2–2, as well as the following:

- Total number of requests

- Total size of response

- Total length of time taken to receive and render response

- Response Header information

*Table 2–2. Firebug Net Tab Column Description*

| Column Name | Description |
| --- | --- |
| URL | Resource (content) fetched as well as the HTTP request used |
| Status | HTTP Response Code |
| Domain | Domain name resource was fetched from |
| Size | Total size of resource |
| Timeline | Color-coded bar representing when the resource was requested by the browser |

Using the Net tab on a web page, we load the Google home page once more and receive the results shown in Figure 2–5.

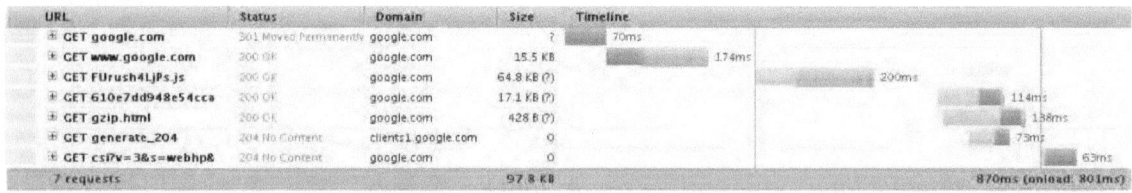

*Figure 2–5. Net results for Google.com*

The table contains an itemized list of calls made by the browser to resources the browser requires for rendering. Using your mouse, you can hover over each of the resources in the Timeline column to see a detailed breakdown of what the browser was doing while retrieving the specific resource, as well as what each color represents. Table 2–3 describes what each of the colors represents.

***Table 2–3.*** *Net Results Description of Colors*

| Color | Description |
| --- | --- |
| Purple | Browser Waiting for Resource |
| Grey | Receiving Resource |
| Red | Sending Data |
| Green | Connecting |
| Blue | DNS Lookup |

Reading the results from top to bottom, we begin with a redirect. I entered the URL google.com instead of www.google.com and was redirected to www.google.com. The redirection took 70ms to complete, and while the redirection was occurring, the browser was waiting for a response and receiving no data. This is the initial row shown in Figure 2–6. After 70ms, the browser was redirected but asked to wait an additional 64ms before receiving data. Keep in mind that as the browser waits, so is your user waiting on something to render to the browser's window. At the 322ms mark, the browser blocks all actions while the JavaScript executes and 72 ms later begins to receive content, shown in the third row in Figure 2–6. Skipping a few resources, we look at the last item, and based on results, we determine that the last resource was fetched 807ms later.

With the information the Net tab provides us, we can begin to not only save on the number of resources called but also reduce the size of the response, among other things. Performance engineers have established a few rules we can apply to our web pages to speed up the rendering process for our users. Let's use a tool that utilizes these rules to help us grade how well a web page conforms to these rules within the next section.

# YSlow

YSlow is a web page performance analyzing tool created by the Yahoo Performance group. The tool is a Firebug add-on and must be used within Firefox. Unlike Firebug, YSlow uses a set of rules, which a web page is graded against. Currently there are two versions of the rules, the default YSlow v2 rules, which grade a web page on all 22 rules, as well as the Classic v1 rules, which grade a web page on 13 of the 23 rules.

## YSlow v2 Rulesets

YSlow v2's 22 web optimization rules cover the following:

- CSS optimization

- Image optimization

- JavaScript optimization

- Server optimization

Using the 22 rules, YSlow calculates a letter grade for each of the rules as well as an overall letter grade on how well the entire web page is optimized. A letter grade of "A" indicates that the web page for the most part follows the 22 rules and is optimized for performance. On the other hand, a letter grade of "F" indicates that the web page is not optimized.

Along with the rules, YSlow also provides references to online tools that can be used to optimize CSS, JavaScript, and HTML. We will use some of these tools later in the chapter.

Since the rule sets are instrumental within the plug-in, let's review some of them now.

### CSS Optimization Rules

Beginning with CSS optimization, a quick snapshot of the rules used follows here:

- Place the CSS styles at the top of the HTML document.

- Avoid certain CSS expressions.

- Minify the CSS files.

By following these three rules, you can both reduce the size of the CSS document by removing any white spaces (minifying) and speed the rendering process within the browser when placing the CSS file at the top of the HTML document.

### Image Optimization Rules

All web sites these days have images for design purposes, and optimizing these images can decrease the load time for the web page by following some of these rules that YSlow grades against:

- Use desired image sizes instead of resizing within HTML using width and height attributes.

- Create sprites when possible.

The first rules allow us to reduce the response size by using an image size fitted for the web page. The second rule reduces the total number of images the browser is required to fetch by combining the images within a page into, in some cases, a single file.

## JavaScript Optimization

As noted in the beginning of this chapter, we can optimize JavaScript. Here are three rules YSlow uses to check JavaScript:

- Place JavaScript at the bottom of the HTML.
- Minify JavaScript.
- Make JavaScript external.

Once again, we look to optimize the size of the response as well as the method in which the browser renders the content for the user. By placing the JavaScript at the bottom of the HTML document, we allow the browser to render the HTML and not become blocked by the loading and execution of the JavaScript. This was seen in our previous example while using the Firebug-Net tab within the Google home page.

By minifying the JavaScript, like minification in CSS, we remove white spaces, thereby reducing the file size and reducing the size of the response.

## Server Optimization

YSlow checks the Server Response Headers within this criterion for a few items such as the following:

- Whether the server utilizes Gzip/bzip2 compression
- Whether DNS lookups are reduced
- Whether ETags are implemented

The rules used were only a sample of the 22 rules used by YSlow. For a complete list of the rules along with a complete description, let's install YSlow now and start grading web pages.

## Installing YSlow

YSlow is available only for Firefox on both Windows and Unix systems. As of this writing, YSlow 1.5.4 was available in stable form on the Mozilla web site, `https://addons.mozilla.org/en-US/firefox/addon/5369/`.

Once on the web page, click the "Add to Firefox" button, and once the plug-in installs, restart your browser. That's all there is to it.

## Starting YSlow

There are two ways to start YSlow. You can either click the YSlow logo on the bottom right-hand corner of the browser, as shown in Figure 2–6, or you can open the Firebug console and click the YSlow tab, as shown in Figure 2–7. Open the YSlow console now, and let's grade the Google home page.

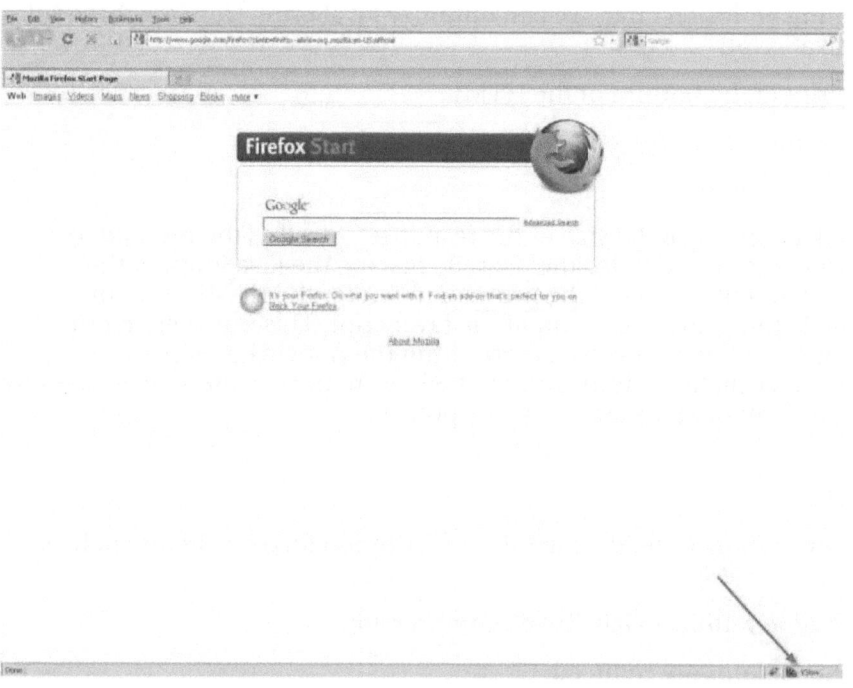

*Figure 2–6. Opening YSlow using YSlow icon*

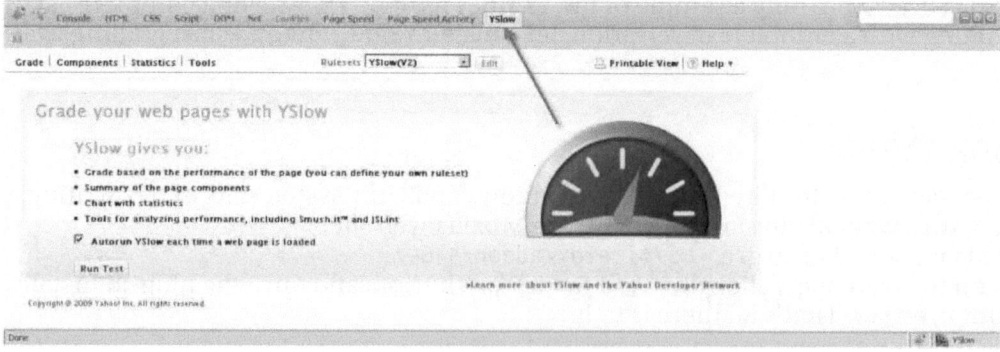

*Figure 2–7. Opening YSlow from Firebug console*

## The Grade Tab

We're going to continue using the Google home page. Load the home page,
www.google.com. Once the Google home page loads, click "Run Test" within the YSlow
tool, and if the Grade tab is not already selected, click it. You will see a screen similar to
that shown in Figure 2–8.

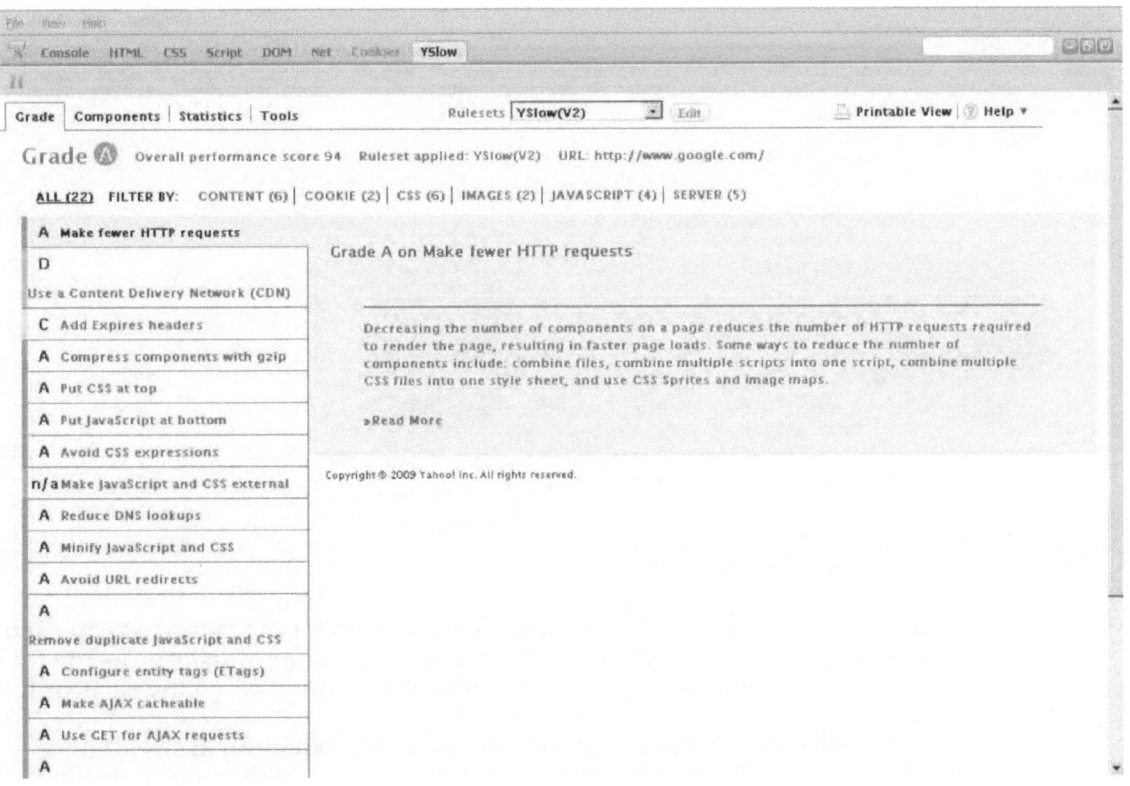

*Figure 2–8. Google.com YSlow results*

Based on the YSlow tool, Google's home page has an overall grade of "A" and a
performance score of 94/100.

YSlow contains six result filters, Content, Cookie, CSS, Images, JavaScript, and Server.
The filter tabs are shown right below the page grade, and when clicked, each of these
filters contains rules that describe the type of optimization to be done, why it's beneficial,
and the overall grade given to the page for the specific filter.

Referring back to the results shown in Figure 2–8, Google received a "D" in
implementing a Content Delivery Network and a "C" in including the "Expires" header
setting, which allows a web page to cache images and content in the browser's cache for
later use.

## Statistics Tab

The Statistics tab, like the Grade tab, provides a bit more insight into how we can improve the rendering performance. The Statistics tab contains information regarding cache usage and provides a very easy way to understand how caching can play an important role in optimizing rendering. Figure 2–9 contains the statistics results for Google.com.

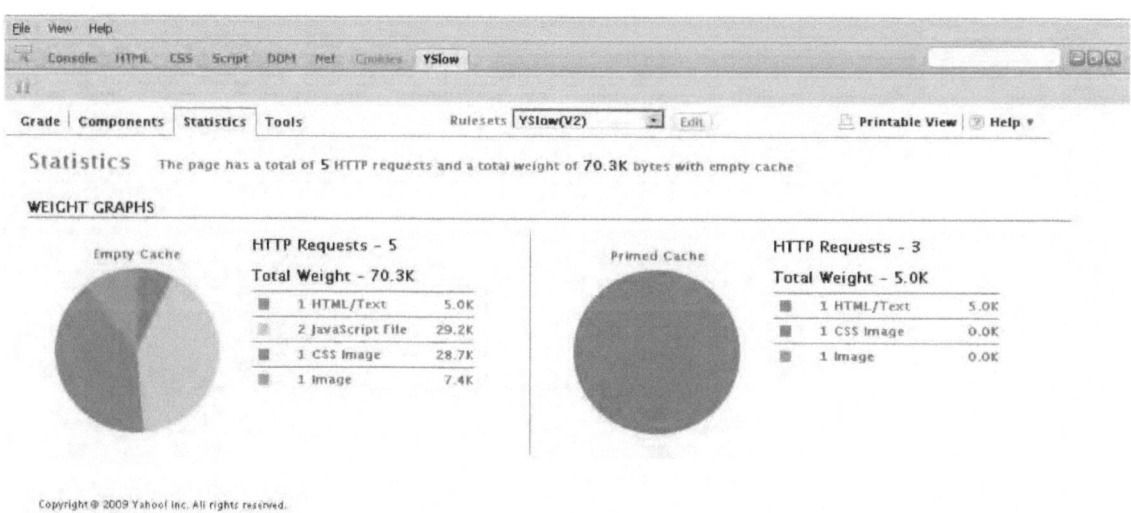

*Figure 2–9.* Google statistics results graphs

Note the pair of graphs. One graph describes the total number of resources requested as well as the total size requested when the cache is empty (the user initially visits the web page). The second graph on the right displays the same information when the cache is full (primed cache).

The results are two resource requests fewer, and a 65.4KB reduction in size. With a primed cache, the browser will download less of the web page from the web server and fetch the cached content stored locally, thereby increasing the speed at which the web page loads. We will further look into caching in Chapters 4 and 5, later in the book.

## Tools Tab

The next tab is the Tools tab. This tab contains a list of tools that help us optimize the JavaScript, CSS, and images we use on our web page. We will refer back to this tab later in the chapter—for now, let's hold off on it.

While YSlow provides a grade and insight on how well we apply optimization techniques within a web page, I primarily use it to grade and read information about a particular performance tweak and how the tweak works. What YSlow lacks is additional information on where I can save on size and what files can be updated. It is not as transparent as one would like it to be, and it acts as a black box of sorts. Let's take a look at a similar tool that acts as a white-box tool—Google's Page Speed.

# Page Speed

Google's Page Speed is also a plug-in for Firefox/Firebug, and like YSlow, Page Speed provides a score on how well a web page has implemented optimization techniques. Unlike YSlow, Page Speed provides information on what files it analyzed, how to optimize the files, where to optimize within your web page, and metrics on how much you can improve by optimizing.

## Installing Page Speed

To install Page Speed, load the URL http://code.google.com/speed/page-speed/download.html, click "Install Page Speed 1.X", follow the instructions on the install window, and once the add-on is installed, restart Firefox.

## Page Speed at Work

Start up Page Speed by clicking the Firebug icon in the lower right corner of the browser. Once the console is open, you will notice two tabs, "Page Speed" and "Page Speed Activity," as shown in Figure 2–10.

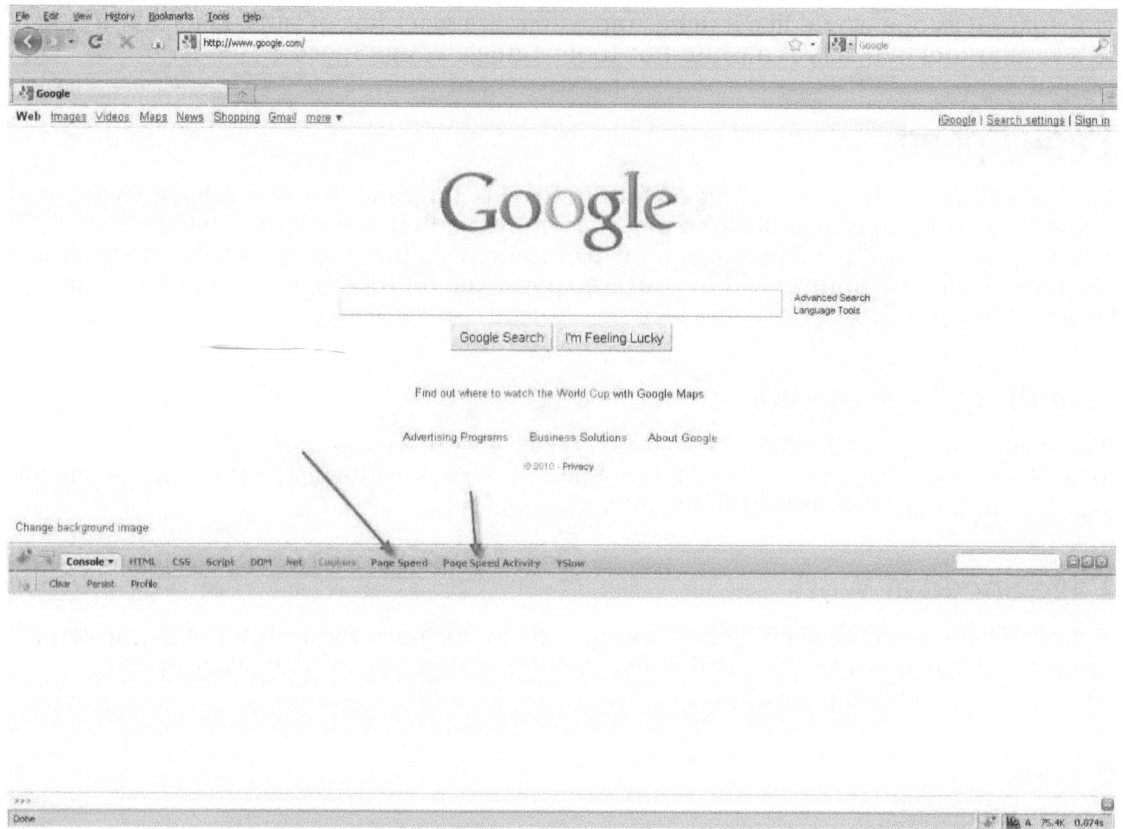

***Figure 2–10.*** *Page Speed tabs in Firebug*

Click "Page Speed", load the Google.com home page, and then click the "Analyze Performance" button. You should see results similar to Figure 2–11.

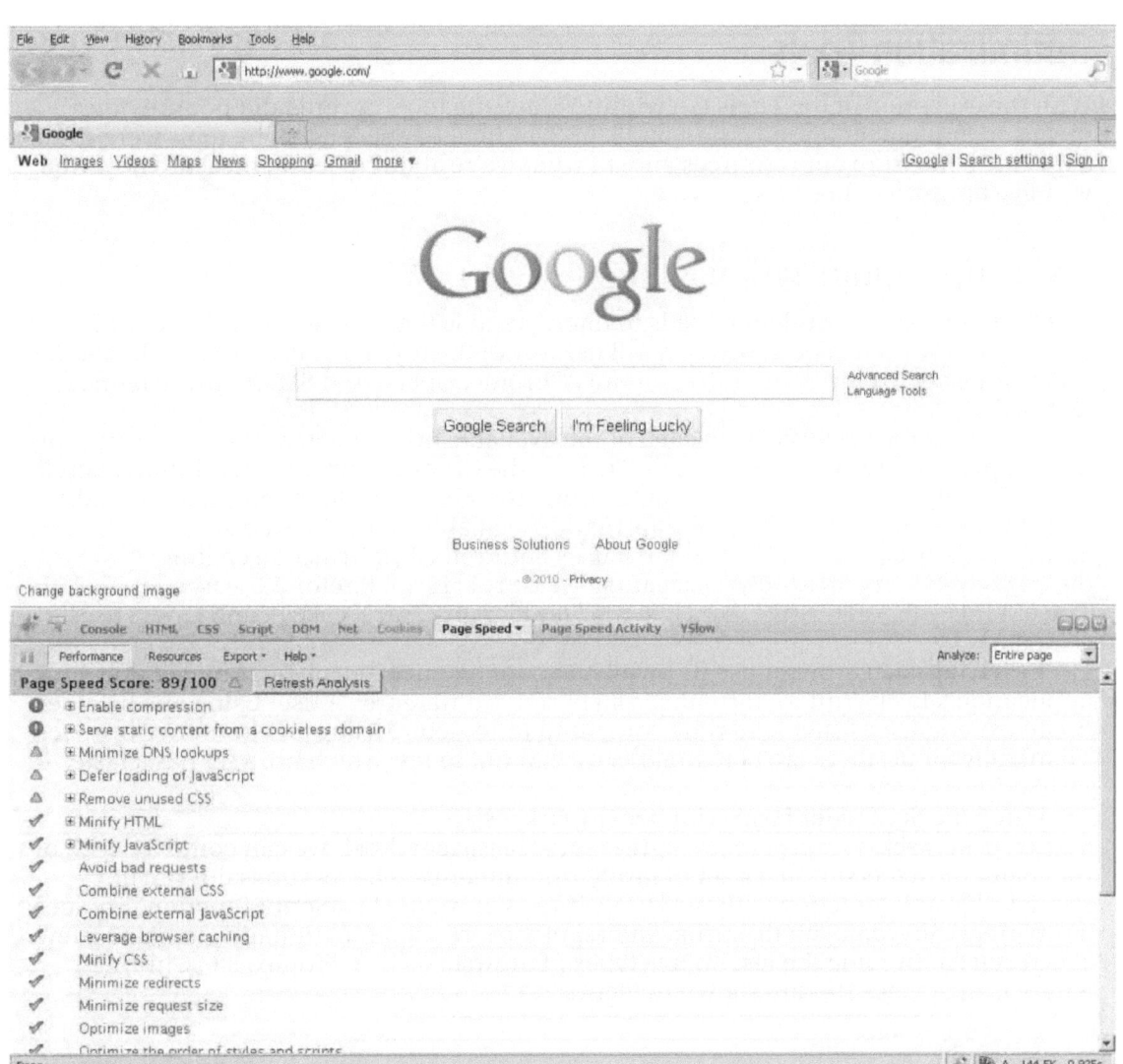

***Figure 2–11.*** *Page Speed results for Google.com*

Page Speed scores Google's home page with an 89/100, and displays a list of rules used to test the single page. Here is why we use Page Speed as a tool for performance optimization on the front end. Click "Remove unused CSS", for example. Page Speed identifies which CSS elements are not in use and estimates that 3.3KB of the file can be removed, reducing the file size by 46.5 percent. Again, reducing the size of the response as well as reducing the number of resources fetched increases the rendering performance for your user.

# Optimization Tools

With the exception of the Tools tab within YSlow, the tools covered did not provide a means to implement optimization on JS, CSS, or images on a page. The tools were simply a means to measure our resources and, in what we're about to learn, measure how well we have optimized these resources.

## JavaScript Optimization

The first thing every developer needs to understand is that your end user is not bound to a single browser. A user can use and will use any of the myriad of browsers in the market today: Internet Explorer (IE) 6/7/8, Firefox, Chrome, Opera, and Safari, just to name a few.

When it comes to JavaScript, each of the available browsers handles JavaScript using its own proprietary JavaScript engine. To date, the Chrome 6 browser has implemented V8, a C++ engine installed directly on Chrome using ECMAScript as outlined in ECMA-262, third edition, with additional information available on the V8 web site, http://code.google.com/p/v8/. Safari 4 uses SquirrelFish, a bytecode engine (http://webkit.org/blog/189/announcing-squirrelfish/), Firefox 3.5+ uses TraceMonkey (https://wiki.mozilla.org/JavaScript:TraceMonkey), and Opera uses Carakan.

By having each browser use its own JavaScript engine, you are guaranteed that your application's JavaScript performance will perform differently. A user using one browser might experience a faster load time compared to someone using an alternative browser. Thankfully for us, there are benchmarks we can run to test which browser has a faster JavaScript engine.

Using the SunSpider JavaScript benchmark tests, http://www2.webkit.org/perf/sunspider-0.9/sunspider.html, we can compare each of the major browsers running a set of JavaScript functions. The test does not run any special APIs or interaction with the DOM. It tests only core JavaScript functionality such as cryptography, date, math, string, and regular expression functionality, to name a few. The results of running the test on five types of browsers—IE 8, Firefox, 3.6, Chrome 7, Safari 5, and Opera 10—are shown in Figure 2–12.

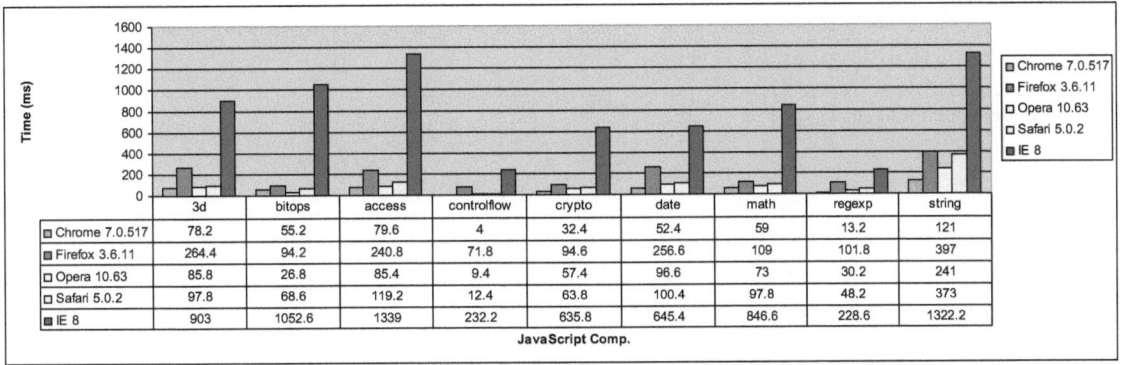

The data shown in the figure:

| | 3d | bitops | access | controlflow | crypto | date | math | regexp | string |
|---|---|---|---|---|---|---|---|---|---|
| Chrome 7.0.517 | 78.2 | 55.2 | 79.6 | 4 | 32.4 | 52.4 | 59 | 13.2 | 121 |
| Firefox 3.6.11 | 264.4 | 94.2 | 240.8 | 71.8 | 94.6 | 256.6 | 109 | 101.8 | 397 |
| Opera 10.63 | 85.8 | 26.8 | 85.4 | 9.4 | 57.4 | 96.6 | 73 | 30.2 | 241 |
| Safari 5.0.2 | 97.8 | 68.6 | 119.2 | 12.4 | 63.8 | 100.4 | 97.8 | 48.2 | 373 |
| IE 8 | 903 | 1052.6 | 1339 | 232.2 | 635.8 | 645.4 | 846.6 | 228.6 | 1322.2 |

*Figure 2–12. SunSpider benchmark results*

The graph shown in Figure 2–12 presents the results from the SunSpider benchmark on five of the major browsers. Based on the results of the five browsers running on a Windows XP, Pentium 4 3.20Ghz system, Chrome has the fastest JavaScript engine, which means your JavaScript will perform faster within this browser.

## JavaScript Placement

As previously mentioned, the placement of JavaScript is important when your application is loading on a browser. The reason for the importance of placement of the JavaScript comes from the way a browser reacts when encountering `<script>` tags. Each time a `<script>` tag is encountered, the browser blocks all further rendering of the page, thereby placing your users and their ability to see content on hold (Listing 2–1). By moving all JavaScript toward the bottom of your HTML file, you are allowing the HTML to render much sooner (Listing 2–2).

*Listing 2–1. Poor Placement of a JavaScript File*

```
<html>
<head>
<title>JavaScript Example</title>

<script type="text/javascript">
function addItems()
{

    var items = ['Apache', 'Nginx', 'Lighty'],
    localDoc = document; //local document object
    var node = '',
    i = 0,
    li = '';

    node = localDoc.getElementById('webservers');
```

```
  for(i; i<items.length; i++)
    {
      li = document.createElement('li');
      li.innerHTML = items[i];
      node.appendChild(li);
    }

}
</script>

</head>
<body>
<div id="main">

        <h3>Technology List</h3>
        <ul id="techlist">
                <li>Javascript</li>
                <li>CSS</li>
                <li>Images</li>
                <li>PHP</li>
        </ul>

        <ul id="webservers"></ul>


</div>


<script type="text/javascript">
addItems();
</script>
</body>
</html>
```

***Listing 2–2.*** *Optimized JavaScript Placement*

```
<html>
<head>
<title>JavaScript Example</title>
</head>
<body>
<div id="main">

        <h3>Technology List</h3>
        <ul id="techlist">
                <li>Javascript</li>
                <li>CSS</li>
                <li>Images</li>
                <li>PHP</li>
        </ul>

        <ul id="webservers"></ul>
```

```
</div>

<script type="text/javascript">
function addItems()
{

        var items = ['Apache', 'Nginx', 'Lighty'],
        localDoc = document; //local document object
        var node = '',
        i = 0,
        li = '';

        node = localDoc.getElementById('webservers');
        for(i; i<items.length; i++)
        {
                li = document.createElement('li');
                li.innerHTML = items[i];
                node.appendChild(li);
        }

}

addItems();
</script>
</body>
</html>
```

The HTML and JavaScript code shown in Listings 2–1 and 2–2 contains a list of web technologies using the ul and li HTML tags. The HTML also contains an empty div tag, which is updated by the JavaScript. The JavaScript contains a single function that creates a DOM element, places each of the web servers inside a li tag, and appends the li to the empty web server's ul tag.

Using Firebug, Listings 2–1 and 2–2 were tested, and the results are shown in Figures 2–13 and 2–14.

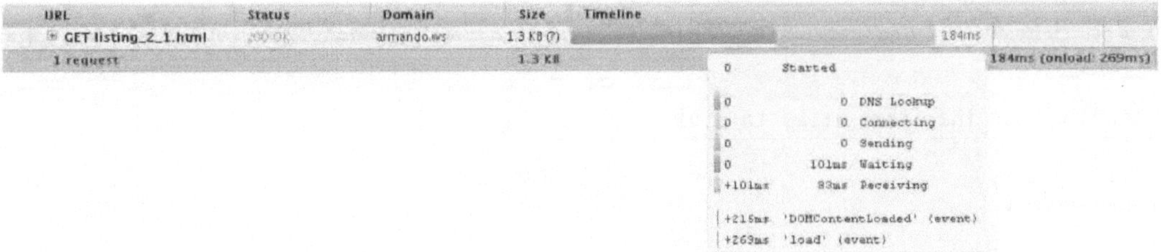

***Figure 2–13.*** *Firebug net results for Listing 2–1*

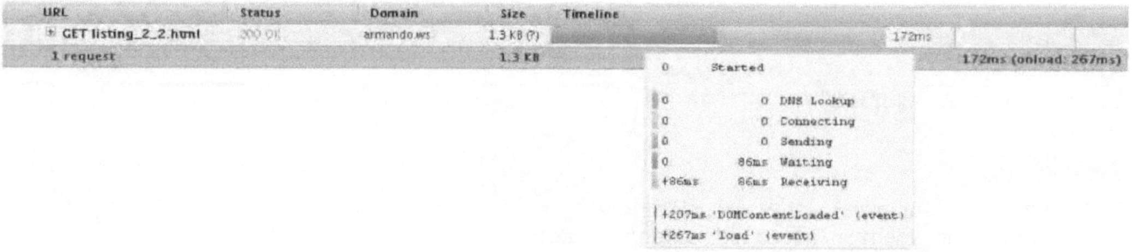

*Figure 2–14.* Firebug net results for Listing 2–2

Both Figure 2–13 and Figure 2–14 use no cache and simulate a user's initial page request. While Figure 2–13 renders the page in 269ms, the code shown in Listing 2–1 renders the page in 267ms. Also the amount of time the browser blocks rendering is reduced from 101ms to 86ms using Listing 2–2. The JavaScript presented, as well as the HTML, is minimal and represents a simplified web page. The improvement will have better effect in heavier HTML/JavaScript pages you create.

## Minification of JavaScript

Reducing the response size increases the performance simply by reducing the length of time the browser needs to wait for the content payload to arrive. The content payload contains every resource required by the browser for the web page. The smaller payload, the faster the download. Minifying reduces the size of a JavaScript file by removing white spaces from the JavaScript file, removing unused code, removing comments, shrinking the size of variables, and in some minification tools, removing unnecessary code.

Using the JavaScript shown in Listing 2–3, we can demonstrate the process of minification. The JavaScript code shown extends the code shown in Listing 2–2 by adding comments and moving the functionality of the for loop into an additional function. The JavaScript code is also removed from the HTML and placed into a separate file, `listing 2_8.js`.

*Listing 2–3.* Add Additional Items to an Unordered List Using JavaScript

```
/**
 * Add Items within the items array to a ul
 * html tag
 */
function addItems()
{
        var items = ['Apache', 'Nginx', 'Lighty'],
        node = '',
        i = 0,
        li = '';

        node = document.getElementById('webservers');
        appendList(items, node);
```

```
}
/**
 * Foreach item within the array, create a li node
 * and append to the node provided.
 */
function appendList(items, node)
{
        for(i; i<items.length; i++)
        {
                li = document.createElement('li');
                li.innerHTML = items[i];
                node.appendChild(li);
        }
}
```

Using one of the available minification tools such as YUI Compressor, we can reduce the file size from 525bytes to 278bytes. The final minified file can be seen in Listing 2–4.

*Listing 2–4. Output File from YUI Compressor*

```
function addItems(){var items=["Apache","Nginx","Lighty"],node="",i=0,li="";⏎
node=document.getElementById("webservers");appendList(items,node);}function⏎
 appendList(items,node){for(i;i<items.length;i++){li=document.createElement("li");⏎
li.innerHTML=items[i];node.appendChild(li);}}
```

Of course, the resulting minified file size isn't that great. Going from 573bytes to 255bytes wouldn't be considered the origins of the bottleneck, but let's take a real-world JavaScript file, such as the JavaScript framework JQuery. The JQuery home page offers two versions of its framework, an unminified version of JQuery with a file size of 155KB and a minified version with a size of only 24KB, which is 131KB less and an 84.51 percent reduction in size.

# Minification Tools

We will cover two JavaScript minification tools, YUI Compressor by Yahoo! and Closure Compiler by Google. Using both tools, we will compress the JQuery JavaScript framework.

# YUI Compressor

Yahoo's YUI Compressor can be used from the YSlow add-on for Firebug or can be downloaded and operated using its Java (.jar) version of the tool. As of this writing, the latest stable release of the tool, 2.4.2, is available for both Linux and Windows systems, and can be downloaded from the official YUI Compressor web site, http://developer.yahoo.com/yui/compressor/. If you do not wish to download the tool, you can open Firebug, click YSlow, click Tools, and then click "All JS Minified". The only drawback to this approach is the need to copy and paste the results into a file of your own.

Once the tool has downloaded, unzip its contents. The jar file will be located within the build directory, build/yuicompressor-2.4.2.jar. To minify a JavaScript file, you can use the command shown in Listing 2–5.

*Listing 2–5. Minifying Using YUI Compressor*

```
java -jar yuicompressor-2.4.2.jar -o js-mini.js js-to-minify.js
```

The command shown in Listing 2–6 executes the YUI Compressor jar file and utilizes the output flag -o. The output flag specifies the location of the desired minified file. The second file presented in Listing 2–6 is the location of the file to minify. In this example, the file to minify is within the current working directory containing the name js-to-minify.js. To see a complete list of available options, run the command java -jar yuicompressor-2.4.2.jar -h.

Using the tool, let's compress the uncompressed JQuery file from the JQuery web site. Unminified, the development file is 155KB, running this command:

*Listing 2–6. Minifying JQuery Using YUI Compressor*

```
java -jar yuicompressor-2.4.2.jar -o jquery-min.js jquery.js
```

This produces a new file—jquery-mini.js—with the file size of 78KB.

# Closure Compiler

An alternative tool to use is the Google Closure Compiler tool. The tool takes a JavaScript file as an input and "compiles from JavaScript to better JavaScript," as the official web site, http://code.google.com/closure/compiler, points out. The Closure Compiler can be used in three ways:

- Using a Java jar file that can be downloaded to your local hard drive
- Via the online tool on the official web site
- Using its RESTful APIs

For additional information, you can visit the official web site.

For the following example, you should download the zip file that includes the tool. To do so, visit the official site, click the "Download the application" link under the "How do I start?" box on the right, and unpackage the content of the download. Once the content has been unpacked, make sure you have the .jar file present; we will use it to compress the JQuery file.

Using the unaltered JQuery file, let's use Closure Compiler on the file. Running the command shown in Listing 2–7 yields the file jquery-min-cc.js with a file size of 71KB.

*Listing 2–7. Compressing JQuery with Closure Compiler*

```
java -jar compiler.jar --js jquery.js --js_output_file jquery-min-cc.js
```

## Reduce Resource Requests

Reducing the number of requests to a web server reduces the number of times the browser must fetch a resource across the Internet. When dealing with JavaScript, this can be easily achieved by combining JavaScript files that are required by your web page into a single file. The caveat here is to make sure the files being merged together are merged in the correct order, where the functionality required by one file is present before the file that uses the functionality.

## Use Server-Side Compression

File compression is another method of reducing the size of JavaScript as well as CSS files. Using compression on an already minified JavaScript or CSS file can reduce the size even further. The most widely used compression to date is GZip. Using a 368.6KB file, we compare the uncompressed, minified, and minified+gzip files and present the results in Table 2–4.

*Table 2–4. Comparative Results of Using Compression*

| Compression | Size |
| --- | --- |
| None | 368.6KB |
| Minified | 88.2KB |
| Minified+gzip | 30.05KB |

The results show the minified+gzip version of the file is much smaller than the other two files. This topic will be covered in greater length in Chapter 8.

# Image Compression

Not all image compressions are alike and should be used to meet specific needs of your web page. When using images, the type of compression used is important in affecting the amount of information the browser is required to download before it begins loading the page. Using the right compression can decrease the size of the response.

We briefly covered this in Chapter 1 by comparing the response size and time using an ab benchmarking test on a small image and a large image, with the results showing that a larger image increased the response time due to its size. The general rule when using the different file types, JPEG, GIF, and PNG, is to use GIF for logos and small icons within a page, JPEGs for photographs or high-quality images, and finally PNGs for everything else. If you're already using this rule, you can take it one step further by compressing the images using a web compression tool such as Yahoo's Smush.it.

# Smush.it

Smush.it is a lossless compression tool created by Yahoo! to reduce the file size of your images even further. The tool is available at `www.smushit.com` and allows you to either upload your files or reference them using a list of URLs (Figure 2–15). There is a file size restriction of 1MB.

*Figure 2–15. Smush.it home page*

As an introduction to Smush.it, we will use the small 300×300 image shown in Figure 2–16.

*Figure 2–16. Original 300×300 image used on a web page*

The original file is a 100KB JPEG. After using Smush.it on the image, the resulting JPEG was reduced to 98.46KB, a reduction of 1.96 percent, as shown in Figure 2–17.

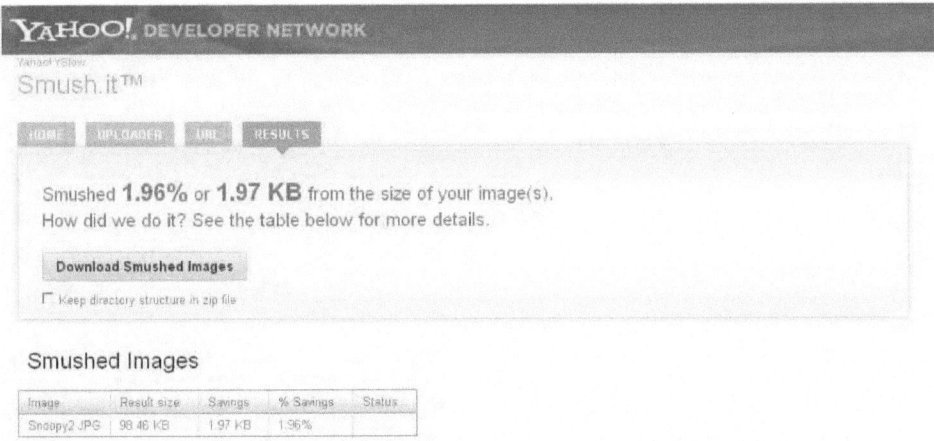

*Figure 2–17. Using Smush.it to compress the original image*

The difference is minimal, using a single image in this case. But what if you had a web site with 15 images? How much could you save by making a small reduction to each image like this? Using Firebug and YSlow, we can test such a case. Using the CNN home page, I ran the Smush.it tool from YSlow by opening Firebug, clicking YSlow, clicking the Tools tab, and finally the "All Smush.it" link. The results are shown in Figure 2–18.

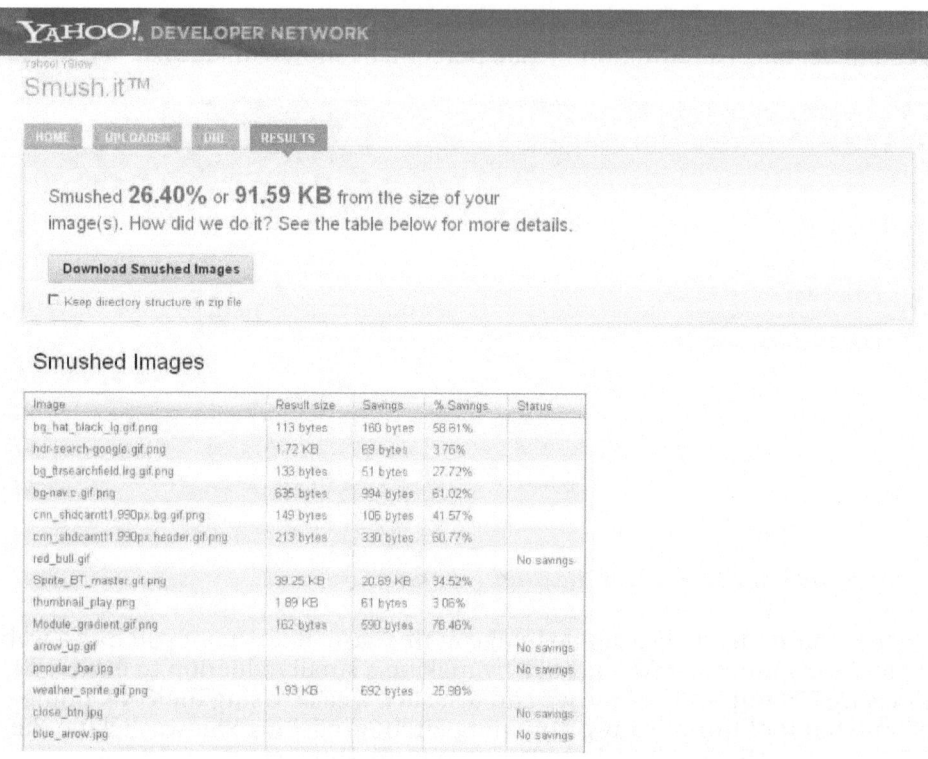

***Figure 2–18.*** *Results of running Smush.it on the CNN home page*

The results demonstrate the total reduction in KB, and in this case, the CNN home page benefits from using Smush.it. There is a 26.4 percent reduction in size for the complete set of images on the home page, which equals 91.59KB removed from the response.

With both guidelines and tools to measure how well we are optimizing our web page on the front end, and tools to implement optimization, we can now move one layer down and look at the PHP code that powers the web page user's view by using profiling tools for PHP and applying the latest best practices in the next chapter.

## Summary

This chapter introduced three additional performance-measuring tools: Firebug, YSlow, and Page Speed. Using the three tools, you learned how to open each of the tools using the quick-open icons on Firefox and within Firebug. You learned how to begin and read the results of the profiling tools while using a small JavaScript example as well as the JavaScript code used within the Google home page. Using Firebug's Net tab, you also learned how to read its output while understanding the behavior of a browser when encountering a `<script>` tag. You also learned how to grade your web page's performance using the YSlow 22–rule grading criteria, and Page Speed's criteria.

With the tools for measuring how well your web page is performing under your belt, you also learned how to implement performance tweaks on JavaScript and images. The performance tweaks covered were minification of JavaScript using the tools YUI Compressor and Google's Closure Compiler. You learned about the benefits of combining JavaScript files into a single file to reduce resource requests, compared server-side compressions using Gzip, and used the image compression tool Smush.it to compress both an example image as well as the images from CNN's home page to understand how much we reduce the response size using such a tool.

■ ■ ■

# PHP Code Optimization

Opcode caching, data caching using Memcached, and optimizing your database are all great optimization tricks you will learn once you're done with this book. But before reaching those chapters, we need to learn how to apply the best coding practices. Knowing when to use a specific PHP function over another and making small incremental changes in your code can change the performance of your PHP code.

In previous chapters, we focused on the tools to optimize the rendering of content and reduce the amount of data the user was required to download, using Firebug, Page Speed, and YSlow. In many cases, optimizing the response and the content returned to the user is enough to make most of your users happy. More than often, though, you want to go the extra mile and optimize the PHP code itself.

I'm going to sound cliché for a bit and reference an old Chinese proverb. "Give a man a fish and you feed him for a day. Teach a man to fish and you feed him for a lifetime." I raise the proverb because that's my intention in this chapter. Yes, we will review and apply the latest best practices, but I will go a step further and teach you how to become a PHP optimization fisherman! You will learn why specific function calls are faster than others by installing and analyzing results from the Vulcan Logic Dumper (VLD). You will learn how to install and use strace to review the system-level operations a PHP script invokes when it's called from the Apache web server. Finally, you will be able to spot bottlenecks within your code using the results from Xdebug, a profiling tool that you will learn how to install and use in this chapter.

## PHP Best Practices

Recently I've seen many great applications miss the mark in speed by not applying some of the basic best practices you're going to learn in this chapter. Some of these techniques have been tried and tested, and have withstood the test of time for years. So, yes, I'm surprised when they are not applied.

To get a better understanding as to how long one of the best practices has been around, Rasmus Lerdof (yes, the creator of PHP) to this day includes a complete section on using the PHP function require instead of require_once, which he initially covered in 2004, within his PHP optimization talks. Yet to this day, very few applications implement it. But you're in luck because we're going to cover it.

---

■ **Tip** For a list of PHP related performance notes, please see `http://talks.php.net/index.php/PHP`.

---

We're going to cover the following best optimization practices using PHP 5.3.2. Since PHP has gone through many performance-tuning enhancements, older versions of PHP will benefit from these coding practices.

- Using `require` vs. `require_once`

- Calculating the length of a `for` loop in advance

- Comparing looping `for` vs. `foreach` vs. `while` to access array elements

- Accessing files using `file_get_contents`

There are other optimization techniques, such as using a comma instead of a period to concatenate strings, as shown in Listing 3–1, or using double quotes instead of a single quote when the string contains a variable, as shown in Listing 3–2. But the performance gains to these are extremely minimal, so we will cover them briefly here only as an example.

***Listing 3–1.*** *Using a Comma to Concatenate a String*

```php
<?php
echo "Hi "."there. "."how are "."you?";   //Slow
echo "Hi ","there. ","how are ","you?";   //Faster…slightly
```

***Listing 3–2.*** *Using Double Quotes When a String Contains a Variable*

```php
<?php
$name = "Snoopy Padilla";
echo 'Hi there, '.$name; //Slower
echo "Hi there, $name"; //Faster..slightly
```

Once again, these options should not be the primary focus when optimizing your PHP code.

Focusing on our PHP performance roadmap, PHP best practices are the initial module within our PHP layer, as shown in Figure 3–1.

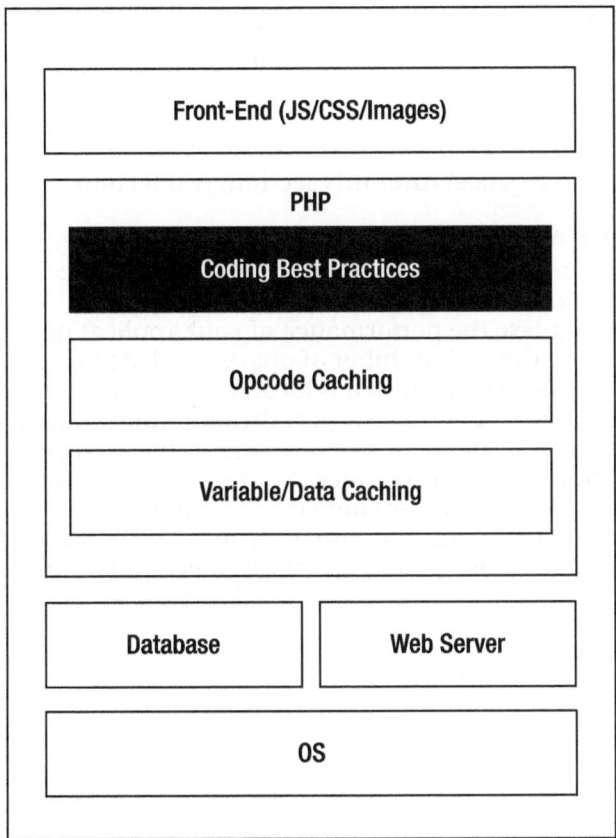

**Figure 3–1.** *PHP performance roadmap*

The PHP layer contains other modules such as variable/data caching and Opcode caching, which we'll cover in other chapters, but we will focus on the small changes we can make to our PHP code in this chapter.

Before we begin, you need to learn about the PHP economy and the trade-off between the cost of calling a function and its response time.

## The PHP Economy

Depending on your PHP script, you may have many calls to internal PHP functions, customized functions, and even instantiating and calling methods within objects. Within the PHP economy, each of these function calls incur a cost, where some function calls are more expensive to call and execute than others. When the script is ready for use in a production setting, you're in essence ready to pay off your cost with the "currency," response time.

The higher the cost incurred (many function calls), the higher your response time will be. In a nutshell, the more function calls you make, the slower your application will be.

## require vs. require_once

The age-old question, to use require or require_once? After this section, you'll know which one to use based on its performance.

require and require_once are both PHP functions that allow developers to import external PHP files for use within a specific script. Depending on the complexity of the application, you could make a single or several require_once/require calls. By using require instead of require_once, you can increase the performance of your application.

require is faster than require_once due to the high number of operational stat calls made when importing the PHP script. If the file you requested is located within the directory /var/shared/htdocs/myapp/models/MyModels/ClassA.php, the operating system will make a stat call within each of the directories before it reaches ClassA.php. In this example, that is a total of six stat calls. While require also issues stat calls, they are fewer in number. So, the fewer function calls there are, the faster your code becomes.

We're going to use the code shown in Listing 3–3 to compare both approaches. Listing 3–3 uses four files that are required and imported using the require_once PHP function.

***Listing 3–3.*** *Base that Loads Four External Class Files*

```php
<?php
require_once("ClassA.php");
require_once("ClassB.php");
require_once("ClassC.php");
require_once("ClassD.php");

echo "Only testing require_once.";
```

The required classes are shown in Listing 3–4 and contain no additional functionality other than declaring themselves.

***Listing 3–4.*** *Classes A–D*

```php
<?php
class A
{
}

class B
{
}

class C
{
}

class D
```

```
{
}
```

Each of the empty classes helps us simulate a PHP script that requires additional external PHP files to use within the main script. By excluding any additional function calls, we focus on the loading of the files using `require_once()`.

Place each of the classes into separate files, `ClassA.php`, `ClassB.php`, `ClassC.php`, `ClassD.php`, and save the files next to the code shown in Listing 3–3. Restart your web server, and using the ab tool covered in Chapter 1, run the ab command shown in Listing 3–5.

***Listing 3–5.** ab Command to Test `require_once` and `require` Functions*

```
ab -c 10 -n 100000 localhost/index.php
```

The ab command shown in Listing 3–5 simulates 100,000 requests with five concurrent requests at a single time. Once the command terminates, you should see results similar to those shown in Figure 3–2.

```
Concurrency Level:      10
Time taken for tests:   9.938 seconds
Complete requests:      1000
Failed requests:        0
Write errors:           0
Total transferred:      217000 bytes
HTML transferred:       29000 bytes
Requests per second:    100.63 [#/sec] (mean)
Time per request:       99.375 [ms] (mean)
Time per request:       9.938 [ms] (mean, across all concurrent requests)
Transfer rate:          21.32 [Kbytes/sec] received

Connection Times (ms)
              min  mean[+/-sd] median   max
Connect:        0     9   8.5      16     47
Processing:    16    89  20.6      94    266
Waiting:        0    60  28.1      63    266
Total:         16    98  21.5      94    266

Percentage of the requests served within a certain time (ms)
  50%     94
  66%     94
  75%    109
  80%    109
  90%    109
  95%    125
  98%    172
  99%    203
 100%    266 (longest request)
```

***Figure 3–2.** ab -n 100000 localhost/index.php results*

Using `require_once()` along with the ab command, we see the resulting data indicates a response time of 99ms. Our results also indicate that the script can support 100.63 requests/second.

Let's now change the require_once() function calls to require(), as shown in Listing 3–6. Restart the web server, and re-run the ab command shown in Listing 3–5. Your results should look similar to Listing 3–6.

**Listing 3–6.** *Optimized Code Using require*

```php
<?php
require("ClassA.php");
require("ClassB.php");
require("ClassC.php");
require("ClassD.php");

echo "Only testing require_once.";
```

Referring to the new results shown in Figure 3–3, we have an increase in the number of requests per second, from 100.63 to 105.44. The results also indicate that our code decreased the response time, from the initial 99.37ms to 94.84ms, a decrease of 5ms.

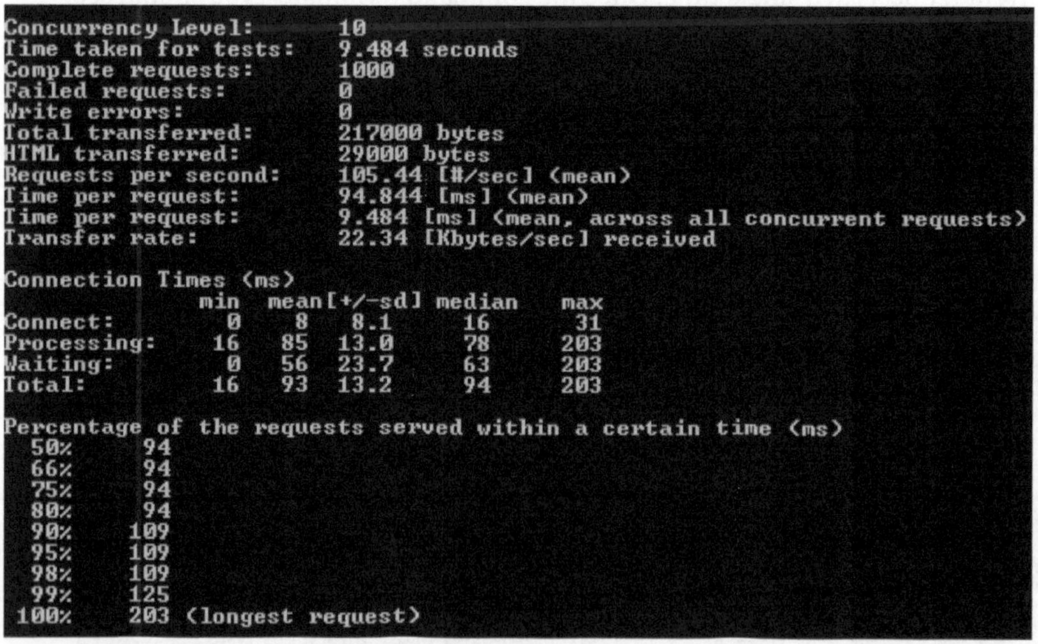

**Figure 3–3.** *ab results using require function*

## Calculating Loop Length in Advance

Calculating the length of the loop before we arrive at the loop is another optimization technique we can use.

The code shown in Listing 3–7 is a simple for loop that will loop through the array, $items, and calculate a numerical value ten times. To identify where we can optimize, and in this case make fewer function calls, you need to analyze what the code is doing step-by-step.

***Listing 3–7.*** *Un-optimized for Loop*

```php
<?php
$items = array(1,2,3,4,5,6,7,8,9,10);
for($i=0; $i<count($items); $i++)
{
    $x = 10031981 * $i;
}
```

Using the code shown in Listing 3–7 and focusing on the for loop logic, PHP executes the for loop in the following way:

1. Initialize $i to 0, start our loop at index 0, check the length of the array using count(), increment $i by 1.

2. Once iteration 0 is complete, start at index 1, check the length of the array using count(), increment $i by 1.

3. Once iteration 1 is complete, start at index 2, check the length of the array using count(), increment $i by 1.

The code continues until we reach the end of the elements within the array. The problem lies when the iteration begins anew. The function call, count(), must be called to determine the length of the array each time the iteration begins on a new index. In the code shown in Listing 3–7, count() is called ten times, nine times too many. These are unnecessary calls that can be replaced with a single call to count() before we reach the for loop. The updated, optimized code is shown in Listing 3–8.

***Listing 3–8.*** *Optimized for Loop*

```php
<?php
$items = array(1,2,3,4,5,6,7,8,9,10);
$count = count($items);

for($i=0; $i<$count; $i++)
{
    $x = 10031981 * $i;
}
```

In Listing 3–8, the code produces the same outcome as Listing 3–7, yet the number of function calls made is reduced from ten to one. The fewer calls made, the faster your PHP script becomes.

Using the PHP function microtime(), we can determine exactly how much faster using nine fewer count() function calls is. Using the code shown in Listing 3–7, we add an additional for loop to execute the code 100,000 times, which represents 100,000 users requesting the PHP script. The changes introduced to the code shown in Listing 3–7 are shown in bold in Listing 3–9.

*Listing 3–9. Un-optimized for Loop Benchmarking–Ready Code*

```php
<?php
$items = array(1,2,3,4,5,6,7,8,9,10);

$start = microtime();
for($x=0; $x<100000; $x++){

    for($i=0; $i<count($items); $i++)
    {
        $j = 100381*$i;
    }

}
echo microtime()-$start;
```

After executing the code ten times and taking the average of the results, the total time to execute the for loop 100,000 times was 0.046ms.

Restart your web server and now test the code shown in Listing 3–10, which contains the optimized for loop.

*Listing 3–10. Optimized for Loop Benchmarking–Ready Code*

```php
<?php
$items = array(1,2,3,4,5,6,7,8,9,10);
$count = count($items);

$start = microtime();
for($x=0; $x<100000; $x++){

    for($i=0; $i<$count; $i++)
    {
        $j = 100381*$items[$i];
    }

}
echo microtime()-$start;
```

Again we're going to run the code ten times to fetch the average. Using this code, we see our average execution time of the for loop is .0095ms, a change of .036ms. The optimized code is faster by .036ms.

# Accessing Array Elements Using foreach vs. for vs. while

The method in which we access data from an array can be optimized by using a foreach loop instead of either a while or for loop. Optimizing how we access data is important due to the number of web applications that pull data from a database or an XML file and must loop through each record to display data to the user. To demonstrate the optimization, we will use the code shown in Listing 3–11.

***Listing 3–11.*** *Using foreach on Code Shown in Listing 3–8*

```php
<?php
$items = array_fill(0, 100000, '12345678910');

$start = microtime();
reset($items);
foreach($items as $item)
{
    $x = $item;
}
echo microtime()-$start;
```

Listing 3–11 creates an array, $items, containing 100,000 elements, with each element containing a 155-byte string representing your typical data from a database. The code then sets the start time and uses a foreach loop to access each element within the array, and finally we display the time, in milliseconds. The code shown in Listing 3–11 is executed ten consecutive times, and after calculating the average of each execution time, the result is 0.0078ms.

Using Listing 3–11 as our foundation, we need to modify the code to use a while loop instead of a foreach loop. The code shown in boldface in Listing 3–12 indicates our modifications to accomplish this.

***Listing 3–12.*** *Using while Loop in Listing 3–11 Code*

```php
<?php
$items = array_fill(0, 100000, '12345678910');

$start = microtime();
reset($items);
$i=0;
while($i<100000)
{
    $x = $items[$i];
    $i++;
}
echo microtime()-$start;
```

Once again, after restarting our web server and running the code ten times, we calculate the average execution time. Using a while loop to access individual elements of the array on average took .0099ms.

Our final loop comparison is the for loop. Using the code shown in Listing 3–13, we follow the same process in benchmarking the loop by restarting our web server, executing the code ten times, and taking the average results.

**Listing 3–13.** *Using a for Loop in Listing 3–11*

```php
<?php
$items = array_fill(0, 100000, '12345678910');

$start = microtime();
reset($items);
for($i=0; $i<100000; $i++)
{
    $j = $items[$i];
}
echo microtime()-$start;
```

The results for all three loop benchmarks are shown in Table 3–1. Using the results shown in the table, accessing array elements using a foreach loop proves to be the best approach.

**Table 3–1.** *PHP Loop Average Execution Times for 100,000-Element Array*

| Loop Type | Average Execution Time |
|-----------|------------------------|
| foreach   | .0078ms                |
| while     | .0099ms                |
| for       | .0105ms                |

## File Access

PHP contains four methods to fetch data from a file: fread(), file_get_contents(), file(), and readfile(). file_get_contents(), readfile(), and fread() return data as a string, while file() returns the data within the file as an array, where each line within the file is an element in the array. Though all four can read the file contents, only file_get_contents places the file in memory for faster read/write access, called memory mapping. Using memory mapping, file_get_contents boosts its performance when reading small files on systems that support it.

We will compare both methods, fread() as well as file_get_contents(), on two scenarios, returning data as a string on a small 3.9KB file, and then returning the data from a large 2.3MB file (Listing 3–14).

***Listing 3–14.*** *Fetching Content from a 3.9KB File Using fread( )—Accessing 100000 Times*

```php
<?php
$fileToFetch = "<YOUR_3.9KB_FILE_STORED_LOCALLY>";

//Access the file 100000 times
$start = microtime();

for($i=0; $i<100000; $i++)
{
    $fileContent = file_get_contents($fileToFetch);
}

$end = microtime()-$start;
echo $end.'ms<br>';
```

Listing 3–14 sets the variable $fileToFetch to a small file we are using for this test containing 3.9KB of data stored locally. Replace the <YOUR_3.9KB_FILE_STORED_LOCALLY> to the path of your locally stored file if you plan to run the code yourself. The code sets our start time using microtime( ) and uses a for loop to run the code, which uses file_get_contents( ) to access the file and read its content 100,000 times. Finally we calculate the execution time and display it on screen.

Once the PHP code is done executing ten times, we calculate the average execution using each run's result. Using file_get_contents had an average execution time of 0.3730ms.

Let's now modify the code shown in Listing 3–14 to use fopen as well as fread( ) to access and read the data from the same 3.9KB file. The updated code is shown in Listing 3–15.

***Listing 3–15.*** *Fetching Content from a 3.9KB File Using file_get_contents( )—Accessing 100,000 Times*

```php
<?php
$fileToFetch = "<YOUR_3.9KB_FILE_STORED_LOCALLY>";

//Access the file 100000 times
$start = microtime();

for($i=0; $i<100000; $i++)
{

    $fileHandler = fopen($fileToFetch, 'r');
    $fileContent = fread($fileHandler, filesize($fileToFetch));

}

$end = microtime()-$start;
echo $end.'ms<br>';
```

The code shown in boldface contains two lines that use the fopen() method to create a read file handler, which is then used by the next line in the method fread(). Running this code ten times and calculating its average execution time results in an execution time of 0.1108ms. Comparing fread() with file_get_contents(), using fread() to read data is .2622ms faster or a 70 percent performance improvement.

Comparing the same functions on a large 2.3MB file using the codes shown in Listings 3–16 and 3–17, we see that file_get_contents has the better performance, with an average execution time of 0.012ms, while fread() has an average execution time of 0.019ms. It is a small benefit, but every bit counts. Table 3–2 compares the average execution times of the four methods.

***Listing 3–16.*** *Fetching Content from a 2.3MB File—Accessing Only Once*

```php
<?php
$fileToFetch = "<YOUR_2.3MB_FILE_STORED_LOCALLY>";

$start = microtime();

$fileHandler = fopen($fileToFetch, 'r');
$fileContent = fread($fileHandler, filesize($fileToFetch));


$end = microtime()-$start;
echo $end.'ms<br>';
```

***Listing 3–17.*** *Fetching Content from a 2.3MB File—Accessing Only Once*

```php
<?php
$fileToFetch = "<YOUR_2.3MB_FILE_STORED_LOCALLY>";

$start = microtime();

$fileContent = file_get_contents($fileToFetch);

$end = microtime()-$start;
echo $end.'ms<br>';
```

***Table 3–2.*** *Average Execution Time Results for Different File Types*

| File Read Type | Average Execution Time | Type of File |
|---|---|---|
| file_get_contents() | 0.3730ms | Small |
| fread() | 0.1108ms | Small |
| file_get_contents() | 0.012ms | Large |
| fread() | 0.019ms | Large |

# Faster Access to Object Properties

This is one of the few topics in this chapter that I was reluctant to write about because it goes against proper object-oriented coding practice, encapsulation. Since the performance gain can reach up to 100 percent, I will let you decide whether to implement it.

With PHP 5.0 and above, you were given the ability to use classes, and as you created complicated objects using a class, you also created class properties, such as the code shown in Listing 3–18.

*Listing 3–18. Benchmarking Person Class Using Encapsulation*

```php
<?php
class Person
{
    private $_gender = NULL;
    private $_age = NULL;

    public function getGender()
    {
        return $this->_gender;
    }

    public function getAge()
    {
        return $this->_age;
    }

    public function setGender($gender)
    {
        $this->_gender = $gender;
    }

    public function setAge($age)
    {
        $this->_age = $age;
    }

}

$personObj = new Person();

$start = microtime();
for($i=0; $i<100000; $i++)
{
    $personObj->getGender();
}
echo microtime()-$start.'ms';
```

As Listing 3–18 demonstrates, the class, Person, contains the class properties, age as well as gender. It also contains two methods, an accessor and a mutator (getter and setter). This class design incorporates encapsulation when we create the methods and set the properties to private. The code also contains our test. The code runs a for loop 100,000 times to instantiate a Person object and access the gender property using its accessor, getGender().

Running the code shown in Listing 3–18 ten times produces the average execution time of 0.0443ms. Let's remove encapsulation now and retest using the code shown in Listing 3–19.

*Listing 3–19. Benchmarking Person Class While Accessing Class Property Directly*

```php
<?php
class Person
{

    public $_gender = NULL;
    public $_age = NULL;

}

$personObj = new Person();

$start = microtime();
for($i=0; $i<100000; $i++)
{
    //Average: 0.0205617ms
    $personObj->_gender;
}

echo microtime()-$start.'ms';
```

The average execution time for the code shown in Listing 3–19 is 0.0205ms, 0.0238ms faster or a 53 percent performance improvement without using encapsulation.

Benchmarking code while applying different functions is a good way to test which function works best for you. The only downside is we still have yet to know why one function is faster than another. To gain this insight, we need to look into the Opcode and analyze what functions are executing and how many operations have been called. To accomplish this, we introduce VLD and strace.

# Looking Under the Hood Using VLD, strace, and Xdebug

You're now at the "learn how to fish" stage. In this section, we look at the Opcode each PHP script is compiled down to before it is executed by your web server. It is the operations within the Opcode that each function in your PHP script is translated into in order for your system to properly execute the script—operations such as ECHO, CONCAT, ADD_VAR, ASSIGN, just to name a few. In the next chapter, we will go into detail on how PHP becomes Opcode, but for now, let's just focus on analyzing it. Using the Vulcan Logic Dumper (a.k.a Disassembler), we will analyze different functions' behavior at the system level.

## Reviewing Opcode Functions with VLD

Written by Derick Rethans and available only for Unix-based systems, VLD is a plug-in for the Zend Engine that displays all Opcodes a script uses when executed. VLD allows us to look under the hood as to what each function is doing and which system calls it's making, and most importantly it allows us to compare what may seem like a similar PHP function on the surface, lighter vs. heavier function calls.

### Installing VLD

Many of the tools covered in this chapter will require you to have PECL installed. If you haven't installed PECL yet, install it—it will save you time and effort in setting up your tools. If you have PECL, let's install the beta version of the tool, vld-0.10.1 as of this writing, by executing the PECL command shown in Listing 3–20.

*Listing 3–20. Installing VLD Using PECL*

```
pecl install channel://pecl.php.net/vld-0.10.1
```

Once VLD is installed, you'll need to add the vld.so file to your php.ini file using the string extension=vld.so. Open your php.ini file, add in the string, and save the changes.

To become accustomed to the tool, we're going use the simple optimization technique we briefly touched on in the beginning of this chapter, using a ',' instead of a '.' when concatenating a string. We will compare the system calls made between the code shown in Listing 3–21 and Listing 3–22, where both code snippets use echo to print identical strings using not-so-identical concatenation values.

*Listing 3–21. Echo Using "."*

```
<?php
echo "Hello"." "."World!";
```

*Listing 3–22. Echo Using ","*

```
<?php
echo "Hello"," ","World!";
```

Save the code shown in Listing 3–21 to a file, echo1.php, and save the code shown in Listing 3–22 to a file named echo2.php. Run VLD using the following commands inside a shell-terminal:

```
php -dvld.active=1 echo1.php
php -dvld.active=1 echo2.php
```

You should see outputs similar to those shown in Figure 3–4 as well as Figure 3–5 after executing each of the commands.

```
function name:  (null)
number of ops:  5
compiled vars:  none
line    # *  op                                  fetch        ext  return  operands
-------------------------------------------------------------------------------------
   2    0  >  EXT_STMT
        1     CONCAT                                                ~0    'Hello', '+'
        2     CONCAT                                                ~1    ~0, 'World%21'
        3     ECHO                                                  ~1
   3    4  >  RETURN                                                 1

branch: #  0; line:     2-   3; sop:     0; eop:    4
path #1: 0,
```

*Figure 3–4. echo1.php VLD output*

Figure 3–4 contains information about the Opcode executed each time the PHP script shown in Listing 3–21 runs. The output contains the number of ops (operations) performed, output of all variables set (compiled vars), and a table containing the line number within your PHP code where the operation was executed, the number of times the operation was executed (#), and the name of the operation executed (op).

By referencing the output provided by VLD, we focus on a number of key items, number of ops, as well as the execution sequence. The number of ops specifies the total number of operations executed at the Opcode level while running. In this example, the total number of operations executed is five. Moving down the results and referencing the table, we can see the complete list of system-level functions executed. To echo "Hello World!" took two CONCAT (concatenation calls) and one ECHO call. Let's now review the VLD output for the code that uses commas to concatenate the string. The output is shown in Figure 3–5.

```
function name:  (null)
number of ops:  5
compiled vars:  none
line    # *  op                                  fetch        ext  return  operands
-------------------------------------------------------------------------------------
   2    0  >  EXT_STMT
        1     ECHO                                                        'Hello'
        2     ECHO                                                        '+'
        3     ECHO                                                        'World%21'
   3    4  >  RETURN                                                       1

branch: #  0; line:     2-   3; sop:     0; eop:    4
path #1: 0,
```

*Figure 3–5. echo2.php VLD output—using commas to concatenate string*

Referring to the number of ops in Figure 3–5, we see the same number of operation calls as Figure 3–4. The difference is the use of only ECHO operations instead of CONCAT operations. Figure 3–5 contains only ECHO calls that are less expensive than CONCAT calls.

VLD can be used to dump the Opcode of your PHP script regardless of how large or small your script is. Using the code shown in Listing 3–11, the Opcode generated is shown in Figure 3–6.

```
filename:        /var/www/foreach_test.php
function name:   (null)
number of ops:   20
compiled vars:   !0 = $items, !1 = $start, !2 = $item, !3 = $x
line    # *  op                          fetch      ext  return  operands
- - - - - - - - - - - - - - - - - - - - - - - - - - - - - - - - - - - - - - - - -
  2     0  >  SEND_VAL                                           0
        1     SEND_VAL                                           100000
        2     SEND_VAL                                           '12345678910'
        3     DO_FCALL                               3           'array_fill'
        4     ASSIGN                                             !0, $0
  5     5     DO_FCALL                               0           'microtime'
        6     ASSIGN                                             !1, $2
  7     7     SEND_REF                                           !0
        8     DO_FCALL                               1           'reset'
  8     9  >  FE_RESET                                    $5      !0, ->15
       10  > > FE_FETCH                                   $6      $5, ->15
       11  >  ZEND_OP_DATA
       12     ASSIGN                                             !2, $6
 10    13     ASSIGN                                             !3, !2
 11    14  >  JMP                                                ->10
       15  >  SWITCH_FREE                                        $5
 14    16     DO_FCALL                               0           'microtime'
       17     SUB                                        ~10     $9, !1
       18     ECHO                                               ~10
 15    19  >  RETURN                                             1
```

*Figure 3–6. Opcode for PHP code shown in Listing 3–11*

## Using strace for C-level Tracing

Another tool we will use is `strace`. `strace` allows you to trace the C-level functions called during an Apache request, including PHP-level processes.

To test the tool, you're going to use one of the sample optimization techniques already covered, using `require` instead of `require_once` or `include_once`. In the following section, you'll learn how to install `strace` on your system.

### Installing strace

One of the requirements to use `strace` is a Unix-based system and having the rights to restart Apache at your whim. I will assume you already have a development Apache installation, so we're going to install `strace` now. You have three options to install `strace`:

- Downloading the source from
  `http://sourceforge.net/projects/strace` and building the files
  directly on your system

- Installing using apt-get: `apt-get install strace`

- Installing using yum: `yum install strace`

Using the second and third options is recommended for its easy installation process. Once you have strace installed, let's hook strace to Apache. You must start Apache by executing this command:

```
apache2clt -X -k [restart OR start].
```

This will start Apache in the debug mode, as well as start Apache using a single process instead of creating children.

Once Apache has started, you will need to bind strace to the Apache process by locating the Apache process ID. To do this, open a shell window and execute this command:

```
ps auxw | grep www-data
```

Finally, using the following command, you can bind strace to Apache. Once these steps are done, keep the terminal window open and visible. While running the next steps, the window will display a steady stream of strace output while a HTTP request is satisfied by Apache.

```
strace -p <processeID>
```

To get accustomed to using strace, load the URL http://<your dev environment running strace>/<code with require_once_usage>.php. You should see output similar to that shown in Figure 3–7.

```
getcwd("/var/www", 4096)                = 9
lstat("/var/www/./ClassA.php", {st_mode=S_IFREG|0644, st_size=24, ...}) = 0
lstat("/var/www/ClassA.php", {st_mode=S_IFREG|0644, st_size=24, ...}) = 0
open("/var/www/ClassA.php", O_RDONLY)   = 10
fstat(10, {st_mode=S_IFREG|0644, st_size=24, ...}) = 0
fstat(10, {st_mode=S_IFREG|0644, st_size=24, ...}) = 0
fstat(10, {st_mode=S_IFREG|0644, st_size=24, ...}) = 0
mmap(NULL, 24, PROT_READ, MAP_SHARED, 10, 0) = 0x7f8de40b4000
munmap(0x7f8de40b4000, 24)              = 0
close(10)                               = 0
getcwd("/var/www", 4096)                = 9
lstat("/var/www/./ClassB.php", {st_mode=S_IFREG|0644, st_size=24, ...}) = 0
lstat("/var/www/ClassB.php", {st_mode=S_IFREG|0644, st_size=24, ...}) = 0
open("/var/www/ClassB.php", O_RDONLY)   = 10
```

*Figure 3–7. Snippet of strace output for require_once usage*

The snippet shown in Figure 3–7 outlines the C-level operations made by our PHP script. Focusing on a single require_once method call, we identify the lines 2, 3, 4 shown in Figure 3–7. These lines highlight the C-level operations executed to satisfy a require_once call. The two lstat calls import ClassA.php into your PHP file.

Now load the URL containing the code shown in Listing 3–6: `http://<your dev environment running strace>/<code with require_usage>.php`. Once again you should see a response similar to that shown in Figure 3–8.

```
getcwd("/var/www", 4096)                = 9
lstat("/var/www/./ClassA.php", {st_mode=S_IFREG|0644, st_size=24, ...}) = 0
open("/var/www/ClassA.php", O_RDONLY)   = 10
fstat(10, {st_mode=S_IFREG|0644, st_size=24, ...}) = 0
fstat(10, {st_mode=S_IFREG|0644, st_size=24, ...}) = 0
fstat(10, {st_mode=S_IFREG|0644, st_size=24, ...}) = 0
mmap(NULL, 24, PROT_READ, MAP_SHARED, 10, 0) = 0x7f8de4135000
munmap(0x7f8de4135000, 24)              = 0
close(10)                               = 0
getcwd("/var/www", 4096)                = 9
lstat("/var/www/./ClassB.php", {st_mode=S_IFREG|0644, st_size=24, ...}) = 0
open("/var/www/ClassB.php", O_RDONLY)   = 10
fstat(10, {st_mode=S_IFREG|0644, st_size=24, ...}) = 0
fstat(10, {st_mode=S_IFREG|0644, st_size=24, ...}) = 0
fstat(10, {st_mode=S_IFREG|0644, st_size=24, ...}) = 0
mmap(NULL, 24, PROT_READ, MAP_SHARED, 10, 0) = 0x7f8de4135000
```

***Figure 3–8.*** *Snippet of* strace *output for require usage*

Figure 3–8 contains a snippet of the C-level operations made to include ClassA.php, and like Figure 3–7, much of the output is identical with the exception of one missing lstat operation. Based on the strace output, the additional lstat call for /var/www/ClassA.php will not be called there by speeding up the inclusion of the file and increasing performance to your PHP script.

# Identifying Bottlenecks

Bottlenecks should be one of the key concerns when writing code. They are layers within your application that take up the most resources in both time and processing relative to the rest of your application. More than often, web applications tend to have their bottlenecks within the database connection layer, connecting to web services, or I/O functions such as opening XML files stored locally. In this section, we will use a tool that helps us identify these bottlenecks within our code.

## Xdebug 2: PHP Debugging Tool

Xdebug is a debugger and profiler tool for PHP. Along with additional debugging information, Xdebug provides developers additional information such as the following:

- Memory consumption of your PHP script

- Total number of calls made to a function

- Total time spent within the function

- Complete stack trace for a function

Now let's install the tool, run it on a number of examples, and spot bottlenecks within our code.

## Installing Xdebug

There are two methods of installing Xdebug on your system—using PECL or building from the source. I will cover the PECL method of installing the tool since it is the much faster approach and the one with fewer pitfalls. To continue you will need PHP 5.0 and above and PECL installed. With both items installed, run the command shown in Listing 3–23.

*Listing 3–23. Installing Xdebug Using PECL*

```
pecl install xdebug
```

Once you install Xdebug, you need a way to allow PHP to profile your script each time it runs. There are two methods to do this.

- Updating the php.ini file

- Adding the declaration at the beginning of the PHP script

We will cover both—the first for users with complete access to their PHP environment, and the latter for users who do not have access to the php.ini file.

## Updating the PHP.ini File

To automatically run Xdebug, you'll need to turn on the extension. Open the php.ini file and add the property zend_extension_ts, shown in Listing 3–24. The text contains the absolute path to the Xdebug thread-safe extension file required to load.

*Listing 3–24. Installing the Xdebug Extension*

```
[PHP_Xdebug]
zend_extension_ts="FULL PATH TO php_xdebug file"
```

Additionally, you will also need to specify five Xdebug specific properties described in Table 3–3 within your php.ini file before using Xdebug.

*Table 3–3. Xdebug Properties*

| Xdebug Property | Description |
| --- | --- |
| `xdebug.profiler_enabled` | Turns on (1) or off (0) the profiler. |
| `xdebug.profiler_output_dir` | Directory to place cachegrind files. Default set to /tmp. |
| `xdebug.profiler_append` | Overwrite files (1) when new request is made on PHP script. By default this setting is turned off (0). |
| `xdebug.profiler_output_name` | File name used. |
| `xdebug.profiler_enable_trigger` | Enable profiler to start using a GET/POST or COOKIE variable, XDEBUG_PROFILE. `Xdebug.profiler_enable` must be set to 0. |

Copy the data shown in Listing 3–24 and Listing 3–25 into your `PHP.ini` file and restart your web server.

*Listing 3–25. `PHP.ini` Properties*

```
xdebug.profiler_enable = 1
xdebug.profiler_enable_trigger = 1
xdebug.profiler_output_dir="ABSOLUTE PATH TO XDEBUG LOGS DIRECTORY"
xdebug.profiler_append=On
xdebug.profiler_output_name = "cachegrind"
```

## Validating Installation

Once your environment is set up, check if the extension is installed by creating a `phpinfo()` file. If the extension was successfully installed, you should see the Xdebug information shown in Figure 3–9.

*Figure 3–9. phpinfo print-out with Xdebug installed*

## Running Our First Profiler

You won't get a sense of how powerful Xdebug is until you apply it to some PHP code. We're going to profile a small snippet of code to become familiar with the process of running Xdebug, as well as analyze some of its output (Listing 3–26).

***Listing 3–26.*** *Example PHP Code*

```php
<?php
function bar($items)
    {
        for($i=0; $i<count($items); $i++)
        {
            if(isInt($items[$i]))
            {
                echo 10*20*$items[$i];
            }
        }
    }

function isInt($value)
{
    if(is_int($value))
    {
        return true;
    }
    else
    {
        return false;
    }
}


$ints  = array(1,2,"E",4,5,6,"T",8,9,"o");
$ints2 = array(0,1,2,3,4,5,6,7,8,9);

bar($ints);
bar($ints2);

echo "Done!";
```

The code shown in Listing 3–26 contains two functions, bar() and isInt(). The function bar() accepts an array as a parameter, checks if the value is an integer by calling the isInt() function, and if the value is an int, we multiply the value with 10 and 20. We do this 20 times, which is also the total number of elements contained within the arrays, $ints and $ints2.

Run the foregoing code with the Xdebug settings turned on, and then check the directory used within the xdebug.profiler_output_dir property. You should have a single file present.

Open the file you see in the directory. You will see a file similar to that shown in Listing 3–27. The files are cachegrind output files, and as you can tell, they seem a bit cryptic. We need a tool that takes the output file and gives us legible information.

**Listing 3–27.** *Example of the Xdebug Profiling Output File*

```
version: 0.9.6
cmd: C:\Program Files\Apache Software Foundation\Apache2.2\htdocs\index.php
part: 1

events: Time

fl=php:internal
fn=php::count
4 1

fl=php:internal
fn=php::is_int
15 1

fl=C:\Program Files\Apache Software Foundation\Apache2.2\htdocs\index.php
fn=isInt
6 110
cfn=php::is_int
calls=1 0 0
15 1
…
```

# Installing the GUI-Based Tool

As a stand-alone tool, Xdebug is great as a debugger but requires an additional tool to be a potent profiling tool. There are two versions of the GUI-based tool—a Windows version, WinCacheGrind, and a Linux (KDE) KDECacheGrind, which can also be installed on Windows using Cygwin.

Unlike KDECacheGrind, WinCacheGrind contains a limited number of features and contains a few bugs. Also, WinCacheGrind lacks the graphs that help us visualize how each function call is made and the amount of time spent in each call.

## Installing WinCacheGrind

Installing the Windows version, WinCacheGrid, is easy to do. Download the executable file at Sourceforge, from http://sourceforge.net/projects/wincachegrind/. Once the download is completed, double-click the executable file and you're ready to load the files.

## Installing KCacheGrind

For Linux users using KDE, download the tar.gz file from http://kcachegrind.sourceforge.net/html/Download.html. Once it's downloaded, un-package the content into a directory of your choosing and run the commands shown in Listing 3–28.

**Listing 3–28.** *KCacheGrind Installation Commands*

```
./configure
make
make install OR sudo make install
```

You're done.

## Analyzing Data

With the cachegrind file created while running the code in Listing 3–27, open the file using one of the tools—WinCacheGrind or KCacheGrind. I will be using WinCacheGrind.

Based on the information provided by the cachegrind output file, the total time taken to process the PHP script was 4.4ms and the PHP script made 64 total function calls.

The first view we will look at contains the function calls made (Figure 3–10), the average time spent within the function, the cumulated average time, the total time within the function, total cumulated time, and the total number of times the function was called.

| Function | Avg. Self | Avg. Cum. | Total Self | Total Cum. | Calls |
|---|---|---|---|---|---|
| (main) | 0.2ms | 4.6ms | 0.2ms | 4.6ms | 1 |
| bar | 1.6ms | 2.2ms | 3.2ms | 4.4ms | 2 |
| isInt | · | · | 1.2ms | 1.2ms | 20 |
| php::count | · | · | · | · | 22 |
| php::is_int | · | · | · | · | 20 |

**Figure 3–10.** *Function profile information for Listing 3–26*

Figure 3–10 contains five total function calls that also include our root, or top-level main function, which invokes the other functions. Based on the information collected, the count() function is called 22 times, isInt() 20 times, and is_int 20 times. Based on these figures, we can quickly identify the functions that contain a high frequency of calls. Another bit of information we could find using this view is the total time a function took to complete. In this example, the php::count() function had the highest frequency of calls.

With the WinCacheGrind tool still open, click the php::is_int function. You should see the window view shown in Figure 3–11. The window contains the time spent within the function, the accumulated time, the callee, the file that called the function, and finally the stack trace.

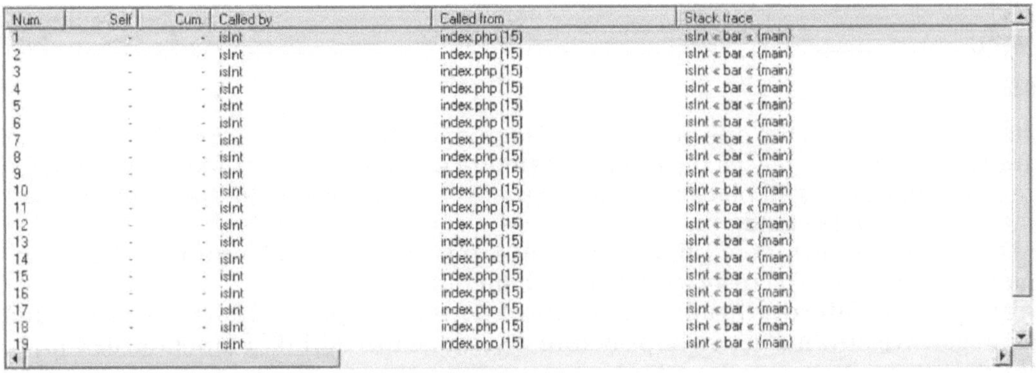

| Num. | Self | Cum. | Called by | Called from | Stack trace |
|---|---|---|---|---|---|
| 1 | - | - | isInt | index.php (15) | isInt « bar « {main} |
| 2 | - | - | isInt | index.php (15) | isInt « bar « {main} |
| 3 | - | - | isInt | index.php (15) | isInt « bar « {main} |
| 4 | - | - | isInt | index.php (15) | isInt « bar « {main} |
| 5 | - | - | isInt | index.php (15) | isInt « bar « {main} |
| 6 | - | - | isInt | index.php (15) | isInt « bar « {main} |
| 7 | - | - | isInt | index.php (15) | isInt « bar « {main} |
| 8 | - | - | isInt | index.php (15) | isInt « bar « {main} |
| 9 | - | - | isInt | index.php (15) | isInt « bar « {main} |
| 10 | - | - | isInt | index.php (15) | isInt « bar « {main} |
| 11 | - | - | isInt | index.php (15) | isInt « bar « {main} |
| 12 | - | - | isInt | index.php (15) | isInt « bar « {main} |
| 13 | - | - | isInt | index.php (15) | isInt « bar « {main} |
| 14 | - | - | isInt | index.php (15) | isInt « bar « {main} |
| 15 | - | - | isInt | index.php (15) | isInt « bar « {main} |
| 16 | - | - | isInt | index.php (15) | isInt « bar « {main} |
| 17 | - | - | isInt | index.php (15) | isInt « bar « {main} |
| 18 | - | - | isInt | index.php (15) | isInt « bar « {main} |
| 19 | - | - | isInt | index.php (15) | isInt « bar « {main} |

***Figure 3–11.** php::is_int function call results*

The data shown in Figure 3–11 is broken up into six columns. We're going to look at the last column, "Stack trace." Since each row represents a unique call to the function, we want to determine how the callee arrived at the function. Based on the data, the flow went from the main PHP flow, to the `bar()` function, and finally arrived at the function `isInt()`. That's a total of three hops to reach our desired function, which checks only whether the value is an integer.

Before you begin refactoring with the goal of reducing hops by consolidating functions, ask yourself if this is worth the effort. Most of the time, functions are broken up into manageable code snippets that help you accomplish a specific task. Combining functional logic will only lead to a mess—so think before you refactor.

In this case, for our example, let's refactor and re-run the script to generate a new output file. The updated code is shown in Listing 3–29.

***Listing 3–29.** Optimized Code—Consolidating Function Logic as Well as Calculating Count Before the Loop*

```
<?php
function bar($items)
{
      $count = count($items);
      for($i=0; $i<$count; $i++)
      {
         if(is_int($items[$i]))
         {
            echo 10*20*$items[$i];
         }
      }
}


$ints  = array(1,2,"E",4,5,6,"T",8,9,"o");
$ints2 = array(0,1,2,3,4,5,6,7,8,9);
```

```
bar($ints);
bar($ints2);

echo "Done!";
```

Listing 3–29 contains the optimized code that moves the function isInt() into the bar() function, as well as places the count() function outside of the for loop. Once you execute the code shown and place the resulting cachegrind output into the GUI tool, the cumulative time should stand out.

The cumulative time is now 1.9ms instead of 4.4ms, and the total number of function calls made dropped from 64 to 44, a very high reduction.

We also removed the overhead of taking three hops to simply check whether the value was an integer. We now make two hops before we invoke the is_int() function, as shown in Figure 3–12.

| Num. | Self | Cum. | Called by | Called from | Stack trace | |
|---|---|---|---|---|---|---|
| 1 | · | · | bar | index.php [7] | bar « {main} | |
| 2 | · | · | bar | index.php [7] | bar « {main} | |
| 3 | · | · | bar | index.php [7] | bar « {main} | |
| 4 | · | · | bar | index.php [7] | bar « {main} | |
| 5 | · | · | bar | index.php [7] | bar « {main} | |
| 6 | · | · | bar | index.php [7] | bar « {main} | |
| 7 | · | · | bar | index.php [7] | bar « {main} | |

*Figure 3–12. Stack trace to reach is_int function*

Xdebug can provide a great amount of insight into your PHP script and fine-tune any application to make it fly. With a few best practices under our belt, let's start to look at how we can optimize even further using cache.

# Summary

This chapter built on top of the foundation of both tools you can use to profile your PHP application, and it also looked into the current PHP best practices, which can increase the performance of your application, such as the following:

- Using require over require_once

- Calculating the length of a for loop in advance

- Using foreach instead of while and for when accessing elements within an array

- Using fread() for small file data access and file_get_contents for large files

- Accessing object properties faster

You also learned how to dig deeper using VLD to analyze the PHP Opcode, and installed and used strace to look at system calls each function makes and determine which function has a better performance. You also learned about Xdebug—how to install it and use the GUI-based tools WinCacheGrind and KDECacheGrind.

We are now going take a deep dive into Opcode—how it's generated, what it is, and how to cache it.

■ ■ ■

# Opcode Caching

Removing any unnecessary process when a request is made to a PHP script is now our goal when speeding up our PHP scripts. By removing a process that does not have to routinely execute during the PHP life cycle, we optimize our application to respond faster to any of our users' requests.

In the previous chapter, we briefly touched on Opcode by analyzing it. Within this chapter, we will take a deeper look at Opcode by reviewing each step of the PHP life cycle in detail and identifying what happens to a PHP script that is executed by the Zend engine. You will also learn about Opcode caching and how caching is used to speed up the PHP life cycle. Finally you'll learn about caching tools, such as the following:

- Alternative PHP Cache (APC)

- XCache

- eAccelerator

We will install each of the caching solutions on both Windows and Unix and provide benchmarking figures to identify the benefits of using Opcode caching. We will also spend some time reviewing each of the caching solution's settings, which will provide valuable insight as to how we can tweak settings to get even better performance from our PHP application.

## Reviewing Our Roadmap

Before continuing we need to take a high-level view of where we're at within our PHP application optimization picture. Figure 4–1 contains the map we started the book with, which shows each layer of most PHP applications today. Within this map, we have moved deeper and deeper into the modern PHP application, and now we are at the PHP Opcode caching section, identified in Figure 4–1 as the shaded region.

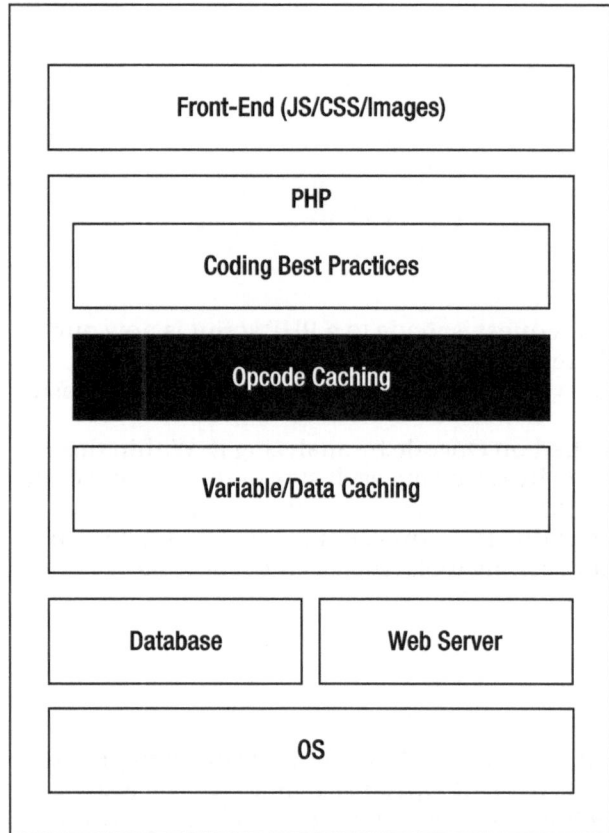

*Figure 4–1. PHP application optimization map*

Opcode is a very important component of PHP, and we need to understand how it's generated before we begin to cache it. In the previous chapter, we identified what Opcode was but not how it was generated. Let's do that now and also review the PHP life cycle in detail.

## The PHP Life Cycle

Each time a request for a PHP script is made, be it from the command line or from a web server, PHP must take the required five steps identified as boxes shown in Figure 4–2. The Zend engine must fetch the file from the file system, scan its lexicon and the expressions, parse the file, create the machine code to execute (called Opcode), and finally execute the Opcode.

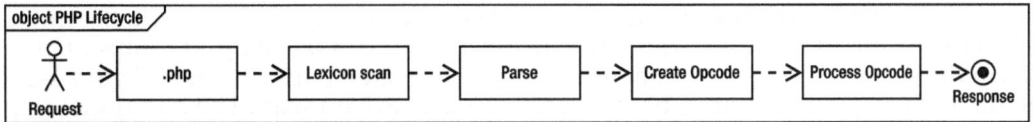

*Figure 4–2. PHP life cycle*

The PHP life cycle is extremely quick, but it must go through each step outlined in Figure 4–2 each time a request for a script is made. As each request arrives for a specific PHP script, the Zend engine must recreate the Opcode for the file, even though nothing has changed within the PHP script. This is necessary for the initial request of the script but unnecessary in subsequent requests. By implementing Opcode caching, we can remove the following three steps to reduce the PHP life cycle, thereby improving performance of our application:

1. Lexicon Scan

2. Parse

3. Create Opcode

The final, optimized PHP life cycle is shown in Figure 4–3.

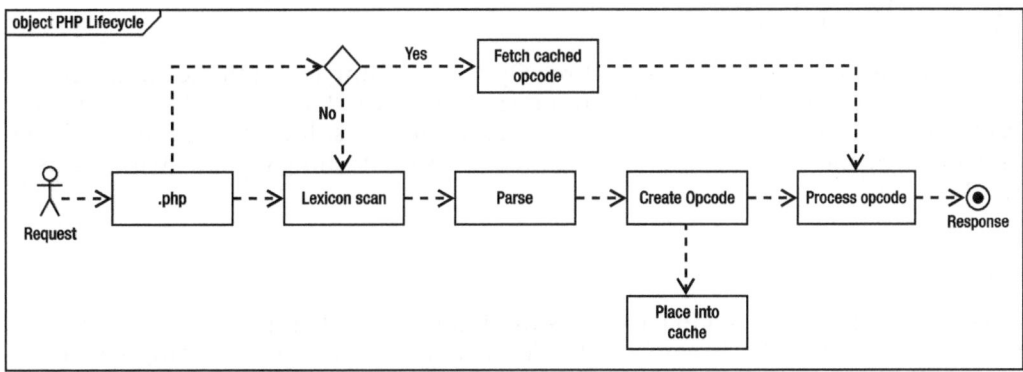

*Figure 4–3. PHP life cycle with Opcode caching*

---

■ **Note** The theory of caching shouldn't be foreign to you, but if it is, don't worry. In a nutshell, caching is the technique of placing data into shared memory to be later fetched at a much faster rate than actually fetching the data from the hard disk.

---

Figure 4–3 contains two paths a request may take when calling a PHP script: the initial path taken by the initial request to the script as well as the path taken by any subsequent requests to the script. During the initial user request, the same path shown in Figure 4–2 is taken but with an extra two steps before performing a Lexicon scan. The additional step the Zend engine performs is a check within the cache for the generated Opcode. If the Opcode was not previously generated, it continues with the Lexicon scan until it reaches the creation of the Opcode. Once the Opcode has been generated, it's placed inside the Opcode cache and then processed. This step allows any subsequent request for the PHP script to fetch the Opcode from shared memory rather than create it. In this path, the process takes two more steps before analyzing and may be a bit slower for the initial request of the PHP script.

The true benefits occur in the subsequent requests within the second path a request takes. During this path, we start at the request to the .php file, followed by a check within shared memory to determine if the Opcode has successfully been cached. Since the initial request created the Opcode and placed the Opcode in cache, the Zend engine retrieves the Opcode from cache and uses that. This allows the PHP life cycle to remove the three steps, Lexicon Scan, Parse, and Create Opcode, shown in Figure 4–3, from its steps to satisfy a user's request.

Let's now look at the caching tools available to PHP.

# Opcode Caching Tools

In the next sections, we're going to cover three Opcode caching technologies that have been used effectively in production PHP projects: Alternative PHP Cache (APC), XCache, and eAccelerator (eA). Though some of these Opcode caching solutions are not restricted to caching only Opcode, such as APC, we will focus only on caching Opcode within this chapter.

## Alternative PHP Cache

Alternative PHP Cache (APC) is a PECL extension that is available for both Unix and Windows servers. APC installs directly on the Zend engine to provide a caching system that redirects the request to the cached Opcode if it's present and has not expired. APC uses shared memory and a mapping table to fetch the Opcode for a specific PHP script.

### Installing APC

As stated before, APC is available for both Windows and Unix-based systems. At the time of this writing, the version for APC was at 3.1.3 and is available for installation using PECL. We will use PECL to install APC and recommend checking if you have PECL installed on your system before continuing. If you do not have PECL installed on your system, a complete step-by-step guide to installing PECL is provided within the appendix.

## Unix Installation

If you have PECL installed, installing APC is very easy to accomplish. On a Unix-based system, open a shell and run the command sudo pecl install apc. This will allow PECL to fetch the required packages and their dependencies from the Internet.

Once the installation is complete, you will be required to update the php.ini file that you are currently using, be it the php.ini that your web server loads or the php.ini file that your command line tool uses. Open the php.ini file and add in the line shown in Listing 4–1. This allows PHP to load the APC extension as a PHP extension, as well as set two APC settings, which we will discuss later in this section. Save the changes to the file, and restart the web server so the changes can take effect.

---

■ **Caution** While writing this book, I came across an issue while trying to install APC on Linux at this specific step. If you encounter an error similar to the following, you can try building the package from source.

```
'/tmp/pear/temp/APC/php_apc.c:959: error: duplicate 'static'
make: *** [php_apc.lo] Error 1
ERROR: `make' failed'
```

Or you can install the beta version of APC using the following command.

```
sudo pecl install apc-beta
```

---

*Listing 4–1. Loading APC Extension in PHP*

```
extension=apc.so
apc.enabled=1
apc.stat=1
```

To make sure APC was correctly installed, open up your favorite editor and create a phpinfo script, which generally looks like Listing 4–2.

*Listing 4–2. Simple phpinfo Script*

```
<?php
phpinfo();
```

If APC was correctly installed, you should see the PHP extension, APC, settings loaded within the phpinfo page, as shown in Figure 4–4.

**apc**

| APC Support | enabled |
|---|---|
| Version | 3.1.3p1 |
| MMAP Support | Enabled |
| MMAP File Mask | *no value* |
| Locking type | pthread mutex Locks |
| Revision | $Revision: 286798 $ |
| Build Date | Jul 25 2010 15:55:58 |

| Directive | Local Value | Master Value |
|---|---|---|
| apc.cache_by_default | On | On |

*Figure 4–4. APC extension displayed within phpinfo page*

## Windows Installation

Installing on a Windows-based machine is a bit trickier. For those of you not on a Windows-based machine, it's OK to skip to the next section. Windows users must find a precompiled (.dll) APC extension for their specific system. Trying to run the PECL install command will more than likely error out with the message shown in Listing 4–3.

*Listing 4–3. Windows PECL Installation Attempt*

```
running: msdev APC.dsp /MAKE "APC - Release"
ERROR: Did not understand the completion status returned from msdev.exe.
```

I have found this link to be useful: http://downloads.php.net/pierre/. It contains the .dll file you will need. For this example, I downloaded the package hp_apc-3.0.19-5.2-Win32-VC6-x86.zip and unzipped its content. Once the content was unzipped, I placed the file php_apc.dll into the PHP extensions folder. Using the default PHP directory location while installing PHP, the full location is C:\Program Files\PHP\ext. If the directory is not present, you can identify the location to the extensions directory by referring to the php.ini file's setting, extension_dir. The directory specified here is used by PHP to load any external module/extension.

Finally, open the php.ini file in use and append the lines shown in Listing 4–4 at the bottom of the file. Save the changes and restart your web server.

*Listing 4–4. Windows php.ini APC Settings*

```
extension=php_apc.dll
apc.enabled=1
apc.stat=1
```

Listing 4–4 will load the .dll file as well as set two APC settings, which we will review in greater detail later in this chapter. The extension setting must contain the full path to the .dll file if it is not present in the PHP ext directory.

To verify the installation, create a phpinfo PHP script containing the code shown in Listing 4–3 and load the page using a web browser. If APC was installed correctly, you should see an entry similar to Figure 4–4.

## Using APC

Using APC is simply a matter of creating your PHP script as you normally do and allowing users to request the script. The initial request to the script will prime the cache, meaning that when the initial request for the script is done or a change to the original PHP script has been made, the Zend engine will create the Opcode in the background and store the generated Opcode within shared memory using APC. APC works in the background of your code and contains no special functions to cache the generated Opcode (though there are functions to cache variable data, which we'll cover in Chapter 5) by the Zend engine.

Let's now run an example using the code shown in Listing 4–5 to determine the benefits of using APC within our application. The code shown in Listing 4–5 creates an array with 10,000 elements and then displays the data on the screen.

***Listing 4–5.*** *Sample Code to Test Using ab*

```php
<?php
$max = 10000;
$x = 0;
$array = array();
while($x < $max)
{

        $array[x] = $x;
        $x++;
}


foreach($array as $z)
{
    echo "$z<br/>";
}
```

We need to check on the improvement APC adds when applied to our PHP script. By taking two tests—the initial test to simulate the speed of our application while APC is turned off and a secondary test to determine the change in performance while APC is turned on—we can accomplish this. We will test this by simulating 1,000 requests with 5 concurrent requests using ab, as shown in Listing 4–6.

***Listing 4–6.*** *ab Command to Test APC*

```
ab -n 1000 -c 5 http://localhost/test.php
```

Before running the ab simulation, we need to disable APC by setting the apc.enabled setting to "0" followed by restarting the web server so the changes can take effect. Make sure that APC is off by loading the phpinfo page and verify that the APC settings are no longer present.

After executing the command five times, I took the best result, shown in Figure 4–5.

```
Concurrency Level:      5
Time taken for tests:   4.013 seconds
Complete requests:      1000
Failed requests:        0
Write errors:           0
Total transferred:      89081000 bytes
HTML transferred:       88890000 bytes
Requests per second:    249.18 [#/sec] (mean)
Time per request:       20.066 [ms] (mean)
Time per request:       4.013 [ms] (mean, across all concurrent requests)
Transfer rate:          21676.93 [Kbytes/sec] received

Connection Times (ms)
              min  mean[+/-sd] median   max
Connect:        0     0    0.1      0      2
Processing:    11    20    5.7     18     47
Waiting:        0     7    3.0      6     26
Total:         11    20    5.7     18     47
```

*Figure 4–5. ab results for Listing 4–4 while using no Opcode caching*

The result shown indicates that the web server can satisfy the simulated load within 30.06 milliseconds and can satisfy 249.18 requests per second, and on average each concurrent request was satisfied in 4.013 milliseconds. Now let's do the same with APC turned on.

Open your php.ini file once more, and update the apc.enabled setting by changing the 0 to a 1. This will enable APC. Restart the web server as well to allow your web server to load the new settings. Run the ab command once more—you should see results similar to Figure 4–6.

```
Concurrency Level:      5
Time taken for tests:   3.934 seconds
Complete requests:      1000
Failed requests:        0
Write errors:           0
Total transferred:      89081000 bytes
HTML transferred:       88890000 bytes
Requests per second:    254.20 [#/sec] (mean)
Time per request:       19.670 [ms] (mean)
Time per request:       3.934 [ms] (mean, across all concurrent requests)
Transfer rate:          22113.60 [Kbytes/sec] received

Connection Times (ms)
              min  mean[+/-sd] median   max
Connect:        0     0    0.5      0     15
Processing:    11    20    5.8     17     50
Waiting:        0     7    2.8      5     24
Total:         11    20    5.8     17     51
```

*Figure 4–6. ab results for Listing 4–4 while using Opcode caching*

The benefits of using APC should be clear. Instead of satisfying 249.18 requests per second with no Opcode caching, our web server can now satisfy 254.20 requests per second with Opcode caching. The web server response time has also decreased. With the initial figure using the default APC settings, we increased performance by a fraction. To determine if we can do better in speed, we need to look into the APC settings in depth and determine what default APC settings can be turned off or on to boost performance.

## APC Settings

APC provides developers settings that can be used to control APC from within the php.ini file. We encountered a few of these settings while setting up APC, as shown in Listing 4–1 and Listing 4–4. In each of the listings, we set the apc.enabled and apc.stat settings.

The apc.enabled setting allows us to turn off or on APC by using an integer value of 0 or 1. By default the setting is set to 1. apc.stat, on the other hand, allows APC to check for any modifications of the PHP script, which has been cached each time the script is requested, regardless of whether it's an initial request or subsequent request. This, of course, is an overhead on the caching life cycle of the Opcode, and in most cases it's a safe bet to turn apc.stat off. Keep in mind that turning this setting off will force you to restart your web server each time you make a change to a PHP script that is cached.

Additional settings are shown in Table 4–1, which contains the most widely used settings as well as their description. The complete list of settings can be found at www.php.net/apc.

*Table 4–1.* *Widely Used APC Settings*

| Setting Name | Description |
| --- | --- |
| apc.cache_by_default | Turns on caching by default. A value of 1 is used for "on" state. A value of 0 is used for "off" state. |
| apc.filters | Files to cache or not cache based on a comma-separated POSIX regular expression. A regular expression containing a + at the beginning will force APC to not cache any file matching the regular expression. A regular expression containing a – at the beginning will force APC to cache any file matching the expression. |
| apc.stat | Turns off or on APC's check of modification of the PHP script that has been requested. The process occurs each time the script is called. If the setting is set to off, any modifications made to the PHP script will require a web server restart, which will clear the cache and allow the change to reflect. A value of 0 will turn off stat. A value of 1 will turn on stat. By default the setting is set to 1. |
| apc.enabled | Turns off or on APC caching. A value of 1 will turn on APC. A value of 0 will turn off APC. By default a value of 1 is set. |
| apc.shm_size | Sets the shared memory size APC is allowed to use. Value is in megabytes. |

| Setting Name | Description |
| --- | --- |
| apc.shm_segments | Sets the total number of shared memory segments to use. |
| apc.include_once_override | Turns on or off optimization of include_once and require_once. When on, the setting will reduce the additional system calls made by these PHP internal functions. A value of 1 will turn on the setting. A value of 0 will turn off the setting. By default this setting is turned off. |
| apc.optimization | Sets the optimization level. Setting the value to 0 will turn off optimization, while setting a high value will increase optimization. |
| apc.num_files_hint | Sets the number of files you believe will need to be cached. By default 1000 is set. A value of 0 is used when unsure of the number. Setting a number close to the figure will tend to provide some performance improvements. |
| apc.ttl | Sets the expiration time in seconds for files stored in cache. When the expiration time is reached, the files meeting the expiration time will be removed from cache. |
| apc.write_lock | When turned on, forces a single process to cache a specific script. Used on heavy traffic web servers or applications that must cache many files. |

Using some of the new settings outlined in the table, we're going to tweak the original settings once again by opening the php.ini file and setting the APC settings shown in Listing 4–7.

*Listing 4–7. Example Use of Configuration Settings*

```
;APC
extension=apc.so
apc.enabled=on
apc.shm_size=16
apc.include_once_override=1
apc.write_lock=1
apc.optimization=9
apc.stat=0
apc.num_files_hint=5
```

The settings along with their values shown in Listing 4–7 turn on APC using the apc.enabled setting, set the size of the shared memory size to 16 megabytes, turn on include_once optimization, turn on write locking, set the optimization level, turn off modification time checking using apc.stat, and set the total number of files to cache to 5 using the APC setting apc.num_files_hint. Save the php.ini file, restart your web server, and verify the new settings have been set using the phpinfo page, as shown in Figure 4–7.

| Directive | Local Value | Master Value |
|---|---|---|
| apc.cache_by_default | On | On |
| apc.canonicalize | On | On |
| apc.coredump_unmap | Off | Off |
| apc.enable_cli | Off | Off |
| apc.enabled | On | On |
| apc.file_md5 | Off | Off |
| apc.file_update_protection | 2 | 2 |
| apc.filters | no value | no value |
| apc.gc_ttl | 3600 | 3600 |
| apc.include_once_override | On | On |
| apc.lazy_classes | Off | Off |
| apc.lazy_functions | Off | Off |
| apc.max_file_size | 1M | 1M |
| apc.mmap_file_mask | no value | no value |
| apc.num_files_hint | 5 | 5 |
| apc.preload_path | no value | no value |
| apc.report_autofilter | Off | Off |
| apc.rfc1867 | Off | Off |
| apc.rfc1867_freq | 0 | 0 |
| apc.rfc1867_name | APC_UPLOAD_PROGRESS | APC_UPLOAD_PROGRESS |
| apc.rfc1867_prefix | upload_ | upload_ |
| apc.rfc1867_ttl | 3600 | 3600 |
| apc.shm_segments | 1 | 1 |
| apc.shm_size | 16 | 16 |
| apc.stat | Off | Off |
| apc.stat_ctime | Off | Off |
| apc.ttl | 0 | 0 |
| apc.use_request_time | On | On |
| apc.user_entries_hint | 4096 | 4096 |
| apc.user_ttl | 0 | 0 |
| apc.write_lock | On | On |

***Figure 4–7.*** *Opimized APC settings*

## APC Admin Tool

APC makes it easy for developers to view how our APC cache is doing by providing an admin tool with information regarding the settings APC is currently running, the total size allocated for caching, the amount in use, the total number of scripts cached along with their names, and the ability to check for updates all within a nice web interface.

## Installing the Admin tool

To install the web interface, each APC installation includes an `apc.php` file. The file is the only item that is required to run the web interface and must simply be installed within the web server to access it.

If you installed APC from source or if you're on a Windows machine, you will need to download the installation package. The file is located within the package. On the other hand, if you were following along and installed from a distribution source, the file can be located using either the `find` command or the `locate` Unix command. You may also try the path `/usr/share/php/apc.php`.

Once you locate the file, copy and paste the file into your web server. This will allow you to access the PHP script from the Web using a browser by visiting the URL `http://YOUR_HOST/apc.php`, where YOUR_HOST can be either localhost or the host you're currently using for development work.

The next step will be to update the script itself by updating the `ADMIN_PASSWORD` constant variable located within the PHP script. By setting the password, you will be able to log into the web interface containing additional functionality, such as clearing the cache. Save the changes and restart your web server. Load the URL `http://YOUR_HOST/apc.php`, and you should see the web interface shown in Figure 4–8.

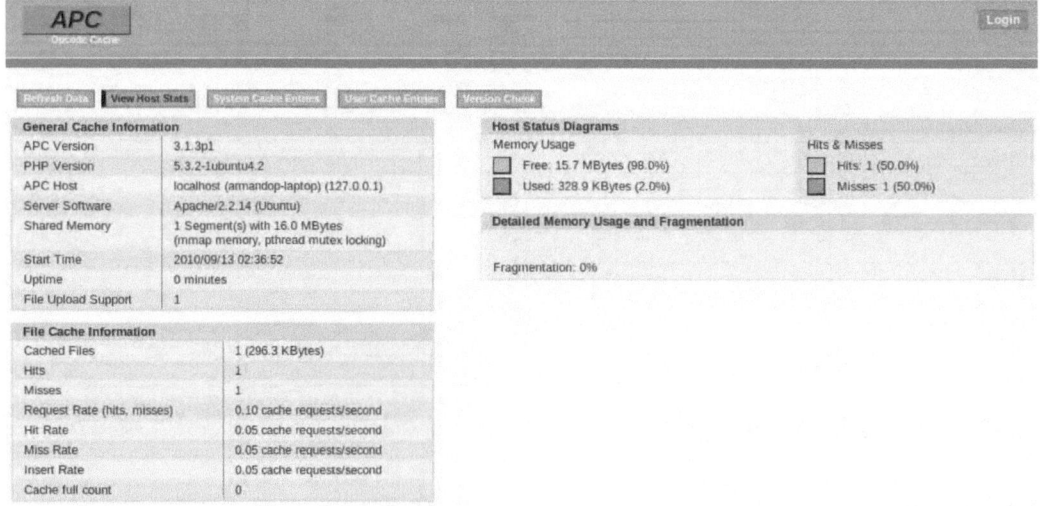

*Figure 4–8.* APC admin tool home page

The home page contains general cache information, such as the version of both APC and PHP the web server is running, the web server software name, the type of shared memory, file caching information, memory usage information, and other useful data you might need. The home page also contains five buttons on the top of the page. Each of these sub-sections provides additional information, such as which scripts have been cached, shown in Figure 4–9, user cached entries information, a check for any updated version section, and when logged in, a section to clear the Opcode cache as well as a list of pre-directory entries, which is also shown in Figure 4–9.

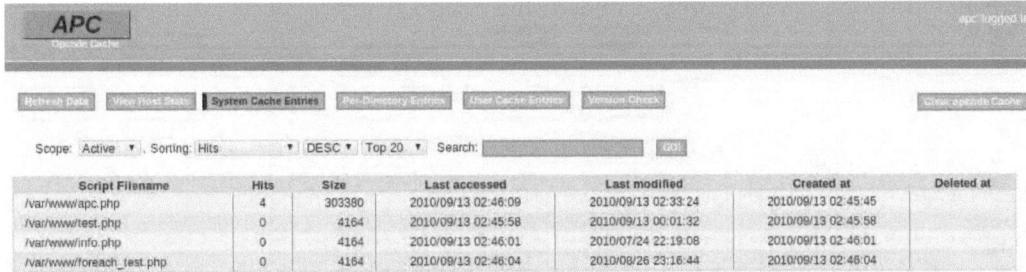

*Figure 4–9. APC admin tool while logged in and within the System Cache Entries section*

APC is a great Opcode caching tool, but it's not the only tool out there. To become good at performance, we must look at alternative tools and determine which one will work best for our requirements. The next tool we'll look at is XCache.

## XCache

XCache is another Opcode caching tool that is used by PHP. XCache, like APC, uses shared memory to store the Opcode and uses this cached Opcode to satisfy a request for a PHP script.

Like APC, XCache is also available for both Unix-based systems and Windows. As of this writing, XCache 1.2.X is the most stable release, and XCache 1.2.2 will be the version I will use to test Opcode caching as well as install.

### Unix Installation

XCache is available to download and install from any repository and is also available from the official site, `http://xcache.lighttpd.net`, when attempting to install from source. I suggest trying to install from a repository before installing from source, using one of the commands shown in Table 4–2. This will automatically download and install any dependencies your system may require.

*Table 4–2. Unix Commands to Install XCache from a Repository*

| Distribution | Command |
| --- | --- |
| Red Hat/Fedora | yum install xcache |
| Debian/Ubuntu | sudo apt-get install php5-xcache |

Once XCache has been installed, make sure to restart your web server as well as verify XCache was properly loaded using a phpinfo script. If the extension was properly installed and loaded, you should see output similar to that shown in Figure 4–10.

**XCache**

| XCache Support | enabled |
|---|---|
| Version | 1.3.0 |
| Modules Built | cacher optimizer coverager assembler encoder decoder |
| Readonly Protection | N/A |
| Cache Init Time | 2010-07-26 21:48:51 |
| Cache Instance Id | 1178 |
| Opcode Cache | enabled, 16,777,216 bytes, 1 split(s), with 8192 slots each |
| Variable Cache | disabled |
| Shared Memory Schemes | mmap |
| Coverage Auto Dumper | disabled |

*Figure 4–10. XCache extension information within phpinfo page*

## Windows Installation

Installing on a Windows system takes a few more steps compared to installing on a Unix system. You will need the compiled extension that matches both your Windows and PHP versions. Since PECL does not contain a Windows installation for XCache, we're going to look for the proper .dll file within the official XCache web site. Load the web site, http://xcache.lighttpd.net/pub/ReleaseArchive, and download the package for your specific PHP version. As an example, to install XCache using a PHP 5.3 installation, we download the latest XCache binary file, XCache-1.3.0-php-5.3.0-Win32-VC9-x86.zip.

Once the file has been successfully downloaded, unzip the package and copy the php_xcache.dll file into the ext directory. Open the php.ini file, and append the text shown in Listing 4–8 to allow PHP to load the php_xcache.dll file as a thread-safe extension.

*Listing 4–8. Windows XCache Settings*

```
[XCache]
Zend_extension_ts=php_xcache.dll
```

Restart your web server, and load the phpinfo script on your browser to make sure the extension was properly loaded. If the extension was properly installed, you should see the XCache extension settings as shown in Figure 4–10.

## Caching with XCache

Applying XCache to any PHP application is, like APC, easy. There are no functions that are required to use to create and store Opcode, and a simple request is enough to create and store the Opcode. To determine how effective XCache Opcode caching is, we're going to use the code shown in Listing 4–4, the ab command shown in Listing 4–5, and both the non-APC results as well as the APC results, Figure 4–5 and Figure 4–6 respectively.

After executing the ab command, the results are shown in Figure 4–11.

```
Concurrency Level:      5
Time taken for tests:   3.852 seconds
Complete requests:      1000
Failed requests:        0
Write errors:           0
Total transferred:      89081000 bytes
HTML transferred:       88890000 bytes
Requests per second:    259.59 [#/sec] (mean)
Time per request:       19.261 [ms] (mean)
Time per request:       3.852 [ms] (mean, across all concurrent requests)
Transfer rate:          22582.66 [Kbytes/sec] received

Connection Times (ms)
              min  mean[+/-sd] median   max
Connect:        0    0   0.3      0       9
Processing:     8   19   6.7     17      53
Waiting:        0    7   3.6      6      30
Total:          8   19   6.7     17      54
```

*Figure 4–11. ab results for Listing 4–4 using XCache*

Comparing our new result to Figure 4–5, our application under no Opcode caching, there are a full ten requests satisfied per second. We also see that the response is much faster on average.

## XCache Settings

XCache also contains a nice set of configuration settings that gives us the ability to customize XCache. The complete list of settings is shown in Table 4–3, and it is extremely important to understand each of the settings for each of the Opcode caching tools covered in this chapter because some settings could possibly speed or slow the process.

*Table 4–3. XCache Configuration Settings*

| Setting | Description |
| --- | --- |
| xcache.admin.user | (String) Admin authentication username. By default it's set to "mOo". |
| xcache.admin.pass | (String) Admin authentication password. By default it's set to "<empty string>". Should be md5(your_password). |
| xcache.admin.enable_auth | (String) Enables or disables authentication for admin site. By default it's "on." |
| xcache.test | (String) Enable or disable testing functionality. |
| xcache.coredump_dir | (String) Directory to place core dump when a crash is encountered. Must be writable by PHP. Leave empty to disable. |
| xcache.cacher | (Boolean) Enable or disable Opcode caching. Default is on. |
| xcache.size | (int) Size of shared cache to use. If using 0, caching will not be used. |
| xcache.count | (int) Number of "chunks" to split cache into. Default set to 1. |
| xcache.slots | Hash table hints. The higher the number, the faster the search within the hash table is made. The higher the value, the more memory is required. |
| xcache.ttl | (int) Time to live value for Opcode file. By leaving value as 0, it will cache indefinitely. |
| xcache.gc_interval | (Seconds) Interval garbage collection is triggered. By default it's set to 0. |
| xcache.var_size | (int) Variable size |
| xcache.var_count | (int) Variable count |
| xcache.var_slots | Variable data slot setting |
| xcache.var_ttl | (Seconds) Time to live value for variable data. By default it's set to 0. |
| xcache.var_maxttl | (Seconds) Max time to live when dealing with variables |
| xcache.var_gc_interval | (Seconds) Garbage collection time to live |
| xcache.readonly_protection | (Boolean) Used when ReadonlyProtection is turned on. Beware this slows down tool but is safer. |

| Setting | Description |
|---|---|
| xcache.mmap_path | (String) File path used for read-only protection. It will restrict two groups of PHP to share the same /tmp/cache directory. |
| xcache.optimizer | (Boolean) Enable or disable optimization. By default this setting is off. |
| xcache.coverager | (Boolean) Enables coverage data collection. When enabled it will slow down the processes. |
| xcaceh.coveragedump_directory | (String) Directory location to place data collection information. By default /tmp/pcov is used. |

## eAccelerator

The final Opcode caching tool we will look at is eAccelerator (eA), which works much like APC and XCache. eA was created by Dmitry Stogov and was originally part of the Turck MMcache project. Like APC and XCache, eA stores cached content within shared memory but also allows for a separate option to store cached data on disk.

The most stable version of the tool as of this writing is 0.9.6.1, and it will be used for the remainder of this chapter to demonstrate its installation process as well as measure performance improvements when using PHP. eA 0.9.6.1 is suitable for PHP 4 and all versions of PHP 5, and can be installed on both Windows and Unix-based systems. The full documentation as well as source can be downloaded from its official web site, www.eaccelerator.net.

We are going to install eA on both a Unix and a Windows system before diving into boosting PHP performance using this tool. If you're on a Unix system, continue reading, otherwise skip to the "Windows Installation" section.

### Unix Installation

Installing eA on a Unix system can be accomplished by executing one of the commands shown in Table 4–4 within a shell, or it can be installed by downloading and installing the source code from the official web site. In this section, I will be taking the latter approach, but feel free to install using the distribution commands as well—there is no difference.

*Table 4–4. Commands to Install eA Using Distributions*

| Distribution | Command |
|---|---|
| Red Hat/Fedora | yum install php-eaccelerator |
| Ubuntu | sudo apt-get install php5-eaccelerator |

Open a shell and run the commands shown in Listing 4–9. The commands will download the source code from the eAccelerator web site and unpack the bz2 file using tar.

*Listing 4–9. eA Download and Unpacking Commands*

```
wget http://bart.eaccelerator.net/source/0.9.6.1/eaccelerator-0.9.6.1.tar.bz2
tar xvjf eaccelerator-0.9.6.1.tar.bz2
```

Once the source code is unpacked, place the content in your preferred location and execute the commands shown in Listing 4–10 within the directory containing the source code.

*Listing 4–10. eA Installation Commands*

```
phpize
./configure
make
sudo make install
```

As soon as the command is complete, you should have two directories presented within the output, as shown in Figure 4–12. One path contains the location of the libraries installed, and the second path contains the path to the shared location. You will need these two directory locations for the next steps, if you're installing as a Zend extension.

```
-----------------------------------------------------------------
Libraries have been installed in:
   /home/armandop/Downloads/eaccelerator-0.9.6.1/modules

If you ever happen to want to link against installed libraries
in a given directory, LIBDIR, you must either use libtool, and
specify the full pathname of the library, or use the `-LLIBDIR'
flag during linking and do at least one of the following:
   - add LIBDIR to the `LD_LIBRARY_PATH' environment variable
     during execution
   - add LIBDIR to the `LD_RUN_PATH' environment variable
     during linking
   - use the `-Wl,-rpath -Wl,LIBDIR' linker flag
   - have your system administrator add LIBDIR to `/etc/ld.so.conf'

See any operating system documentation about shared libraries for
more information, such as the ld(1) and ld.so(8) manual pages.
-----------------------------------------------------------------
Installing shared extensions:     /usr/lib/php5/20090626+lfs/
```

*Figure 4–12. eA installation output*

## Creating the Cache Folder

As mentioned earlier, there are two options to store cached content. We can either store the cache within shared memory or use the disk by saving the cache within a locally stored directory. By setting the value of eaccelerator.keys to either shm_and_disk, shm_only, or disk_only, we can specify these options. Using the default value, shm_and_disk, eA will initially attempt to store cached content within shared memory, but if there is no space within shared memory, eA will place the cached content on the disk. Using the other two options, shm_only and disk_only, will force eA to use only the specified location.

We are going to use the default value, so we need a location to place the cached Opcode. By default eA will attempt to store the content within the directory, /tmp/eaccelerator. It is recommended that this location be changed and removed from the /tmp directory because the directory is cleared each time the system is rebooted. eA recommends creating a directory within the /var/ location, with the complete directory location being /var/cache/eaccelerator.

Create the directory location by running the command mkdir -p /var/cache/eaccelerator, which creates the complete directory path followed by changing the directory security rights using the command chmod 0777 /var/cache/eaccelerator.

Once the eA has been installed and a cache directory has been created, you are ready to integrate eA into PHP.

## Installing eAccelerator As a PHP Extension

There are several methods to use when installing eA. We can install eA as a PHP extension, as a zend_extension, or as a zend_extension_ts (thread safe). Within this book, we will install eA as a PHP extension.

To allow PHP to use eAccelerator, we must update the php.ini file. Locate the php.ini file you are currently using, and append the text shown in Listing 4–11.

*Listing 4–11. php.ini Settings for eA*

```
extension="eaccelerator.so"
eaccelerator.shm_size="16"
eaccelerator.cache_dir="/var/cache/eaccelerator"
eaccelerator.enable="1"
eaccelerator.optimizer="1"
eaccelerator.check_mtime="1"
eaccelerator.debug="0"
eaccelerator.filter=""
eaccelerator.shm_max="0"
eaccelerator.shm_ttl="0"
eaccelerator.shm_prune_period="0"
eaccelerator.shm_only="0"
eaccelerator.compress="1"
eaccelerator.compress_level="9"
```

Listing 4–11 contains a list of settings that need to be defined before running eA. The .so file to load along with 13 eA settings are some of the ideal settings to set, but you are not limited in setting only these. A complete list of settings along with their descriptions is shown in Table 4–5. We will go over these settings in greater detail later in this section.

## Making Sure eA Is Installed

To make sure eA was successfully installed takes two steps. The initial step is to use a phpinfo script to identify if the PHP extension was successfully installed. Once you create, save, and load the phpinfo script within a browser, you should see the eA information present within the page, as shown in Figure 4–13.

**eAccelerator**

| eAccelerator support | enabled |
| --- | --- |
| Version | 0.9.6.1 |
| Caching Enabled | true |
| Optimizer Enabled | true |
| Check mtime Enabled | true |
| Memory Size | 16,777,176 Bytes |
| Memory Available | 16,772,488 Bytes |
| Memory Allocated | 4,688 Bytes |

*Figure 4–13. eA phpinfo() settings*

The second step is to make sure the caching directory structure has been created successfully. This will test if the permission levels on the caching directory are set properly. If you have been following along, open the directory /var/cache/eaccelerator—otherwise open the cache directory you have specified within the eaccelerator.cache_dir setting within the php.ini file. If everything was set up correctly, you should see a collection of directories named 0,1,2,3,...,9. The directories shown here will contain the files created by eA when saving to disk. Let's go ahead and use eA for caching Opcode.

The next section will describe how to install eA within Windows. Skip to the next section to begin benchmarking and identifying the benefits of using eA.

## Windows Installation

The official eAccelerator web site contains an up-to-date list of web sites that provide the compiled version of many eA binaries for each version of PHP you might be running on Windows. To install eA on Windows, you need to download one of the binary files that match your installed PHP version using the URL http://eaccelerator.net/wiki/InstallFromBinary.

Click one of the links, and download the appropriate .dll file you need for your PHP version. Once the file has downloaded, place it inside the PHP extensions folder. You are not required to place the file in this location, but it's a good practice to keep all your extensions in the same location. If you installed PHP in the default location using the installation wizard from the php.net web site, the location of the extension folder will be C:\Program Files\PHP\ext. If you have a custom directory, place the file there.

### Creating the eA Directory

eA provides us with two methods of storing the cached content: storing it to shared memory or storing the content within a specific directory on the web server. Using the default behavior, we will allow eA to initially attempt to store the data within shared memory. But if there is no free space within shared memory, eA will store the content within a directory that we will create now.

Create the directory cache\eaccelerator within the location C:\Program Files\Apache Software Foundation\Apache2.2. This will allow other applications to also use the cache directory and will keep it secure by not allowing access from the Web. Once the directory has been successfully installed, you need to make changes to the php.ini file.

### Updating php.ini

Open the php.ini file your web server is using, append the eA settings shown in Listing 4–12, save the changes, and restart your web server. The settings shown in Listing 4–12 will allow PHP to load the .dll file using the zend_extension_ts key as well as set a few settings to get our eA running. The settings presented here are only suggestions and can be replaced with settings that you find useful. We will review each of the settings presented in Listing 4–12 later in this section. The complete list of eA settings available to you is shown in Table 4–5.

*Listing 4–12. php.ini eA Settings for Windows*

```
[PHP_eA]
zend_extension_ts="C:\Program Files\PHP\ext\eAccelerator0961_5.3.3_ts.dll"
eaccelerator.shm_size="16"
eaccelerator.cache_dir="C:\Program Files\Apache Software Foundation\Apache2.2\cache"
eaccelerator.enable="1"
eaccelerator.optimizer="1"
eaccelerator.check_mtime="1"
eaccelerator.debug="0"
eaccelerator.filter=""
```

```
eaccelerator.shm_max="0"
eaccelerator.shm_ttl="0"
eaccelerator.shm_prune_period="0"
eaccelerator.shm_only="0"
eaccelerator.compress="1"
eaccelerator.compress_level="9"
```

If all the settings were set correctly and the .dll file was located when restarting the web server by PHP you should see output similar to that shown in Figure 4–13 when creating and loading a phpinfo file.

With eA properly set up, let's look at the settings available to us and make a few changes to the initial setup.

## eA Settings

eA, like other Opcode caching software, contains many settings that allow you to control eA. eA allows us to set up the size of the shared memory to use and the expiration time for files stored within cache, and even allows us to cache only specific files using the filter setting, just to name a few. We encountered some of the settings while installing eA, and using the same list of settings we will focus on some of the key settings outlined in both Listing 4–7 and Listing 4–8. Along the way, we will also update our installation to increase our performance.

The initial setting we'll look at is eaccelerator.check_mtime, which allows eA to check the modified times between the cached content and its non-cached content counterpart. If the modified times do not match, eA attempts to cache the updated file. When turned on, this setting forces eA to run this check each time a request for a file is made, even if there has been no update. Of course, this is an overhead on the request due to the comparison of the modified times, so we should turn this off. The drawback when turning this setting off will be restarting eA each time there is an update to your PHP scripts.

The next setting we want to look at is the eaccelerator.filter setting. This setting helps us narrow down the type of files your eA should cache. If you wanted to cache only .phtml files, for example, you would set the value of the key to *.phtml. On the other hand, we can negate this behavior by placing a '!' before the pattern, such as !*.phtml *.php. The value allows eA to cache only files that contain the extension .php but not files with the extension .phtml.

Controlling the size of the cache as well as knowing how to treat cached content when there is no additional space available can be accomplished using the next three settings: eaccelerator.shm_max, eaccelerator.shm_ttl, and eaccelerator.shm_prune_period. eaccelerator.shm_max sets the amount of space available eA can use for caching. This setting is measured in megabytes, and when exhausted, the next two settings, eaccelerator.shm_ttl and eaccelerator.shm_prune_period, will be used.

eaccelerator.shm_ttl and eaccelerator.shm_prune_period determine which content will be removed when the shm_max size has been reached. The first setting, eaccelerator.shm_ttl, contains the last access time, in seconds. If a file is not requested after eaccelerator.shm_ttl seconds, the content will be removed from cache when there is no additional space. On the other hand, `eaccelerator.shm_prune_period` contains the length of time content should remain in cache.

There are additional settings you can use within the `php.ini` file, and they are shown in Table 4–5. The table contains the setting name, a short description of when to use the setting, as well as its default settings. I recommend you read through the table and determine which features you should turn off or on.

***Table 4–5.*** *eA Settings*

| Setting | Description | Default Value |
| --- | --- | --- |
| eaccelerator.shm_size | Sets the shared memory size. Size is in megabytes. | 0 megabytes |
| eaccelerator.cache_dir | Sets the location of the cached directory. eA places the precompiled code, session data, as well as content within this directory when disk caching is turned on. | /tmp/eaccelerator |
| eaccelerator.enable | Turns off or on eA. Using 0 turns eA off. Using 1 turns eA on. | On, 1 |
| eaccelerator.optimizer | When on may speed up code execution. The optimizer runs when the script is compiled. Use 1 to turn on optimization. Use 0 to turn off optimization. | On, 1 |
| eaccelerator.debug | Turns on logging for eA. Log messages are placed inside the file specified within the `eaccelerator.log_file` setting. Using 1 turns on logging. Using 0 turns off logging. | Off, 0 |
| eaccelerator.log_file | Specifies the location of the file that eA will use to log messages. When a log file is not specified, any log entries will be placed in stderr or within the Apache log file, if the Apache web server is used. | No value present. |
| eaccelerator.name_space | String to append to the beginning of keys generated by eA. | Web server's hostname |
| eaccelerator.check_mtime | Allows eA to check if the file has been modified since last cached each time the script is requested. | On, 1 |
| eaccelerator.filter | Specify which files to cache or not cache. Example: '*.php' will cache all files that end with a `.php` extension. To exclude patterns, use '!' in front of the pattern. | "", Cache all php files. |

| Setting | Description | Default Value |
|---|---|---|
| eaccelerator.shm_max | Sets the max size of content to place in cache. Any file that is larger than the size specified will not be cached. Size is in bytes. A value of 0 will disable max size and allow any size. | 0, Max size off. |
| eaccelerator.shm_ttl | When max space within shared memory has been reached, the file that has *not been accessed* in the time specified by this setting will be removed. Value is an integer in seconds. A value of 0 will set no expiration time. | Off, 0 |
| eaccelerator.shm_prune_period | When max space within shared memory has been reached, the file that was created shm_prune_period seconds ago will be removed. When a value of 0 is used, no cache will be removed. | Off, 0 |
| eaccelerator.shm_only | Enable or disable saving cached scripts on disk. Using a value of 0 will allow disk caching. | On, 0 |
| eaccelerator.compress | Enable or disable compression. A value of 1 will enable compression. A value of 0 will turn off compression. | On, 1 |
| eaccelerator.compress_level | Set the compression level for cache. A value of 9 will use max compression. | 9 max compression |
| eaccelerator.keys | Set the type of caching for this type of caching. Possible values are shm_and_disk (will store in both shared memory and disk), shm (shared memory storage, if available, otherwise on disk), shm_only (shared memory storage only), disk_only (disk caching only), none (no caching). | shm_and_disk |
| eaccelerator.sessions | Set the type of caching for this type of caching. Possible values are shm_and_disk (will store in both shared memory and disk), shm (shared memory storage, if available, otherwise on disk), shm_only (shared memory storage only), disk_only (disk caching only), none (no caching). | Shm_and_disk |

| Setting | Description | Default Value |
|---------|-------------|---------------|
| eaccelerator.content | Set the type of caching for this type of caching. Possible values are shm_and_disk (will store in both shared memory and disk), shm (shared memory storage, if available, otherwise on disk), shm_only (shared memory storage only), disk_only (disk caching only), none (no caching). | Shm_and_disk |
| eaccelerator.admin.name | Username used for the eA admin tool | N/A |
| eaccelerator.admin.password | Password used for the eA admin tool | N/A |

# Summary

Chapter 4 covered the PHP life cycle, which gave you an overview on how Opcode is generated. You also learned how Opcode caching can increase performance by removing three steps within the PHP life cycle during subsequent requests to the file. With the foundation established in Chapter 3 and now Chapter 4 concerning Opcode, we learned about the tools available for us in caching Opcode. We installed, benchmarked the benefits of caching Opcode, and reviewed each setting to identify which settings can be modified to boost performance with the following caching tools:

- APC
- XCache
- eAccelerator

Specifically we covered turning off file modification checks for both APC and eA due to the extra process taken when creating Opcode as well as optimization levels we can use within APC. Finally, we reviewed and installed the APC admin tool, which allows us to control and view memory consumption and PHP files that have been cached, and provides easy access to clear the Opcode cache, all within a web interface.

In the next chapter, we will look at caching content, eliminating heavy processes like connecting to a database, and fetching content for each use request.

# CHAPTER 5

■ ■ ■

# Variable Caching

Modern, rich web applications all contain some type of method that allows users to interact with the application. The most popular method these days is updating a status within your favorite social network web application. In almost all cases, these user interactions are saved within an external non-volatile storage solution, and in almost all cases, the saved content is redisplayed to users within a listing page.

Within such a request, there are countless areas to improve, from the database software that we will cover in Chapter 9, to the way we connect to the database, and to the way we handle the results of such a process. In this chapter, we focus on optimizing the fetching of content and how to reuse the results from a database query, a heavy algorithm, or any arbitrary data using cache.

We're going to cover two different caching softwares, APC and Memcached. You will learn how to install Memcached (you installed APC in Chapter 4), apply variable caching using code examples, and benchmark their impact on an application we will create. The application will utilize a MySQL database to store 10,000 records, a medium-sized record set, and our application will display these records on a page. We will also take a high-level view of where caching occurs within a request for a web application to further understand where caching comes into the picture.

## Application Performance Roadmap

We're moving away from the PHP life cycle of caching the Opcode, the logic and code of your PHP script, and moving into caching data that the user has requested. By doing so, we move deeper into our application stack to find bottlenecks that can be removed entirely or partially. Within the application stack shown in Figure 5–1, this chapter will focus on variable caching, shown in the gray box.

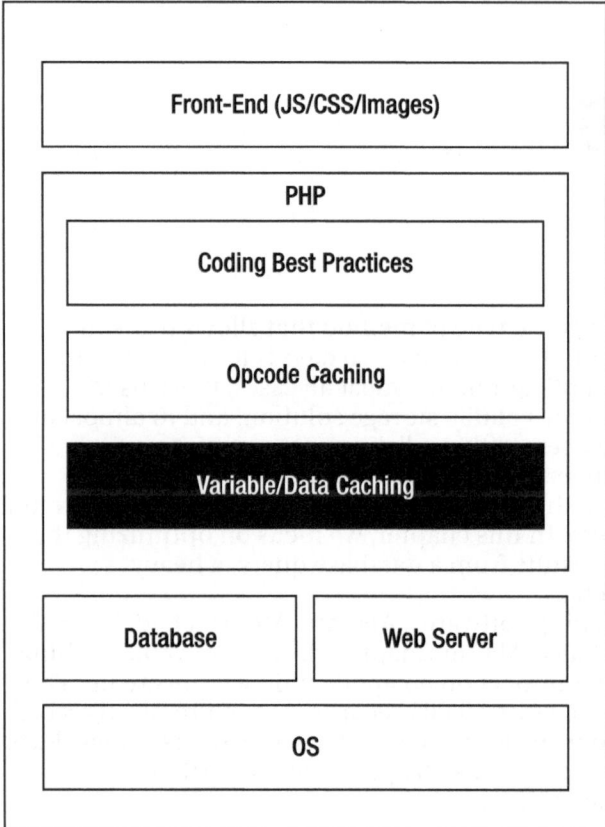

*Figure 5–1. Application stack*

Variable caching, as mentioned previously, allows us to cache arbitrary data and not PHP logic or source code, which is done by Opcode caching. Variable caching is a means to cache the results of the PHP logic within methods, database query calls, and generally any data results from a process.

## The Value of Implementing Variable Caching

The importance of variable caching can be seen at a high level by using a generic web application. Most web applications to date use some type of non-volatile storage solution in the form of a database (includes the cloud), and/or a flat file. Consequently, when fetching data from these external sources, you end up with a slower-running application (refer to "The PHP Economy" section in Chapter 3). To understand, we need to refer to Figure 5–2.

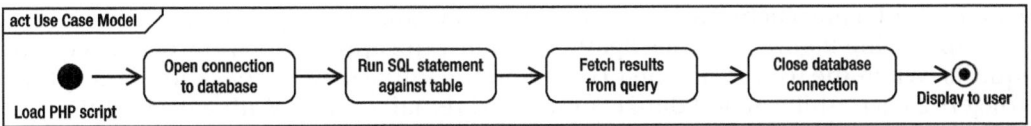

**Figure 5–2.** *Fetching data from a database without cache*

Figure 5–2 contains the typical application flow of a PHP script fetching data from a database. The figure begins by opening the connection to a database, running an arbitrary SQL statement, fetching the results found by the SQL statement, closing the connection to the database, and finally displaying the content to the user via an HTML page. In this example, there are bottlenecks in each of the steps outlined. The database software might be un-tuned to run its optimal settings, the table used by the SQL statement might not be optimized, or the database drivers might not be the most optimal—there simply are too many areas to worry about. Without cache a user encounters each of these bottlenecks when requesting the PHP script and each time a performance hit is incurred. By using cache to store the results of the SQL statement, the performance hit is negated.

PHP performance improves by using cache and by the extra steps taken on behalf of the application flow. Referring to Figure 5–3, our simple application flow now contains extra steps each request must make. There are two steps that both our initial request and subsequent requests must make. On our initial request, the application checks cache to determine if data has been stored for the database query. Because it is an initial request, there is no data to fetch from cache and a cache-miss is triggered. A cache-miss is encountered when there is no cached data found. Due to the cache-miss, the normal steps of opening a connection to the database, executing a SQL statement, fetching results from the query, etc. are taken. Within this sequence, the second new step is encountered. Once the data is fetched from the result set, the data is placed into cache for subsequent user requests to use.

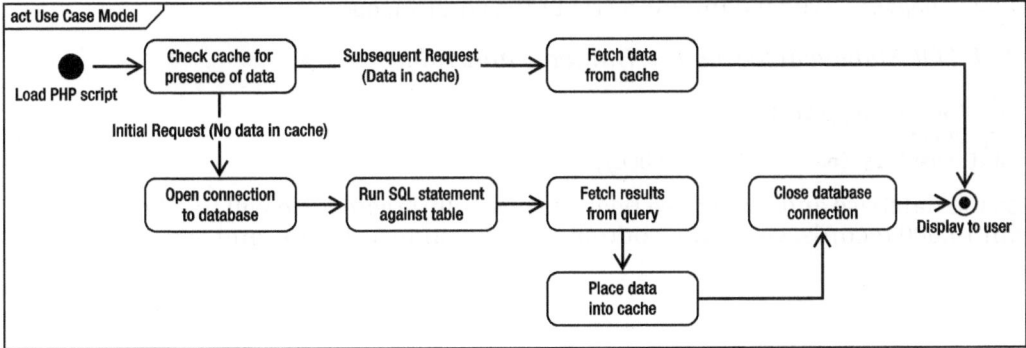

**Figure 5–3.** *Fetching data from cache*

The benefits of using cache can be seen when analyzing subsequent user requests to the PHP script. Using Figure 5–3 once again, we follow the application flow of subsequent user requests. When the user loads the PHP script, the initial step to check for data within cache triggers a cache-hit; cached data is found and remains valid. With a cache-hit triggered, a number of steps are ignored, specifically, opening the connection to the database, executing the SQL statement, fetching the data from the result set, adding the data to cache, and closing the database connection. Instead we fetch the data from shared memory, a much faster and optimal way to fetch content since there are no external drivers, network issues, and software to deal with.

This approach isn't limited to fetching data from a database exclusively. As stated before, we can apply caching to data stored in flat files, and results of a process-intensive function/method. In the next sections, we will create a small application that utilizes a database to apply the application flow outlined in Figure 5–3.

## A Sample Project: Creating the Table

To get the full effect of using cache, we're going create a small database-driven web application. The application will simply display 10,000 records stored within a database using an HTML table. By creating a very simple application, we will easily see how applying a caching solution will help with performance. We will benchmark the application while it has no database layer, followed by benchmarks with a database layer, and finally benchmark the application while using cache. Let's start by creating and prepping our database and table.

Installing a database is not the primary focus of this book, so I will not cover the topic in detail here. But instructions on how to install MySQL can be found in Appendix A. I suggest installing a database now since you will also require a database in Chapter 8. You can download the free installer from www.mysql.com. For the remainder of this example, I will use MySQL 5.1 for testing.

Using the SQL statement shown in Listing 5–1, create the database along with a single table, called chapter5, which contains a single int column, num.

*Listing 5–1. SQL Statement to Create a Database and Table*

```
CREATE DATABASE pro_php_perf;
USE pro_php_perf;
CREATE TABLE chapter5 (num int(8) NOT NULL);
```

Once the database and table have been successfully created, we will need to seed our table with 10,000 records. Using the code shown in Listing 5–2, copy and execute the code.

*Listing 5–2. PHP to Insert 10,000 Numerical Values into the Table*

```php
<?php
/**
 * Insert 10,000 random numerical values into table.
 *
 */
$username = 'YOUR_USERNAME_HERE';
$password = 'YOUR_PASSWORD_HERE';
$host     = 'YOUR_DB_HOST_HERE';
$dbName   = 'YOUR_DATABASE_NAME_HERE';

//Open connection.
$dbHandler = mysqli_connect($host, $username, $password, $dbName)
        or die('Connection error: '.mysqli_error());

//Connect to db.
mysqli_select_db($dbHandler, $dbName)
    or die ('Could not connect to db: '.mysqli_error());

//Add in 10000 records into db.
$i=0;
while($i<10000)
{
        //Generate random number
        $num = rand(1,1000000);

        //Insert into table
        $statement = "INSERT INTO chapter5 (num) VALUES ($num)";
        mysqli_query($dbHandler, $statement)
            or die ('Error executing statement: '.mysqli_error());

        ++$i;
}

//Close connection.
mysqli_close($dbHandler);
```

The code shown in Listing 5–2 sets the connection information and uses the mysqli PHP functions to open a connection to the database, insert 10,000 random numerical values using the INSERT statement, and finally close the connection. Once the code is executed, make sure the data is present within the table by running the SQL statement shown in Listing 5–3.

*Listing 5–3. SQL Statement That Counts the Number of Records in the Table*

```sql
SELECT COUNT(num) FROM chapter5;
```

If everything looks OK, continue on. If you run into any issues, make sure you have updated the connection information to match your database user settings and check for any SQL errors.

## Fetching the Records

With the seed data in the table, it's time to create the code to fetch all, yes all, 10,000 records from the table as shown in Listing 5–4. We're first going to measure the performance of the PHP code without using the database layer and only iterate though an array containing 10,000 elements. This will help us measure the cost incurred when using the database.

***Listing 5–4.** PHP Code with No Database Overhead*

```php
<?php
$records = array_fill(0, 10000, 50000);

$table = "<table border='1'><tr><td>Array Elements</td></tr>";

//Display the data.
foreach($records as $record)
{

    $table .= "<tr><td>$record</td></tr>";

}

$table .= "</table>";

echo $table;
```

Listing 5–4 contains the PHP code as well as the HTML markup to display our records but contains no database connection and fetching overhead. Instead the code creates 10,000 elements within the $records array, followed by a foreach loop that loops through the elements within the array and displays the data using an HTML table.

Our initial benchmark will analyze the code shown in Listing 5–4 and will be our baseline measurement for further results. Using the ab command shown in Listing 5–5, we will simulate a traffic load of 1000 requests with 5 concurrent requests.

***Listing 5–5.** ab Command*

```
ab -n 1000 -c 5 http://localhost/Listing5_4.php
```

Once the command has executed, you should see an ab result similar to that shown in Figure 5–4.

```
Concurrency Level:      5
Time taken for tests:   3.759 seconds
Complete requests:      1000
Failed requests:        0
Write errors:           0
Total transferred:      230265384 bytes
HTML transferred:       230074193 bytes
Requests per second:    266.06 [#/sec] (mean)
Time per request:       18.793 [ms] (mean)
Time per request:       3.759 [ms] (mean, across all concurrent requests)
Transfer rate:          59829.11 [Kbytes/sec] received

Connection Times (ms)
              min  mean[+/-sd] median   max
Connect:        0    0    0.1      0       2
Processing:     8   19    6.5     17      43
Waiting:        7   16    5.7     14      42
Total:          8   19    6.5     17      43
```

*Figure 5–4. ab results for code shown in Listing 5–2*

The results indicate the web server can satisfy 266.06 req/sec, and each request can be satisfied in 18.79ms when a database layer is not present. The results also indicate that across our concurrent requests, the request was satisfied in 3.75ms. Let's now add the database layer and benchmark.

## Calculating a Database Fetch

We will now benchmark the PHP script shown in Listing 5–6. The code shown will use a database layer to not only connect to a database but also fetch all records within the table we created, table chapter5. The code, however, will not display or create the HTML table from the result set. Instead we will continue to utilize the $records array. This will allow us to benchmark the overhead of using a database.

Update your code as shown in Listing 5–6.

*Listing 5–6. PHP Script That Fetches 10,000 Records from a Table*

```php
<?php
/**
 * Benchmark Database overhead
 *
 */
$username = 'YOUR_USERNAME_HERE';
$password = 'YOUR_PASSWORD_HERE';
$host     = 'YOUR_DB_HOST_HERE';
$dbName   = 'YOUR_DATABASE_NAME_HERE';

//Open connection.
$dbHandler = mysql_connect($host, $username, $password, $dbName)
        or die('Connection error: '.mysql_error($dbHandler));
```

```
//Connect to db.
mysql_select_db($dbName, $dbHandler)
        or die ('Could not connect to db: '.mysql_error($dbHandlder));

//Fetch the records from the Database.
$statement = "SELECT num FROM chapter5 ORDER BY num DESC";
$results   = mysql_query($statement, $dbHandler)
        or die ('Could not run SQL: '.mysql_error($dbHandler));

//Close connection.
mysql_close($dbHandler);

$records = array_fill(0, 10000, 50000);

$table = "<table border='1'><tr><td>Array Elements</td></tr>";

//Display the data.
foreach($records as $record)
{

    $table .= "<tr><td>$record</td></tr>";

}

$table .= "</table>";

echo $table;
```

Listing 5–6 begins by setting our connection information. If you're following along, change the values within these settings to your personal database settings. The code opens the database connection, creates the SQL statement to fetch all values in descending order, closes the database connection, populates the $records array with 10,000 elements, and finally invokes a foreach loop that will eventually display all the results within an HTML table. Running the ab command shown in Listing 5–5 on the updated code produces the results shown in Figure 5–5.

```
Concurrency Level:       5
Time taken for tests:    4.786 seconds
Complete requests:       1000
Failed requests:         0
Write errors:            0
Total transferred:       230249000 bytes
HTML transferred:        230058000 bytes
Requests per second:     208.96 [#/sec] (mean)
Time per request:        23.928 [ms] (mean)
Time per request:        4.786 [ms] (mean, across all concurrent requests)
Transfer rate:           46985.91 [Kbytes/sec] received

Connection Times (ms)
              min  mean[+/-sd] median   max
Connect:        0    0   0.1      0       1
Processing:    10   24   8.9     22      60
Waiting:        9   21   7.9     19      59
Total:         10   24   9.0     22      60
```

***Figure 5–5.** ab results for Listing 5–4*

The new results show a significant performance hit. The web server can support only 208.96 requests per second, and the time in which a request can be satisfied is 23.92ms. Compared to the results shown in Figure 5–4, when the database connectivity and record fetching are introduced, it reduces the requests per second by 21.46 percent, or 58 fewer requests per second and a 27.32 percent increase in the response time. What this shows is the cost associated with fetching data from an external source, in this case, a database.

Before moving on, let's now update the code to fully use the result set and use its content to display the data within an HTML table. The complete code is shown in Listing 5–7.

***Listing 5–7.** Fetching and Displaying All 10,000 Records from Database*

```php
<?php
/**
 * No Database overhead.
 *
 */
$username = 'root';
$password = 'password';
$host     = 'localhost';
$dbName   = 'pro_php_perf';

//Open connection.
$dbHandler = mysql_connect($host, $username, $password, $dbName)
        or die('Connection error: '.mysql_error($dbHandler));

//Connect to db.
mysql_select_db($dbName, $dbHandler)
        or die ('Could not connect to db: '.mysql_error($dbHandlder));

//Fetch the records from the Database.
```

```
$statement = "SELECT num FROM chapter5 ORDER BY num DESC";
$results   = mysql_query($statement, $dbHandler)
        or die ('Could not run SQL: '.mysql_error($dbHandler));

//Close connection.
mysql_close($dbHandler);

//Add to collection
$records = array();
while($record = mysql_fetch_object($results))
{

        $records[] = $record->num;

}

//Display
$table = "<table border='1'><tr><td>Array Elements</td></tr>";

foreach($records as $record)
{

        $table .= "<tr><td>$record</td></tr>";

}

$table .= "</table>";

echo $table;
```

Benchmarking the full implementation using the ab command shown in Listing 5–5, once again the results are shown in Figure 5–6.

```
Document Path:          /Chapter5/Listing_5_7.php
Document Length:        238932 bytes

Concurrency Level:      5
Time taken for tests:   13.614 seconds
Complete requests:      1000
Failed requests:        0
Write errors:           0
Total transferred:      239123000 bytes
HTML transferred:       238932000 bytes
Requests per second:    73.46 [#/sec] (mean)
Time per request:       68.067 [ms] (mean)
Time per request:       13.614 [ms] (mean, across all concurrent requests)
Transfer rate:          17153.45 [Kbytes/sec] received

Connection Times (ms)
              min  mean[+/-sd] median   max
Connect:        0    0   0.2      0       4
Processing:    26   68  23.2     66     136
Waiting:       24   62  21.5     59     123
Total:         26   68  23.2     66     136
```

***Figure 5–6.*** *ab results for Listing 5–7 code*

Adding the full logic to the sample application we'll be using reduces the total number of requests per second to 73.46, and a request is satisfied in 68.067ms. Not a very ideal set of numbers—that's a 65 percent decrease in total requests per second and a 184 percent increase to satisfy a single request. Let's go ahead and use APC to improve these numbers.

# APC Caching

In Chapter 4, we implemented APC to exclusively cache PHP Opcode. In this chapter, we will use APC to store information. To do so, we're going to focus on a subset of internal PHP APC methods shown in Table 5–1. Before we begin, make sure you have the APC PHP extension fully installed. The complete steps to install APC are shown in Chapter 4.

***Table 5–1.*** *APC Functions*

| Function | Parameters | Description |
|----------|-----------|-------------|
| apc_add() | apc_add(String key, Mixed var, int Expiration Time) | Adds content into cache using specific key if key does not already exist. |
| apc_fetch() | apc_fetch(Mixed key) | Fetches content of a specific key within cache. Returns false if key not found. |
| acp_store() | apc_store(String key, Mixed var, int Expiration Time) | Stores a value in cache using a specific key. Will replace value if key exists. |

| Function | Parameters | Description |
|----------|-----------|-------------|
| apc_exists() | apc_exists(mixed keys) | Checks if the key is present in cache. Returns true if key exists, false otherwise. |
| apc_delete() | apc_delete(String key) | Removes a specific key from cache. Returns true if successful, false otherwise. |

■ **Note** Additional APC functions can be found at www.php.net/apc.

The functions outlined in the table allow us to add data into shared memory, fetch data from shared memory using a specific key, check to determine if the key is present, and finally remove content from cache that is associated to a specific key.

## Adding Data to Cache

Using some of the functions outlined in Table 5–1, we're going to create a small page counter, shown in Listing 5–8, before applying it to our database-driven web application.

*Listing 5–8. Page Counter: Adding Content to APC Cache*

```php
<?php
/**
 * Example visitor counter using APC.
 *
 **/
if(!$counter = apc_fetch('myCounter'))
{
    $counter = 1;
    //Add the new value to memcached
    apc_add('myCounter', $counter, 120);

}
else
{

    $counter++;

    //Update the counter in cache
    apc_store('myCounter', $counter, 120);

}

echo "Your visitor number: ".$counter;
```

Using Listing 5–8 as only an example to introduce us to using APC data caching, the code contains a working page counter that keeps a running count of users visiting this PHP script within two minutes of the initial visit. The page counter begins by calling apc_fetch() to both fetch and check if the specified key, myCounter, exists within cache. If the key does not exist, the $counter variable is set equal to 1, and a new key, myCounter, is inserted into shared memory, APC cache. On the other hand, if the key is found, it simply fetches the data currently in cache, increments the value by 1, and uses apc_store() to update the data stored within the myCounter key. Finally, we present the visitor count to the user.

In this example, we also make use of the third parameter, apc_add(). By specifying an integer value of 120 seconds (2 minutes), we request the cache information to remain valid for 2 minutes. Once the data has expired, the cache key will update during a request.

Let's apply caching using APC to our sample database-driven application.

## Benchmarking APC

Using the APC functions you just learned, we are going to apply them to our database-driven application by placing the functions where our bottlenecks are within the code, connecting, and fetching data from the database. Update the code as shown in Listing 5–9.

***Listing 5–9.*** *APC Caching Applied to Listing 5–7 Code*

```php
<?php
/**
 * Listing 5.7 with APC applied.
 */
$username = 'YOUR_USERNAME_HERE';
$password = 'YOUR_PASSWORD_HERE';
$host     = 'YOUR_DB_HOST_HERE';
$dbName   = 'YOUR_DATABASE_NAME_HERE';


if(!$records = apc_fetch('orderedNumbers'))
{

        //Open connection.
        $dbHandler = mysql_connect($host, $username, $password, $dbName)
                or die('Connection error: '.mysql_error($dbHandler));

        //Connect to db.
        mysql_select_db($dbName, $dbHandler)
                or die ('Could not connect to db: '.mysql_error($dbHandlder));

        //Fetch the records from the Database.
        $statement = "SELECT num FROM chapter5 ORDER BY num DESC";
        $results   = mysql_query($statement, $dbHandler)
                or die ('Could not run SQL: '.mysql_error($dbHandler));
```

```
        //Close connection.
        mysql_close($dbHandler);

        //Place into array.
        $records = array();
        while($record = mysql_fetch_object($results))
        {

                $records[] = $record->num;

        }

        //Add to cache for 2 minutes
        apc_store('orderedNumbers', $records, 120);


}

//Display
$table = "<table border='1'><tr><td>Array Elements</td></tr>";

foreach($records as $record)
{

        $table .= "<tr><td>$record</td></tr>";

}

$table .= "</table>";

echo $table;
```

---

■ **Note** If you've been following each code example in the book, make sure you have removed the ; from your php.ini file to turn on APC and then restarted your web server.

---

The code has only minor updates shown in bold. Like the code shown in Listing 5–7, we have added the apc_add() as well as the apc_fetch() functions. Using the code, let's use ab once again and determine what APC caching offers in terms of performance. The results for our ab simulation are shown in Figure 5–7.

```
Concurrency Level:      5
Time taken for tests:   7.891 seconds
Complete requests:      1000
Failed requests:        0
Write errors:           0
Total transferred:      259047000 bytes
HTML transferred:       258856000 bytes
Requests per second:    126.73 [#/sec] (mean)
Time per request:       39.454 [ms] (mean)
Time per request:       7.891 [ms] (mean, across all concurrent requests)
Transfer rate:          32059.41 [Kbytes/sec] received

Connection Times (ms)
              min  mean[+/-sd] median   max
Connect:        0    0   0.7      0      18
Processing:    15   39  13.3     39      86
Waiting:        0   19   9.1     17      61
Total:         15   39  13.4     39      86
```

***Figure 5–7.** ab results for APC cache enabled*

Figure 5–7 displays our results for the ab run. Comparing the results shown in Figure 5–7 with those shown in Figure 5–6, we see an improvement in the number of requests the server can satisfy and a decrease in the speed in which the web server can satisfy a single request. The number of users the server can now satisfy increased by 72.51 percent, while the total time to satisfy a single request decreased by 42 percent. Using APC improved the performance of our application.

The drop in time and the increase in the number of users now supported can be attributed to a fetch from memory rather than the recurring three-step process of opening the database connection, executing the SQL statement, and fetching the data. By fetching the data, your users no longer have to execute these steps until after two minutes, in this example. To further improve the performance of our script, we can also cache the HTML that is generated, allowing the complete table to be fetched from memory.

APC is not the only tool out there that can help in caching data. Memcached is another tool that can be used.

# Memcached

Unlike other caching tools covered in this chapter and in Chapter 4, Memcached was the original caching solution for PHP. Memcached was originally developed by Brad Fitzpatrick for the web application Livejournal in 2003 and then found great backing within the open source community. It now has wide use in major web applications such as Wikipedia, Flickr, Twitter, and YouTube, just to name a few.

In the following sections, we will cover the install process, review the PHP Memcached functions, and fine-tune our setup to get the most from it.

## Installing Memcached

Memcached's stable release is currently at version 1.4.5 and can be found and downloaded from the web site www.memcached.org. There are two methods to install Memcached. You can either download the source .tgz file from the listed web site, or use a distribution port using apt-get or yum.

If you're on a system that has apt-get installed, run the command apt-get install php5-memcached.

The command will install all necessary dependencies and packages for Memcached. Restart your web server and verify PHP successfully loaded the Memcached extensions by creating a phpinfo() PHP script, and load the file using your web browser. If everything was installed correctly, you should see the Memcached PHP settings as shown in Figure 5–8.

### memcached

| memcached support | enabled |
|---|---|
| Version | 1.0.0 |
| libmemcached version | 0.31 |
| Session support | yes |
| igbinary support | no |

*Figure 5–8. Memcached info within phpinfo page*

The alternative method to install Memcached is by using the source. Download the source and execute the commands shown in Listing 5–10 within a terminal.

*Listing 5–10. Installing Memcached from Source*

```
./configure
make
make install
```

Once Memcached has been installed, restart the web server and load a phpinfo script to make sure all was installed correctly. You should see the Memcached settings as shown in Figure 5–8.

## Starting Memcached Server

Turn on Memcached by specifying the amount of memory to allocate to it as well as its port to run on. By default Memcached listens on port 11211, but you can change this behavior using the –p parameters. Execute the command /usr/bin/memcached –m 512 –p 11211 to begin Memcached.

# Using Memcached with PHP

PHP has bundled a list of Memcached methods within the PHP Memcached class. We will focus on the subset of methods listed in Table 5–2 to get you familiar with the tool. The methods shown allow you to add content to the cache, fetch content from the cache, update content within cache, flush all the content, and delete a specific item from cache.

*Table 5–2. Memcached Methods*

| Method | Parameters | Description |
| --- | --- | --- |
| Memcached::add() | add(String key, mixed Value, int Expiration Time in seconds) | Adds a new key/value into cache. Will fail if key present. |
| Memcached::get() | get(String key, Callback function, float cas_token) | Get content from cache for a specific key. Returns false if key is not present. |
| memcached::set() | set(String key, Mixed value, int Expiration Time in seconds) | Set the content for a specific key. Unlike add(), it will not fail if key is present. |
| memcached::flush() | flush(int time) | Removes all keys and content from cache. |
| memcached::delete() | delete(String key, int Time in seconds) | Removes a specific key from cache. If time is present, any attempt to add the key into cache will be ignored until time expires. |

■ **Note** The complete list of Memcached available methods can be found within the PHP documentation at www.php.net/memcached.

## Connecting to Memcached Server

Before we save data into our new Memcached server, we need to open a connection to it, much like opening a connection to a database or creating a handler to a file. Listing 5–11 contains a simple PHP 5 code example that connects to the Memcached server running locally.

*Listing 5–11. Connecting to Memcached Server*

```php
<?php
/**
 * Example visitor counter using Memcached.
 *
 **/
$memHost = 'localhost';
$memPort = 11211;

$memCached = new Memcached();
$memCached->addServer($memHost, $memPort);
```

We store the server we plan to connect to in the $memHost variable, and place the port the Memcached server is listening on in the $memPort variable. We then instantiate the Memcached class and use its method addServer() to add the localhost server into the Memcached server pool.

## Adding Data into Cache

As in the previous APC section, you're going to use the visitors counter code shown in Listing 5–8 as an introduction to using the Memcached functions. The updated visitor counter code is shown in Listing 5–12.

*Listing 5–12. Using Memcached for a Page Counter*

```php
<?php
/**
 * Example visitor counter using Memcached.
 *
 **/
$memHost = 'localhost';
$memPort = 11211;

$memCached = new Memcached();
$memCached->addServer($memHost, $memPort);

if(!$counter = $memCached->get('myCounter'))
{
    $counter = 1;
    //Add the new value to memcached
    $memCached->add('myCounter', $counter, 120);

}
else
{

    $counter++;

    //Update the counter in cache
```

```
$memCached->set('myCounter', $counter, 120);
}

echo "Your visitor number: ".$counter;
```

The logic is identical to Listing 5–8: we check if the cache has a value for myCounter using an if-else statement. If the cache does contain a value, we increment the value and store the new value into cache. Otherwise we initialize the content to store and place the value into a new key within cache.

While using Memcached, we begin by creating the Memcached object, adding a Memcached server using the method addServer(), identify if there is data within shared memory using the Memcached method get(), and if there is no data present, we initialize the data using the $counter variable and add the data into a new key, myCounter, along with the initial value of 1, using Memcached::add().

## Benchmarking Memcached

Using the code shown in Listing 5–7, we're going to benchmark the results when we apply Memcached to it. Listing 5–13 contains the updated code.

*Listing 5–13. Implementing Memcached to Listing 5–5 Code*

```php
<?php
$username = 'YOUR_USERNAME';
$password = 'YOUR_PASSWORD';
$host     = 'YOUR_HOST';
$dbName   = 'YOUR_DB';

$memHost = 'localhost';
$memPort = 11211;

$memCached = new Memcached();
$memCached->addServer($memHost, $memPort);


if(!$records = $memCached->get('myRecords'))
{
        //Open connection.

        $dbHandler = mysql_connect($host, $username, $password, $dbName)
                or die('Connection error: '.mysql_error($dbHandler));

        //Connect to db.
        mysql_select_db($dbName, $dbHandler)
                or die ('Could not connect to db: '.mysql_error($dbHandlder));

        //Fetch the records from the Database.
        $statement = "SELECT num FROM chapter5 ORDER BY num DESC";
        $results   = mysql_query($statement, $dbHandler)
                or die ('Could not run SQL: '.mysql_error($dbHandler));
```

```
        //Close connection.
        mysql_close($dbHandler);

        $records = array();
        while($record = mysql_fetch_object($results))
        {

                $records[] = $record->num;

        }

        //Add the data into Memcached
        $memCached->add('myRecords', $records, 120);
}

//Display
$table = "<table border='1'><tr><td>Array Elements</td></tr>";

foreach($records as $record)
{

        $table .= "<tr><td>$record</td></tr>";

}

$table .= "</table>";

echo $table;
```

Using the ab command shown in Listing 5–5 the results show an increase in performance when using a caching solution. Caching makes your application support more users and speeds up your script. In these new results, shown in Figure 5–9, the request per second jumped to 215.46, an increase of 193 percent from the application using no cache. The time per request also decreased from 68.06ms to 23.20ms, a 65 percent performance improvement in regards to speed.

```
Concurrency Level:      5
Time taken for tests:   4.641 seconds
Complete requests:      1000
Failed requests:        0
Write errors:           0
Total transferred:      259047000 bytes
HTML transferred:       258856000 bytes
Requests per second:    215.46 [#/sec] (mean)
Time per request:       23.206 [ms] (mean)
Time per request:       4.641 [ms] (mean, across all concurrent requests)
Transfer rate:          54505.72 [Kbytes/sec] received

Connection Times (ms)
              min  mean[+/-sd] median   max
Connect:        0    0   0.2      0       6
Processing:    10   23   7.8     22      47
Waiting:        0   11   4.9      9      37
Total:         10   23   7.8     22      47
```

***Figure 5–9.*** *ab results for Listing 5–13*

# Summary

This wraps the focus on the PHP code itself. As you'd expect from reading Chapter 2, optimization isn't just about PHP—it's about all the layers PHP runs on. To push our app to the best performance possible, we started with the tool sets to measure, followed by the client-side JavaScript and CSS optimization, and then used caching for PHP. With Chapter 4 and Chapter 5 introducing and applying a caching solution for not only our Opcode but also large sections of data that is required for our application to run, we have covered the foundation of what caching is and what it can do within our PHP application.

In Chapter 5, we focused on APC as well as Memcached. You learned the terminology behind caching, used the built-in PHP functions to store, retrieve, and clear cache from APC, installed and used Memcached, and most importantly created small experiments to test how well APC as well as Memcached increased performance. In the remaining chapters, we'll focus on the software our application runs on.

# CHAPTER 6

■■■

# Choosing the Right Web Server

Since it is the responsibility of the web server software to look for any incoming requests, delegate what the request is trying to accomplish to the PHP engine, and finally send a response, a portion of the measured speed of our PHP application is tightly coupled with the performance of your web server software. Therefore, we need to prevent the web server from slowing down our application by eliminating unnecessary processing.

This chapter will help you understand how a web server works "under the hood" and will help you to determine which of the major web server packages would be the best one to use for your application. We will look at the ever-popular Apache web server with mod_php, and examine some more recent newcomers—lighttpd as well as Nginx. We will be analyzing why each of the alternatives are beneficial to use, and how to install FastCGI PHP on each one. We will also look at few simple benchmarks for each server type, covering both static and PHP content.

Before we get too far, though, we will look at some general guidelines in selecting an appropriate web server package, along with some aspects of web servers that are common to all types, such as usage, request handling, and hardware.

But first, to get our bearings, please refer to Figure 6–1, which shows that we are now in the web server component of the application performance roadmap.

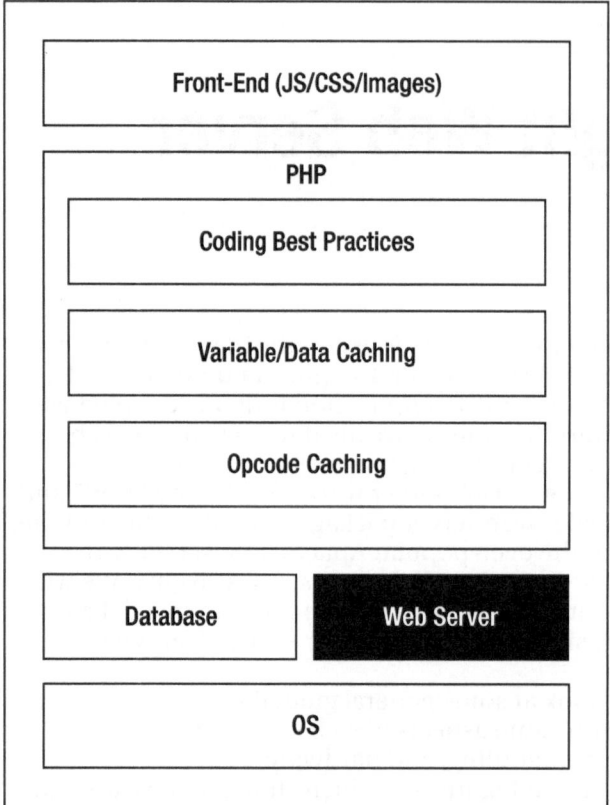

*Figure 6–1. PHP Application component stack*

This section of the application stack is important because the speed at which our web server performs will impact how slow a response to the user will be. Now, let's move on to some of the common considerations of all web servers.

# Choosing Which Web Server Package Is for You

There are no hard rules that allow you to decide which package you should use. We will, however, attempt to give you a few pointers that will help you make the choice.

## Security and Stability Are Important to You

Apache is without a doubt the most "exercised" web server package available. This popularity means that there is a continuous stream of stability and security patches being produced to track any exploit that is discovered. If you need to be able to guarantee the security of your installation and track that as new exploits are discovered, then Apache is probably the best bet.

## Availability of Engineers with Detailed Knowledge Is Important to You

Nginx and lighttpd, while mainstream, are not as well known in the community as the venerable Apache server. If you rely on being able to locate and hire engineers with guru-level web server skills, then Apache is again probably the best bet.

## Your Site Is Predominantly Static Content

If you are running a photo or video hosting site, then the enhanced static object serving performance that lighttpd or Nginx can bring to the table is probably a good reason to take a long, hard look at these newer alternatives.

## You Are Hosting in a Managed Service

Many managed hosting services are traditional in the components that they provide for hosting applications. Before committing yourself to a design that relies on servers other than Apache, check with your hoster to see if it is supported.

## You Are Using Unusual PHP Extensions

Most PHP extension writers assume that PHP will be running on Apache with mod_php. Testing of extensions under FCGI, which is the mechanism used by lighttpd and Nginx to host the PHP interpreter, is often not done. Before committing to using these alternative web server packages, check that all the PHP extensions your application requires work correctly in FCGI mode.

# Usage Figures for Web Servers

One of the factors that should be considered when choosing a web server package is its popularity. If a web server is popular, it means there are a lot of people using it, shaking out bugs, providing support services, etc. Web servers that are lower in the popularity stakes may not have the same exposure as their more popular brethren (see Table 6–1).

***Table 6–1.*** *Web Server Package Popularity (Source: Netcraft 2010)*

| Vendor | Product | Web Sites Hosted (millions) | Percent |
|--------|---------|------------------------------|---------|
| Apache | Apache | 111 | 54 |
| Microsoft | IIS | 50 | 24 |
| Igor Sysoev | Nginx | 16 | 8 |
| Google | GWS | 15 | 7 |
| lighttpd | lighttpd | 1 | 0.46 |

Before dismissing servers such as Nginx or lighttpd, you should, however, understand that because of their nature, and reputation for use as fast static asset servers, they are often used as "supporting servers" for larger domains, serving just static assets (images, .css, .js), and will not necessarily register in the Netcraft figures.

# Web Server Request Handling

Web servers have to perform a set of well-defined processes on an incoming request as specified by the HTTP specifications. In order to produce the required output, this sequence of events is known as the "Request Processing Pipeline," as it describes a sequence or pipeline of actions that need to be performed to handle a request.

Although the details of how this occurs in each web server package vary greatly, they all generally follow the same pattern.

- *Request Listener*: This component is responsible for picking up an inbound network connection from the browser, and reading the request from the socket.

- *Request Parsing*: Takes the request and parses it into a data structure that can be easily interpreted by the rest of the web server components; most web servers expose this parsed data as a "Request Object" to applications running on it. It is also responsible for decoding things such as the cookie jar and making it available as a dictionary of values.

- *Input Filter*: This component is responsible for any transformations that need to be applied to the request. If the web server is capable of performing any URL rewriting, then it is typically done at this stage.

- *URI Mapping*: This is where the URIs in the input request are mapped to physical directories and files in the web server. Any security, location, or directory options are applied at this stage.

- *Request Handling*: The web server picks up the contents of the page from the disk. It could be a cached file if the web server supports object caching.

- *Output Filter*: For dynamic languages like PHP, this is where the source of the file is transformed into the output HTML, or where compression is applied if relevant. Other output encodings such as chunking can also be applied at this point.

- *Output Transmission*: The final stage in the pipeline; oversees the transmission of the contents back to the user's web browser

Figure 6–2 shows a typical request to a hosted document.

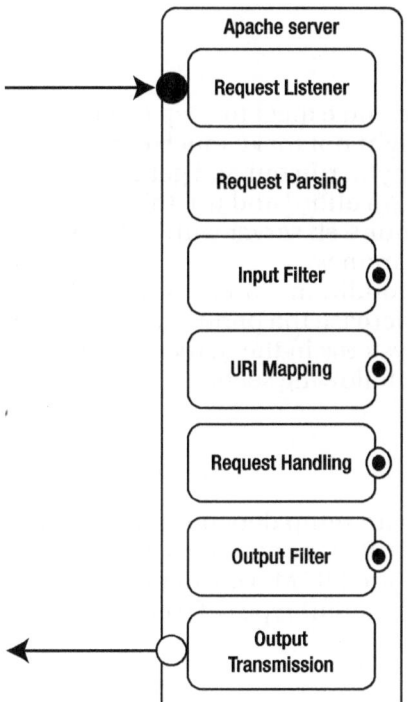

***Figure 6–2.*** *The request processing pipeline*

As the browser performs a request for a hosted document at a specific URL, the web server will listen for any incoming requests under a specific port number. When the web server encounters a request for a PHP file, it will either open a connection, if it hasn't already reached its limit, or satisfy the request with any of the current open connections. The web server will then process the request with the PHP engine, send the response, and finally close the connection once it's done. Along the process, there are other items that a web server can perform, such as logging the request within the access log writing error logs, if any, and compressing the data before it's sent to the browser.

The process described can quickly become a speed bottleneck if connections must be opened and closed numerous times or if "other" steps outlined are non-essential yet consume valuable CPU time.

Though these steps can take fractions of a second, they all add up, and it is not until these steps have completed that the user's browser receives the results. If we could speed this process up by removing some of the steps or reducing the number of times some of the steps are done, we could speed up the response and thereby increase the application speed.

## Web Server Hardware

Hardware does matter. If you have non-optimal hardware and expect to keep thousands of visitors at once satisfied, the changes in this chapter might not make much of a difference. But by the same token, I'm also not suggesting you run out and get the cream-of-the-crop hardware. What I am saying is buy what you can afford and use this book to squeeze the last bit out of the hardware. By configuring your web server with optimal settings and using your current hardware, it can save you money.

With that said, having spare RAM allows you to create additional processes to handle incoming requests, and having more than one CPU can increase the performance of your web server. Since there are different types of web server systems in the market, we are going to look into the different types of web servers in the following sections.

## Classifying Web Servers

Not all web servers are alike. As stated before, your hardware setup depends on how you will run your web server. Some web servers have multiple CPUs, containing GB of RAM, while other web servers contain a single CPU with very limited RAM. Due to these different permutations of server hardware, there are two different types of web servers worthy of further discussion:

- Prefork/Fork
- Threaded

Apache is the most well-known web server and is generally deployed as a prefork web server, although other models are available (see the "Apache Multi-processing Modules" ahead). A prefork web server allows the web server to create a separate process (fork) based off an original process. Web servers that operate as a prefork server type tend to create a pool of processes for incoming users to use. This type of web server has been recommended for single CPU servers. A complete description of each type of web server can be found in Table 6–2. This type of web server is also recommended for any application that is making use of linked libraries, such as database integration, text processing, etc., as many of these third-party extensions are not proven to be thread-safe, and could result in issues when run under heavy load.

On a single CPU, when comparing prefork to threading and to workers, there is favorable performance in the preforking server type. As the concurrency level increases, preforking remains at a constant, while the other server types increase. Once again this all depends on the type of server you are using and its configuration.

*Table 6–2.* Web Server Types

| Web Server Type | Description |
| --- | --- |
| Prefork | Process-based web server; for each incoming request, a forked process is used to satisfy the request. |
| Threaded | Thread-based web server; for each incoming request, a thread is used to satisfy the request. |

Next we'll discuss the similarities and differences of these two types of servers. Depending on the strengths of each style, your hardware and your serving need may determine which style you choose to configure Apache as.

# Apache HTTPD

The Apache web server is by far the most widely used web server for both development and production environments. The most up-to-date version of the Apache web server at the time of writing is version 2.2, and is available for Unix and Windows systems. What makes Apache appealing is the array of settings you are allowed to tweak within its configuration file. By default the configuration file contains settings that can get you off and running with your application, but when your site experiences an increase in traffic, some of these settings might not be ideal.

■ **Note** There is often some confusion about the naming used for the Apache service and the configuration files it uses. For Debian-based distributions, such as Ubuntu, the package is called "apache2," which is used in both its service name and the name of its configuration file, "apache2.conf." For Red Hat–based distributions, such as Fedora, etc., the process name is "httpd" and has a corresponding configuration file of "httpd.conf." This difference is maintained throughout, including the names of directories used for configuration, logging, etc. We will refer to "apache2" in this text, but on Red Hat–derivative systems please substitute "httpd."

There are two ways of installing Apache: from a package, or from source. We will examine how to install from packages for the two most common distribution families, Debian (SUSE, Ubuntu) or Red Hat (Red Hat, CentOS, Fedora).

Appendix A has full instructions for installing Apache as part of a full LAMP stack on windows, while Appendix B provides the same instructions for installing on Linux servers or workstations.

## Apache Daemon Command Line

We are going to briefly look over the command-line options before diving into modifying the configuration file. By using the command-line option, we can gain insight into which modules are loaded, check the web server type, and test whether the changes we will make to our configuration file are valid, among others. Table 6–3 contains the full list of command-line options available to you.

*Table 6–3. Apache 2 Command-Line Arguments*

| Argument | Description |
| --- | --- |
| -D name | Set name to use within the <IfDefine name> directives |
| -d directory | Set a ServerRoot |
| -f file | Set a ServerConfigFile |
| -C "directive" | Process directive before reading configuration files |
| -c | Process directive after reading configuration files |
| -e level | Show startup errors of loglevel "level" |
| -E file | Log startup errors to file "file" |

| Argument | Description |
|---|---|
| -v | Show version number |
| -V | Show compile settings |
| -h | Show available command-line options |
| -l | List compiled-in modules |
| -L | List available configuration directives |
| -t -D DUMP_VHOSTS | Show parsed settings, currently only VHOSTS |
| -S | A shortcut for -t -D DUMP_VHOSTS |
| -t -D DUMP_MODULES | Show loaded modules |
| -M | A shortcut for -t -D DUMP_MODULES |
| -t | Run syntax check on configuration files |

One of the reasons to know the commands is to understand what has been installed if you did not install the web server. To check the modules, run the command apache2ctl -M. You should receive a listing of all of the modules loaded in your system, i.e., core.c, prefork.c, and http_core.c. This also provides us with additional information regarding the type of web server Apache is currently configured to run as, such as prefork.

By default Apache installs the most important files within its installed directory. On a Unix system, that directory is /etc/apache2, while for Windows users, the directory is C:\Program Files\Apache Software Foundation\Apache2.2—that's if you used the default installation values.

Within this directory, you will find apache2.conf. This file contains a list of configuration settings from the directory where your files will be loaded, DocumentRoot, to the number of users your web server can support at a single moment. By making modifications to some of the settings, discussed in the following section, you can configure the web server to match your needs.

Later, in Chapter 7, we will also look at the settings that can be changed to optimize your web server to achieve higher performance.

## Apache Multi-processing Modules

Apache uses a set of multi-processing modules (MPMs) to determine what process and memory model it will use to handle each request. Requests are first placed into the request queue and then dispatched to the processes that will handle them via the MPM. Apache is shipped with a set of MPMs for different OS architectures and processing models.

Make sure your system is using the correct MPM by first identifying which modules it's loading using `apache2ctl -M` or `httpd -M`. Within the output, you should see one of the modules shown in Table 6–4.

***Table 6–4.*** *List of Available MPM Within Apache*

| Operating System | MPM |
| --- | --- |
| BeOS | BeOS |
| Netware | Mpm_netware |
| OS/2 | Mpmt_os2 |
| Unix | Prefork, Perchild, Threadpool, Worker |
| Windows | Mpm_winnt |

If your system is not running the correct module, this setting is changed during compile time using the `-with-mpm=<MPM Value>`.

The possible Unix MPMs available are as follows:

- *Prefork*: Apache pre-creates a set of child processes.

- *Perchild*: A variant of Prefork that allows setting of separate process permissions for the child processes.

- *Threadpool*: Apache uses multithreading to implement request handlers—not recommended for most Unix systems because of the lack of guaranteed thread safety.

- *Worker*: A hybrid of Prefork and Threadpool, where each child process supports multiple threads.

On Unix-based systems, there is almost a 99 percent use of the Prefork MPM, with some use of the Worker MPM in specialist applications. Any multithreaded MPM is generally not recommended because many libraries bound to Apache and the PHP interpreter are not certified to be thread-safe, and may produce erratic results when executed in a multithreaded environment. For the purposes of brevity, we will restrict discussion to the Prefork MPM.

### The Prefork MPM

Prefork is by far the most common form of MPM in general use, and is the default installed in most Unix Apache distributions. On startup Apache will create a fixed number of child processes to handle requests, will route requests to each of the child processes as required, and will grow and shrink the pool of children between defined limits as the number of requests hitting your server goes up and down.

Apache will recycle child processes in the pool up to a maximum number of requests per child, at which point it will tear down the child and spawn a new one to replace it. This mechanism is designed to stop processes that have developed memory or other corruptions from becoming permanently locked into the system. Once a child has processed its quota of requests, it dies and is reborn.

# Understanding Apache Modules

MPMs are loadable components that control how requests are dispatched and handled, and which memory/process model is used to handle the requests. Apache modules actually perform the processing of the requests. Apache has a built-in module called core_module that handles the basic function of serving static content. It is responsible for locating the object to be served on the disk, and sending it back to the client.

Apache uses a set of "hooks" at each stage that allows dynamically loaded or compiled-in modules to insert themselves into the chain of execution and add additional functionality. Figure 6–3 shows how an Apache module attaches itself to the processing pipeline and either adds or replaces components in the standard core processing. Generally Apache modules are named after their loadable file name, i.e., mod_php, mod_rewrite, or mod_deflate.

Multiple modules can be loaded and invoked in each request, each module placing itself in the correct part of the processing chain to allow it to handle the output of a previous module.

For example, mod_php, the module that converts PHP source into HTML output, can pass its output via the output filter stage to mod_deflate, the module that compresses the output using gzip compression. Each provides an output filter stage that is chained together in the correct order.

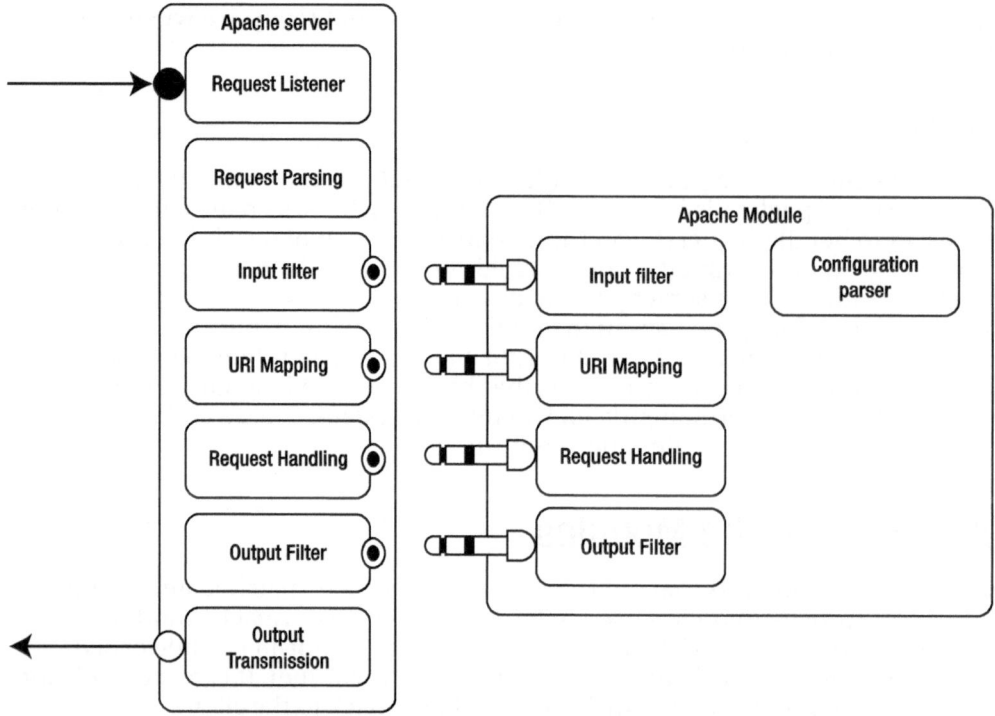

*Figure 6–3. Apache module attachment to processing pipeline*

## Adding Dynamic Apache Modules

There are several ways to enable dynamic modules, depending on how your system has deployed Apache. In general the way that a module is enabled is to add a "LoadModule" statement to your Apache configuration file. However, there are several "conventions" that can be used that make this easier, and your particular installation may have used one or the other.

### Using a conf.d Directory

Red Hat–based distributions have a directory called /etc/httpd/conf.d, which is included into the configuration file immediately after the LoadModule section. Any file with the extension .conf placed into this directory is included automatically when Apache starts. This allows you to maintain separate files in this directory that has both the "LoadModule" line and any default global directives needed to configure the module.

## Using a Module Management Helper

Debian-based distributions like Ubuntu have a mechanism that extends the example of the separate module configuration directory just described, and adds a tool for managing its contents. The directory `/etc/apache2/mods-available` contains individual configuration files for each module that is available in the distribution. A second directory, `/etc/apache/mods-enabled`, contains symlinks to the modules in `/etc/apache2/mods-available`. To enable a module, for example, `mod_rewrite`, a module for mapping URLs, you would execute the following command.

`$sudo a2enmod rewrite`

This will create the required symlinks in the `/etc/apache2/mods-enabled` directory.

# Removing Dynamic Apache Modules

While adding the correct modules to your installation of Apache is important, keeping the list of modules short and using only the modules you need to run your application is important. Once again using the `-M`, you can check which modules are installed or you can check the configuration file. Using a Windows Apache configuration, you can check the list of modules by looking for the word "LoadModule" within the file. To remove the module look for a "LoadModule" line with the name of the module you want to disable to the right, and just place a comment marker code '#' on the start of the line, so that it is not loaded any further. It's probably not a good idea to delete the line, as you may wish to restore the module at a later date, commenting it out of the file is a far safer approach. Once you're done, save the changes and restart Apache.

## Removing a Module Using a conf.d Directory

If your distribution is using a `conf.d` directory, then this makes it easy to remove a module, simply by renaming the file to something like `mod_rewite.conf.bak`, and restarting Apache.

## Removing a Module Using a Module Management Helper

On Debian (Ubuntu) distributions, use the module helper to unlink the modules configuration file.

`$sudo a2dismod rewrite`

Then restart Apache.

# Final Words on Apache

Apache is without a doubt the most comprehensive web server package available today; it has a strong following and is used extensively across the Internet to provide most of the biggest sites.

It is a good comprehensive all-rounder, with excellent support; however, that comprehensiveness comes at a price. It is not the fastest solution available. If your application does not need the flexibility and extensive support that Apache brings, then one of the other web servers we will now examine may be the one for you.

# lighttpd

lighttpd can be best summed up with the description that appears as the very first paragraph of the web site that supports its distribution (`www.lighttpd.org`): Security, speed, compliance, and flexibility—all of these describe lighttpd (pron. *lighty*), which is rapidly redefining efficiency of a web server, as it is designed and optimized for high-performance environments. With a small memory footprint compared to other web servers, effective management of the CPU load, and advanced feature set (FastCGI, SCGI, Auth, Output-Compression, URL-Rewriting, and many more), lighttpd is the perfect solution for every server that is suffering load problems.

lighttpd was originally written by Jan Kneschke as an experimental system to explore the "c10K" problem, or how to create a web service that could support 10,000 concurrent connections on a single server. Because of this, it has earned a reputation as being a fast web server for static content.

## Installing lighttpd

Installing lighttpd is done using either a package from a repository or the source code available on the web site. There are two versions of the web server; one is Unix-based and the other is a Windows binary. I will go over the process of installing the web server for each system. Skip to the section that best suits you—you will not lose any information in doing so.

### lighttpd on Unix

As previously stated, lighttpd is available for most Unix-based systems within a repository. It's currently available for Debian, Ubuntu, OpenSUSE, and others, just to name a few. The full list of repositories and the commands to install the package is shown in Table 6–5.

**Table 6–5.** *Available Repositories for lighttpd Installation*

| Repository | Command |
|---|---|
| Zypper | zypper install lighttpd |
| Aptitude | apt-get install lighttpd lighttpd-doc |
| Yum | yum install lighttpd |
| Emerge | emerge lighttpd |

I'm going to do a fresh install on my Ubuntu system by using the Aptitude repository by running the command on the second row.

By default lighttpd is installed with the following features if you install using the repository:

- IPv6
- Zlib
- Bzip2
- Crypt
- SSL
- mySQL
- Memcached
- SQLite

Furthermore you can take a close look at the web server's configuration and other settings by using the command lighttpd -V. A complete list of lighttpd commands is shown in Table 6–6; they will come in when modifying the configuration file.

The directories that you should be made aware of are the log, www, and the configuration directories. In my installation, the www, or the directory where all web applications will need to be placed, is located at /var/www. The log directory is located at /var/log/lighttpd/, and the directory that contains the web server's configuration settings is located at /etc/lighttpd/.

## lighttpd on Windows

Until recently the lighttpd version for Windows required the system to also have Cygwin installed. Most recently a binary version of the web server installation became available on the web site http://en.wlmp-project.net/downloads.php. The site has the latest stable release, 1.4.X, and it is available for Windows 2000, XP, 2003, Vista, and 2008, as well as Windows 7.

For a fast and seamless install, download the setup wizard and follow the steps shown. Once you have installed the web server, you will have a directory with the items shown in Figure 6–4.

*Figure 6–4. lighttpd directory structure*

The contents of the directory contain a number of files that are important. LightTPD.exe allows you to start the web server. The htdocs directory is the location to place your web application, the logs directory contains the error and access logs, and the conf directory contains all the available configuration options.

To start the web server, open the directory bin and double-click the Service-Install.exe file. (It's important to note that this will install a service, and thereby start lighttpd every time the operating system boots.)

The file will open a command-line prompt and run through a set of items as shown in Figure 6–5.

```
============================================================
WLMP Project ToolKit - LightTPD Service Installation Tool
============================================================

Copyright (C) 2006-2009.
WLMP Project TEAM / D-Club Soft.

- Copy Service executable to 'C:\WINDOWS\LIGHTSRC.exe'
- Install LightTPD Service
- Add Service values to Registry
- Add LightTPD to Windows Firewall

LightTPD Service installation succesfull.

Do you want to start LightTPD Service? [Y/N] Y

- Start LightTPD Service
The LightTPD service is starting.
The LightTPD service was started successfully.

Press any key to continue...
```

***Figure 6–5.** Windows install process window*

Once the process is done, press any key and open the URL `http://localhost/` to see the welcome lighttpd page shown in Figure 6–6.

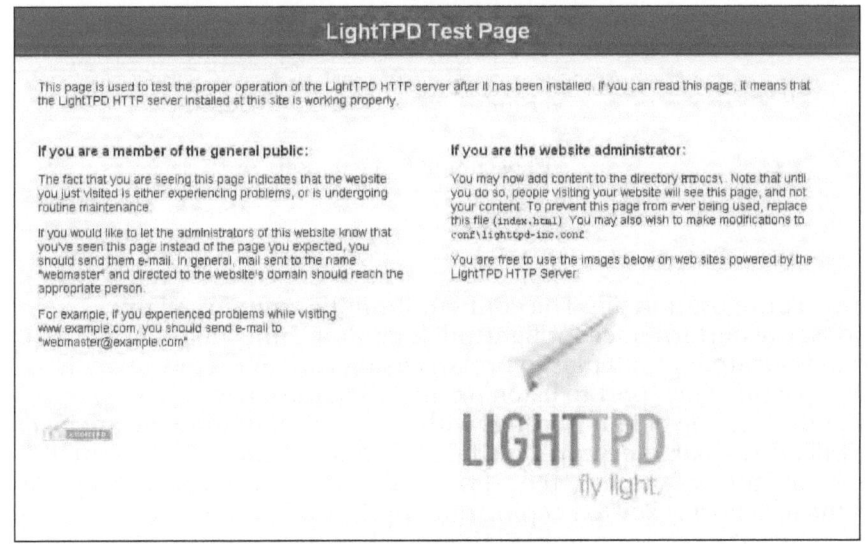

***Figure 6–6.** Windows lighttpd welcome page*

## lighttpd Configuration Settings

Because the configuration file is the primary location where we will spend much of our time in this section, we need to get familiar with it as well as the tools to test our configuration changes. You're going to learn the lighttpd command-line commands next.

Open a shell window, and type in lighttpd -h. On Windows-based systems, type in LightTPD.exe -h. This will display a list of available commands you can run. For example, to load a different configuration file, you could use the -f flag. By using the flag, you can load any configuration file located anywhere in your system. To view the version of lighttpd, you could use the -v flag. The complete list of commands is shown in Table 6–6.

*Table 6–6. Command-Line Options for lighttpd*

| Flag | Description |
| --- | --- |
| -f <name> | Full path to configuration file |
| -m <name> | Full path to module directory |
| -p | Display parsed configuration file |
| -t | Test the configuration file used with –f |
| -D | Don't go to background |
| -v | Version |
| -V | List of compile time options |
| -h | Help menu |

Let's now go over the configuration file. The configuration file contains all the available options to boost the performance for lighttpd. It contains information such as where the web directory is located, which files to process using PHP or exclude, which module to load on startup, and which port to listen on, just to name a few.

Open the configuration file. The default settings within the configuration file are just a small snapshot of the full array available. server.modules contains a comma-separated list of modules to use. By default mod_access, mod_alias, mod_accesslog, and mod_compress are installed. Keeping the list short is key to keeping our application performing optimally. The server.document-root settings contain the full path to the web directory, and server.errorlog contains the full path to the web server's error log. Some of settings that are not placed into the configuration file are server.max-connections, server.max-fds, and server-max-keep-alive-idle. Using these settings, we can set the total number of maximum connections, set the maximum number of file descriptors (file handlers), and maximum number of seconds an idle connection is dropped.

The complete list of configuration settings is shown at
http://redmine.lighttpd.net/projects/lighttpd/wiki/Docs:ConfigurationOptions.

## Comparing Static Load Content

We want to optimize our web server, so we need to know how fast it is out of the box. To do so, I'm going to run a benchmark on lighttpd, using my machine running Ubuntu with the same specifications previously mentioned at the beginning of the book. This is the same machine I've been running the other benchmarks on, making sure to restart the web server each time I run a test.

I will be running the following ab test, which simulates 1,000 requests with 500 concurrent requests at a time on both Apache and lighttpd. The goal is to select the web server that will run our application at an optimal speed.

Listing 6–1 shows the command line used to run the benchmark test.

***Listing 6–1.** ab Test Command Simulating 1,000 Connections with 500 Concurrent Requests*

```
Ab -n1000 -c 500 http://localhost/
```

The results of the simulated load on lighttpd are shown in Figure 6–7.

```
Concurrency Level:      500
Time taken for tests:   0.074 seconds
Complete requests:      1000
Failed requests:        0
Write errors:           0
Total transferred:      435000 bytes
HTML transferred:       177000 bytes
Requests per second:    13450.80 [#/sec] (mean)
Time per request:       37.172 [ms] (mean)
Time per request:       0.074 [ms] (mean, across all concurrent requests)
Transfer rate:          5713.96 [Kbytes/sec] received

Connection Times (ms)
              min  mean[+/-sd] median   max
Connect:        0     5   5.1      1      14
Processing:     6    10   4.4      8      22
Waiting:        4    10   4.6      8      22
Total:          7    15   7.2     15      29
```

***Figure 6–7.** Benchmark results on static HTML file*

Why are we testing static content? If you have a server cluster of four servers, one server (notably the lightweight server) can serve all your images and static content while the remaining three servers can share the load in server PHP content.

Now let's compare the web server running a PHP script. To do so, we need to install PHP using FastCGI.

## Installing PHP on lighttpd

Installing PHP on lighttpd is straightforward and can be accomplished using the CGI or FastCGI PHP versions. I suggest going with the FastCGI version for obvious reasons (it's in the name).

FastCGI PHP is available for both Unix and Windows, and I will go over both methods. To start we'll look at the Unix version to install. Windows users, go ahead and skip to the next section on installing FastCGI PHP in that environment. Unix users, you'll need to install the php5-cgi package available in most of the repositories. You can run the command shown in Listing 6–2 if you are using Ubuntu or Debian.

***Listing 6–2.** Installing FastCGI PHP Using Aptitude*

```
apt-get install php5-cgi
```

If the package encountered no issues, you should have a new directory within your /etc/php5 directory. Open the /etc/php5/cgi/php.ini file, append the text shown in Listing 6–3, and save the changes. This change is required to make sure that the fcgi version of PHP sets the value of php variable $_SERVER['PATH_INFO'] correctly, some applications make use of this variable and the default behavior was to replicate an old bug in early fcgi implementations.

***Listing 6–3.** Turn on FastCGI Within the php.ini File*

```
#[FastCGI PHP]
cgi.fix_pathinfo = 1
```

Now we need to configure the web server to process all files using FastCGI when it encounters files with .php extensions. Open the lighttpd.conf file located in the conf directory. In my installation, the file is located in the /etc/lighttpd/ directory. Open the file, and append the text in Listing 6–4.

***Listing 6–4.** Update to lighttpd.conf Adding FastCGI Module*

```
...
server.modules = (
        ...
        "mod_fastcgi"
)
...
```

Within the same file, append the text shown in Listing 6–5 at the end of your file.

***Listing 6–5.** fastcgi.server Settings*

```
...
fastcgi.server = (."php" => ((
        "bin-path" => "/path/to/your/php-cgi",
        "socket" => "/tmp/php.socket"

))
...
```

Listing 6–5 sets the fastcgi.server setting. The text states that all .php files should use the php-cgi binary located at the location set in the "bin-path". Save the file and restart the server.

## Verifying PHP Installation

To verify the installation was a success, create a phpinfo.php PHP file and place it inside the web-root directory. Request the file from within a browser, and if everything was successful, you should see something similar to Figure 6–8.

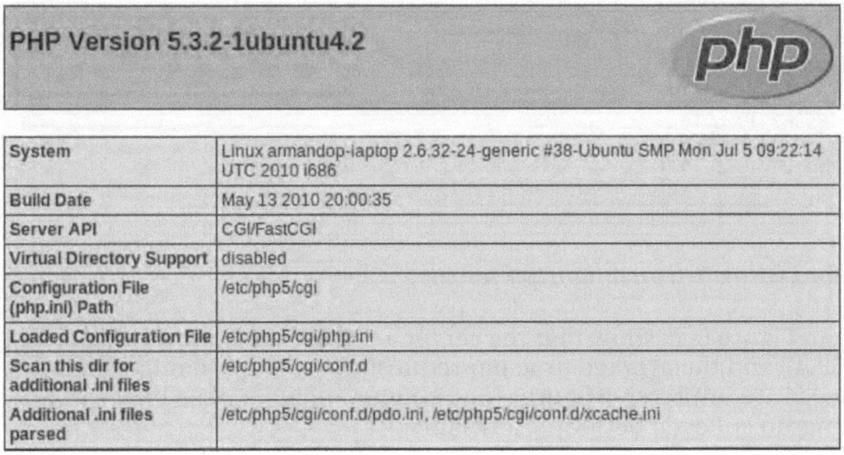

| PHP Version 5.3.2-1ubuntu4.2 | |
|---|---|

| System | Linux armandop-laptop 2.6.32-24-generic #38-Ubuntu SMP Mon Jul 5 09:22:14 UTC 2010 i686 |
|---|---|
| Build Date | May 13 2010 20:00:35 |
| Server API | CGI/FastCGI |
| Virtual Directory Support | disabled |
| Configuration File (php.ini) Path | /etc/php5/cgi |
| Loaded Configuration File | /etc/php5/cgi/php.ini |
| Scan this dir for additional .ini files | /etc/php5/cgi/conf.d |
| Additional .ini files parsed | /etc/php5/cgi/conf.d/pdo.ini, /etc/php5/cgi/conf.d/xcache.ini |

*Figure 6–8. lighttpd phpinfo page*

## Benchmarking PHP Content

Using the code shown in Listing 6–6, we're now going to run our ab test and fetch results. These results will help us not only compare the results using the default settings of each web server, but also gauge how well our tweaks in the next section are working.

The ab command I will use for this test is shown in Listing 6–1, and the code is shown in Listing 6–6.

*Listing 6–6. Code Snippet to Test*

```
<?php
$max = 10000;
$x = 0;
$array = array();

while($x < $max)
{
```

```
    $array[$x] = $x;
    $x++;
}

foreach($array as $z)
{
    echo "$z<br/>";
}
```

After running the test five times, I took the highest results, which are shown in Figure 6–9.

```
Concurrency Level:        500
Time taken for tests:     3.945 seconds
Complete requests:        1000
Failed requests:          0
Write errors:             0
Total transferred:        89124898 bytes
HTML transferred:         88963530 bytes
Requests per second:      253.47 [#/sec] (mean)
Time per request:         1972.640 [ms] (mean)
Time per request:         3.945 [ms] (mean, across all concurrent requests)
Transfer rate:            22060.80 [Kbytes/sec] received
```

***Figure 6–9.*** *ab results for Listing 6–6 on a lighttpd server*

The results shown in Figure 6–8, show that the server achieved a maximum requests per second value of 253.47 and the average time per request was 1,972.640 milliseconds (1.9 seconds). While these are impressive figures for a single server, let's see how we can tweak the servers settings to get even better performance.

## Setting Tweaks

We are going to increase the number of file descriptors, remove the overhead fetching a file, and set the number of PHP processes we need for our system.

The first thing we need to do is increase the number of file descriptors. A file descriptor is a file handler that allows a user/request to access a specific file within the server. If the web server runs out of file descriptors, it will return errors to the user, and your error logs will fill up quickly with the following logs:

```
(server.1345)socket enabled again
(server.1391)sockets disabled, connection limit reached.
```

To remove this issue, we increase the value of server.max-fds. By default lighttpd has this value set to 1,024 (in most cases). With 1,024 file descriptors, our server can handle only 512 connections (1,024/2 = 512). It's recommend by the lighttpd web site to increase this value to 2,048 on busy servers. This will allow for 1,024 max connections. To increase the maximum file descriptors, use the server.max-fds property, server.max-fds=2,048, and also set server.max-connections=1,024.

The next configuration change we can do is remove the overhead of our server calling `stat()` numerous times per request by either disabling, caching, or using FAM to control the stat calls. Using the `server.state-cache-engine` parameter, we can set the value to `disable`, `simple`, or `fam`.

# Nginx

The final HTTP web server we're going to cover is Nginx (engine-x). Nginx not only is an HTTP web server but can also operate as a reverse proxy and an IMAP/POP3 mail server. The goal of installing Nginx is to determine how well a PHP script will perform under this web server. Nginx was created by Igor Sysoev in 2002, according to its official web site, `www.niginx.org`. It also hosts 6.55 percent of the worldwide domains and touts Wordpress.com and Hulu as users. To date the latest stable release of the web server is version 0.7.x. Previous releases remain available as well, and it is available for both Windows and Unix systems.

Nginx is an asynchronous web server, unlike Apache, which is a process-based web server. What this means is Nginx will spawn very few or no threads to support concurrent requests, unlike the Apache web server, which will require a new thread for each concurrent request. Due to this, one of the most stellar features Nginx provides is its low use of RAM under heavy traffic loads.

## Installing Nginx

Nginx is available for both Windows and Unix, and both versions can be found within the official web site. I'm going to first install the web server on a Unix-based system, followed by a Windows-based system. You can skip to the section your system is running without losing any valuable information. In both cases, we will refer to the Nginx web site, `http://wiki.nginx.org`.

## Nginx on Unix

Most of the packages we have installed are available in repositories at this point. We will now be installing Nginx in an Ubuntu-based system by running the `apt-get` command shown in Table 6–7 within a shell. Refer to the table, and use the appropriate command for your OS.

*Table 6–7. Commands to Install Nginx*

| OS | Command |
| --- | --- |
| Red Hat/Fedora | yum install nginx |
| Ubuntu/Debian | apt-get install nginx |

After executing the command for your system, you should have the required packages installed correctly. If you run into problems, read over the output, since many times it will contain information concerning which packages were missing or what issues were encountered.

Installing from source is also an option. For those of you who wish to install Nginx from source, open your browser and load the page http://wiki.nginx.org/NginxInstall. There are three options—stable, development, and legacy. Once you select the appropriate package to download, download it, expand it in your local drive, and run the commands shown in listing 6–7.

*Listing 6–7. Installing Nginx from Source Commands*

```
./configure [compile-time options]
make
sudo make install
```

Nginx should now be installed on your system and ready for use.

## Compile-Time Options

By default installing Nginx using one of the repository commands will install the configuration settings shown in Listing 6–8.

*Listing 6–8. Default Configuration Settings*

```
conf-path=/etc/nginx/nginx.conf
    --error-log-path=/var/log/nginx/error.log
    --pid-path=/var/run/nginx.pid
    --lock-path=/var/lock/nginx.lock
    --http-log-path=/var/log/nginx/access.log
    --http-client-body-temp-path=/var/lib/nginx/body
    --http-proxy-temp-path=/var/lib/nginx/proxy
    --http-fastcgi-temp-path=/var/lib/nginx/fastcgi
    --with-debug
    --with-http_stub_status_module
    --with-http_flv_module
    --with-http_ssl_module
    --with-http_dav_module
    --with-http_gzip_static_module
    --with-http_realip_module
    --with-mail
    --with-mail_ssl_module
    --with-ipv6
    --add-module=/build/buildd/nginx-0.7.65/modules/nginx-upstream-fair
```

The default configuration contains valuable information such as the path to our error logs, the path to the access logs, configuration file, SSL support, mail support, and server status page enabled, just to name a few. To change these settings, you have two options: make modifications to the configuration file specified in the conf-path, or recompile using some of the compile-time options. A list of the most used compile-time options is shown in Table 6–8 as well as a description of the configuration options installed by default. The complete list is available on the web site `http://wiki.nginx.org/NginxInstallOptions`.

*Table 6–8. Nginx Compile-Time Settings*

| Setting | Description |
| --- | --- |
| `--prefix=<path>` | Relative path all other settings will use; by default it's set to `/usr/local/nginx`. |
| `--conf-path=<path>` | Location to the configuration file; defaults to `<prefix>/conf/nginx.conf` |
| `--pid-path=<path>` | Path to the `nginx.pid`; defaults to `<prefix>/logs/nginx.pid` |
| `--error-log-path=<path>` | Path to the error log used; defaults to `<prefix>/logs/error.log` |
| `--http-log-path=<path>` | Path to the access log used; defaults to `<prefix>/logs/access.log` |
| `--user=<user>` | Default user Nginx will run as; defaults to "nobody" |
| `--group=<group>` | Default group Nginx will run under; defaults to "nobody" |
| `--lock-path=<path>` | Path to lock file |
| `--http-client-body-temp-path=<path>` | Path to the HTTP client temporary request file; defaults to `<prefix>/client_body_temp` |
| `--http-proxy-temp-path=<path>` | Path to HTTP temporary proxy files; defaults to `<prefix>/proxy_temp` |
| `--http-fastcgi-temp-path=<path>` | Path to FastCGI temporary files; defaults to `<prefix>/fastcgi_temp` |
| `--without-http` | Turns off HTTP server |
| `--with-debug` | Turns on debug logs |
| `--with-http_stub_status_module` | Turns on server status page |
| `--with-http_flv_module` | Turns on flv module |

| Setting | Description |
|---|---|
| --with-http_ssl_module | Turns on ssl module |
| --with-http_dav_module | Turns on dav module |
| --with-http_gzip_static_module | Turns on gzip module |
| --with-http_realip_module | Turns on realip module |
| --with-mail | Turns on IMAP4/POP3/SMTP proxy module |
| --with-mail_ssl_module | Turns on mail ssl module |
| --add-module=<path> | Third-party modules located within the path specified |

## Verifying Installation and Starting Up Nginx

To start Nginx, execute the command shown in Listing 6–9 within a shell. A list of additional command-line options can be found in Table 6–9.

*Listing 6–9. Starting Nginx*

```
Nginx
```

Once the web server is running, load the URL http://localhost/. You should see a page similar to that shown in Figure 6–10.

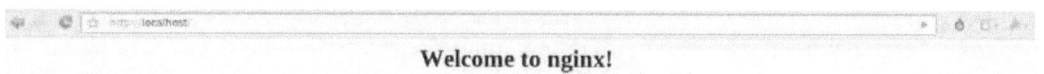

**Welcome to nginx!**

*Figure 6–10. Welcome screen for Nginx*

*Table 6–9. Nginx Command-Line Options*

| Option | Description |
|---|---|
| -s [stop\|quit\|reopen\|reload] | Allows you to stop, quit, reopen, or reload Nginx web server |
| -h | List of options available for use |
| -v | Display version number |
| -V | Display configuration options |
| -t | Test a configuration file; useful when making changes |
| -p <prefix> | Sets the prefix path |
| -c <filepath> | Sets the configuration file to use |
| -g <directives> | Sets global directives |

■ **Caution** If you have any other web server turned on, make sure you turn it off at this point.

## Windows Installation

Nginx is available in binary format for Windows systems. Like the Unix version, Nginx is available in three versions—stable, development, and legacy. The latest stable release is 0.7.67 and can be found at http://ngingx.org/en/download.html , Download the file to a suitable directory, preferably one that does not contain a space in its pathname and unzip it. C:\nginx is probably a good location to use.

Once the content has been unzipped, you should have the directory structure shown in Figure 6–11.

***Figure 6–11.*** *Windows Nginx directory structure*

Within the directory, you will find the `nginx.exe` executable, with six different directories:

- `conf`
- `contrib`
- `docs`
- `html`
- `logs`
- `temp`

The `conf` directory contains the configuration file, which contains Nginx settings as well as FastCGI settings. The `html` directory is where you will place your application. The `logs` directory contains all the logs Nginx outputs, and the `temp` directory will contain any temporary files Nginx needs to create.

To start the server, simply double-click the `nginx.exe` file located within the directory and wait for it to load. Once the web server has started, make sure the web server was installed correctly by visiting the URL `http://localhost/` within a browser. Verify that Figure 6–9 is shown.

## Nginx As a Static Web Server

With Nginx now installed, let's now compare Nginx and Apache web servers and see which web server will perform best for our application. We will test the default installation of Apache against the default installation of Nginx on an Ubuntu system by running the command shown in Listing 6–10.

*Listing 6–10. ab Command*

```
ab -n 1000 -c 500 http://localhost/
```

The command shown in Listing 6–10 will test our servers by requesting the static HTML page 1,000 times while maintaining 500 concurrent connections. Given this load, the results for the Apache web server are shown in Figure 6–12, and the results for Nginx are shown in Figure 6–13.

```
Concurrency Level:      500
Time taken for tests:   4.207 seconds
Complete requests:      1000
Failed requests:        0
Write errors:           0
Total transferred:      487596 bytes
HTML transferred:       190098 bytes
Requests per second:    237.67 [#/sec] (mean)
Time per request:       2103.724 [ms] (mean)
Time per request:       4.207 [ms] (mean, across all concurrent requests)
Transfer rate:          113.17 [Kbytes/sec] received
```

***Figure 6–12.*** *ab results for Apache web server*

```
Concurrency Level:      500
Time taken for tests:   0.074 seconds
Complete requests:      1000
Failed requests:        0
Write errors:           0
Total transferred:      372860 bytes
HTML transferred:       155530 bytes
Requests per second:    13535.83 [#/sec] (mean)
Time per request:       36.939 [ms] (mean)
Time per request:       0.074 [ms] (mean, across all concurrent requests)
Transfer rate:          4928.68 [Kbytes/sec] received
```

***Figure 6–13.*** *ab results for Nginx web server*

We are interested in two items within the results: time per request and requests per second. For our optimization focus, we focus on time per request. Nginx web server decreases the response time of a static file from 2,103.724 milliseconds (2 seconds) (using Apache) to 36.939 milliseconds, a decrease of 2.06 seconds.

For those interested in getting the biggest bang for your buck on each of your web servers, Nginx also allows you to satisfy additional users. Referring back to the results for the requests per second, Nginx can satisfy 13,535.83 users, while Apache can satisfy 237.67 users. That's an increase of 13,298. Since we're testing these results using only static content, let's now see how well Apache and Nginx measure up while running PHP using their default settings. To do so, we need to install PHP on Nginx.

---

■ **Note** This is not an invitation to a "my web server is better than your web server" conversation. These are only benchmark tests on my local machine, as well as using each of the web server's default settings.

---

## Installing FastCGI PHP

To use PHP with Nginx, we need to use the FastCGI version of PHP. In order to install the FastCGI version of PHP, you will need to install the php5-cgi package as well as spawn-fcgi onto your system. For Unix users, use the command shown in Listing 6–11.

*Listing 6–11. Command to Install php5-cgi*

```
apt-get install php5-cgi
apt-get install spawn-fcgi
```

Once the package has been installed, you should have the path /etc/php5/cgi available. Move into the directory, and open the php.ini file. Make the modifications shown in Listing 6–12 at the bottom of the file. This change is required to make sure that the fcgi version of PHP sets the value of php variable $_SERVER['PATH_INFO'] correctly, some applications make use of this variable and the default behavior was to replicate an old bug in early fcgi implementations.

*Listing 6–12. Modifying the php.ini File*

```
Cgi.fix_pathinfo=1
```

Once both packages are installed, we need to start up the FastCGI process. To do so, run the command in Listing 6–13.

*Listing 6–13. Starting FastCGI*

```
/usr/bin/spawn-fcgi -a 127.0.0.1 -p 9000 -u www-data -g www-data -f /usr/bin/php5-cgi -P↵
/var/run/fastcgi-php.pid
```

The command shown in Listing 6–13 uses six optional commands. The first, -a, specifies the IP of the host we will run the process on. Since I'm running the process locally, I entered the local IP. The second option, -p, specifies the port number to listen on. The third option specifies the user the process will run as, the fourth option is the group the process belongs to, the fifth option specifies the location to the binary file, and the last option specifies the location of our .pid file to use.

Once the process spawned successfully, you will need to update the Nginx configuration file. To do so, open the Nginx configuration file, located at /etc/nginx/sites-available/default. Remove the commented-out FastCGI information, which is similar to the text in Listing 6–14.

*Listing 6–14. Removing the Commented-Out FastCGI Information*

```
location ~\.php$ {

    fastcgi_pass    127.0.0.1:9000;
    fastcgi_index   index.php;
    fastcgi_param   SCRIPT_FILENAME /var/www/nginx-default$fastcgi_script_name;
    include fastcgi_params;

}
```

The snippet of code shown specifies Nginx to use the FastCGI for any .php files using the FastCGI process listening in 127.0.0.1:9000. Save the changes and restart the server.

## Verifying FastCGI Installation

Create a phpinfo page and place it into the /var/www/nginx-default/ directory. Once done, load the file http://localhost/info.php. You should see Figure 6–14.

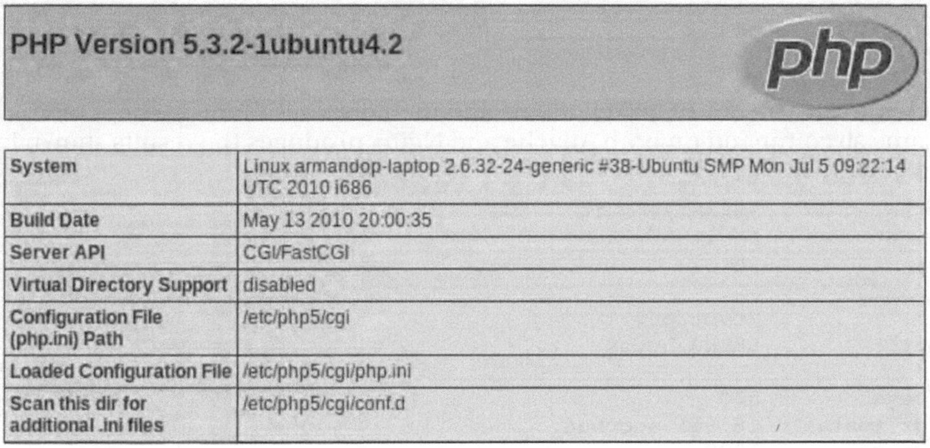

**PHP Version 5.3.2-1ubuntu4.2**

*php*

| System | Linux armandop-laptop 2.6.32-24-generic #38-Ubuntu SMP Mon Jul 5 09:22:14 UTC 2010 i686 |
| --- | --- |
| Build Date | May 13 2010 20:00:35 |
| Server API | CGI/FastCGI |
| Virtual Directory Support | disabled |
| Configuration File (php.ini) Path | /etc/php5/cgi |
| Loaded Configuration File | /etc/php5/cgi/php.ini |
| Scan this dir for additional .ini files | /etc/php5/cgi/conf.d |

*Figure 6–14. PHP information page with FastCGI PHP installed*

If everything was properly installed, you should see "CGI/FastCGI" as the value for the Server API row, as shown in Figure 6–14.

## NGinx Benchmarking

To test how well a script will perform, we'll use the previously tested code shown throughout this book, shown in Listing 6–15.

*Listing 6–15. PHP Snippet to Test*

```php
<?php
$max = 10000;
$x = 0;
$array = array();

while($x < $max)
{
   $array[$x] = $x;
   $x++;
}

foreach($array as $z)
{
   echo "$z<br/>";
}
```

The code creates an array of 10,000 elements and then displays them on the screen. Running the same ab command on both Apache and Nginx produces the results shown in Figure 6–15 and Figure 6–16.

```
Server Software:        Apache/2.2.16
Server Hostname:        localhost
Server Port:            80

Document Path:          /test.php
Document Length:        88890 bytes

Concurrency Level:      500
Time taken for tests:   16.961 seconds
Complete requests:      1000
Failed requests:        0
Write errors:           0
Total transferred:      89081000 bytes
HTML transferred:       88890000 bytes
Requests per second:    58.96 [#/sec] (mean)
Time per request:       8480.315 [ms] (mean)
Time per request:       16.961 [ms] (mean, across all concurrent requests)
Transfer rate:          5129.12 [Kbytes/sec] received
```

*Figure 6–15. ab results for Listing 6–15 running on an Apache web server using default settings*

```
Server Software:        nginx/0.7.67
Server Hostname:        localhost
Server Port:            80

Document Path:          /test.php
Document Length:        88890 bytes

Concurrency Level:      500
Time taken for tests:   9.152 seconds
Complete requests:      1000
Failed requests:        0
Write errors:           0
Total transferred:      89048000 bytes
HTML transferred:       88890000 bytes
Requests per second:    109.27 [#/sec] (mean)
Time per request:       4575.926 [ms] (mean)
Time per request:       9.152 [ms] (mean, across all concurrent requests)
Transfer rate:          9502.00 [Kbytes/sec] received
```

**Figure 6–16.** *ab results for Listing 6–15 on an Nginx server using default settings*

The results shown in Figure 6–15 once again show two important items that we need to look at when dealing with optimization: requests per second and time per request. In this result, the time per request for the apache server stood at 8,480.315 milliseconds or 8.5 seconds. That would mean that a user would wait for almost ten seconds for a response from the server before the browser could begin displaying the data. When we compare that figure to the Nginx results shown in Figure 6–16, Nginx had a time per request of 4,575.926 milliseconds or 4.5 seconds, which is 50 percent faster.

## Summary

Chapter 6 took you another step down into the PHP application. You learned about the different types of servers: prefork, threaded, and event. You also learned about why hardware is important in serving content to the user at a much faster rate.

The chapter also covered topics such as useful Apache configuration settings and commands, and how to remove steps within the Apache process to speed up load time. We also touched on two of the most popular alternative web servers, lighttpd and Nginx. You learned to install, configure, and run a few ab tests to test how well they withstood your application requirements.

You are encouraged to use the information presented in this chapter to determine which web server package would be best for your particular application. You are also encouraged to experiment and verify that the choice you have made is the correct one using some of the mechanisms outlined here.

# CHAPTER 7

■ ■ ■

# Web Server and Delivery Optimization

One of the most important components of your application is the web server it is hosted on. No matter how much you optimize your application, if your web server is not optimized too, you are not going to get the full performance that you may be looking for.

In this chapter, we are going to learn how to create an "application profile" for our web service and use that profile to ensure our web servers are correctly configured.

We will look at how to overcome some common problems that result in a reduction in performance, by eliminating unnecessary file operations.

There may also come a time where the performance levels you require exceed the performance or throughput that a single web server can deliver, so you may need to scale up by dividing your application across multiple servers. We will examine some of the requirements of an application that enable it to grow so it can run on a farm of Apache web servers operating as a cluster.

We will also examine some of the methods you can use to partition your application to achieve higher performance levels.

Monitoring is also an important requirement for a professionally hosted application; we will look at some of the systems available that you can install to make sure you are always aware of the status of your system.

Finally we will look at some infrastructure choices and services you can use to speed delivery of your content, and help you understand what some of the common pitfalls are, and how to overcome them.

---

■ **Note** We are still locked into the web server layer, so please refer back to Figure 6-1 for a visual of where this falls in the application stack model.

---

# Determining the Performance of Your Web Server

In Chapter 1, we saw how to use benchmarking tools to determine the performance of your web service. The method outlined works well for static tests, and will give you a good idea about how well your service should run. But load testing is not suitable for frequent use on a production server, and we often need to determine how our server is performing under real-world load before making decisions about optimization. ApacheTop is the main tool we will use to inspect the performance of our web server.

## Using ApacheTop, a Real-Time Access Log File Analyzer

ApacheTop can be installed via apt-get on Debian systems, and is available in .rpm form for Red Hat/CentOS/Fedora systems. You can install ApacheTop on a Debian-based (Ubuntu) system with the following command:

```
$sudo apt-get install apachetop
```

Installation on Red Hat/CentOS/Fedora is available via a source install. Use the following instructions.

```
mkdir ~/maketemp
cd ~/maketemp
wget http://www.webta.org/apachetop/apachetop-0.12.6.tar.gz
sudo yum install readline-devel
sudo yum install ncurses-devel
sudo yum install pcre-devel
tar xvzf apachetop-0.12.6.tar.gz
cd apachetop-0.12.6
./configure
make
sudo make install
```

ApacheTop is a real-time access log analyzer; it behaves in a similar fashion to tailing the access log, but provides a level of analysis, too.

Start up ApacheTop by specifying the path to your web server access log file, as shown in Listing 7–1.

*Listing 7–1. ApacheTop Output*

```
$sudo apachetop -f /var/log/apache2/access_log
```

```
last hit: 13:48:40        atop runtime:  0 days, 00:01:25          13:49:02
All:              68 reqs (   1.2/sec)      1462.5K (   25.7K/sec)     21.5K/req
2xx:      67 (98.5%) 3xx:      0 ( 0.0%) 4xx:      1 ( 1.5%) 5xx:     0 ( 0.0%)
R ( 30s):         15 reqs (   0.5/sec)       288.9K ( 9859.7B/sec)     19.3K/req
2xx:      15 ( 100%) 3xx:      0 ( 0.0%) 4xx:      0 ( 0.0%) 5xx:     0 ( 0.0%)


REQS REQ/S    KB KB/S URL
   1  0.05   4.7  0.2 */tags/view/tag/Lincoln+Smart+Dodge+Lotus+Subaru
   1  0.05  20.9  0.9 /media/4c7b73ba0dc48dc965820300
   1  0.05  27.7  1.3 /media/4c7b74f90dc48d7668200000
   1  0.05  35.0  1.6 /media/4c7b72680dc48dc965770200
   1  0.05  20.2  0.9 /media/4c7b78270dc48d7668240200
   1  0.05  25.1  1.1 /media/4c7b778d0dc48d7668b10100
   1  0.03  17.5  0.6 /media/4c7b6de30dc48dab64840000
   1  0.03  29.3  1.0 /media/4c7b6c6d0dc48d0e5f370500
   1  0.03  25.3  0.8 /media/4c7b6dbd0dc48dab64670000
   1  0.03  16.1  0.5 /media/4c7b6e240dc48dab64a20000
   1  0.03  31.6  1.1 /media/4c7b6e690dc48dab64a20000
   1  0.03  24.9  0.9 /media/4c7b6e8f0dc48dab64ec0000
   1  0.03   5.6  0.2 /
   1  0.04   2.4  0.1 /feed/top
   1  0.04   2.6  0.1 /tags/top
```

ApacheTop will display the accumulated request rate since it was started for all 2xx, 3xx, 4xx, and 5xx status codes; it will also provide those same stats for the last 30 seconds, allowing you to determine if load is rising or falling. It also provides a breakdown of the top URLs being hit and the rate at which they are being hit. This information is useful for working out which pages you should focus your optimizations on first.

You can change the period that ApacheTop accumulates results for in the R display by using the -T n command-line option. This allows you to change the period from the default 30 seconds to a longer period if you have a low-traffic web server. The aim is to get a representative amount of traffic displayed so you can determine the top ten URLs hit on your site and what their frequency is.

Use the "?" key once ApacheTop has finished loading to display a list of commands that can be used to modify the display, switch from URLs to referrers, zoom in, and examine detail statistics for a single URL.

The most notable feature that will help with determining the distribution of top URLs in your site is the filter mechanism; for example, if you type "f", "a", "u" (for filter=>add=>url) and then type ".php", ApacheTop will then restrict the URLs displayed to those ending with ".php".

It is suggested that you spend some time with ApacheTop to get to know the profile of your application and work out what the top pages being hit are, so you can focus your optimization effort where it will generate the most benefit. You should be aware of what your top ten pages are by usage. Make sure you have identified what these pages are, and what percentage of use they get.

For example, you might find you get something like that shown in Table 7–1.

*Table 7–1.* *Top Ten URLs by Requests for an Example Application*

| Page | Requests | Percentage (rounded) |
|------|----------|----------------------|
| / (home page) | 2,000 | 33 |
| /news.php | 1,500 | 25 |
| /blog.php | 1,000 | 17 |
| /video.php | 600 | 10 |
| /topuser.php | 400 | 6 |
| /message.php | 150 | 2 |
| /message_send.php | 100 | 2 |
| /message_read.php | 90 | 2 |
| /user_profile.php | 80 | 2 |
| /feedback.php | 15 | 1 |
| Totals | 5,935 | 100 |

This kind of map will tell you where all the "action" is in your application and let you know where you will need to focus your attention.

## Understanding the Memory Footprint of Your Application

Using ApacheTop, we have built an understanding of what the "profile" of our application is. Now we need to work out what the memory footprint is, so you can either ensure you have sufficient memory installed in your web servers, or configure the server to avoid swapping.

If you have a common footer included in your application, you can add a comment that allows you to visualize the peak memory usage of each of the high-profile pages you identified previously.

Add something like the following:

```
<!-- Memory usage: <?php echo memory_get_peak_usage(1); ?> -->
```

This will place a comment at the end of each page that shows how much memory was used to create the page. Access each of your pages that you identified as your high-profile pages, use view source to get the value, and record the peak memory used. The weighted average is the percentage expressed as a factor times the request memory usage (33 percent => 0.33), as shown in Table 7–2.

*Table 7–2. Adding the Memory Consumption and Weighting to Our Top Ten URLs*

| Page | Requests | Percentage (rounded) | Per request mem | Weighted average mem |
|---|---|---|---|---|
| / (home page) | 2,000 | 33 | 10MB | 3.3MB |
| /news.php | 1,500 | 25 | 15MB | 3.75MB |
| /blog.php | 1,000 | 17 | 16MB | 2.72MB |
| /video.php | 600 | 10 | 8MB | 0.8MB |
| /topuser.php | 400 | 6 | 17MB | 1.02MB |
| /message.php | 150 | 2 | 9MB | 0.18MB |
| /message_send.php | 100 | 2 | 6MB | 0.12MB |
| /message_read.php | 90 | 2 | 8MB | 0.16MB |
| /user_profile.php | 80 | 2 | 14MB | 0.28MB |
| /feedback.php | 15 | 1 | 3MB | 0.03MB |
| Totals | 5,935 | 100 | 106MB | 12.36MB |

What this tells us is that for a normal mix of traffic, the weighted average memory consumption per request is 12.36MB. So if you had a web server that had 1GB of RAM, and you were reserving 200MB for the operating system, etc., then the amount of memory left over for the application would be 800MB. Dividing this value by the weighted average gives 800/12.36 = 64.72. This is the number of concurrent requests in the top ten that you can process at the same time without running the risk of exhausting memory and causing the system to swap.

It should be noted that we have used the top ten here as a general rule of thumb. If you find that the percentage of requests for your URLs has not fallen off to a small number—say, 1 percent—at the end of your table, then you may need to extend the table to include a larger number of URLs. ApacheTop automatically ignores any query string parameters after a URL when creating its sorted-by-request view, so variations in the

URLs due to query strings won't create a lot of extra entries. The intention is not to provide a 100 percent accurate assessment for all of the possible URLs in your system, which could run to many hundreds of pages on a large site, but to rather to provide sufficient coverage of the major paths.

# Optimizing Processes in Apache

In Chapter 6, we saw how the Apache web server processes requests and uses the MPM to dispatch the requests to your application.

In this section, we will see how we can optimize the settings for the Prefork MPM (the most common MPM) to ensure it does not overuse memory and start swapping.

## Controlling Apache Clients (Prefork MPM)

The request handling behavior just described for the Prefork MPM is controlled by a number of configuration directives. The default values shown in Table 7–3 are from the Ubuntu distribution of Apache; other distributions may have chosen alternative values for their defaults.

Most distributions set these values in the main httpd.conf configuration file; however, some distributions such as Ubuntu place them in a separate file in the "extra" subdirectory in the Apache configuration folder. For example, on Ubuntu they are found in /etc/apache2/conf/extra/httpd-mpm.conf. You may also need to uncomment an include file line in httpd.conf to get them to load.

*Table 7–3. Apache Directives for Controlling Prefork MPM Behavior*

| Directive | Description | Default value |
|---|---|---|
| StartServers | This directive controls the number of clients that Apache will spawn when it starts up. Because there is a cost to creating a client, it is a good idea to have sufficient clients available to handle your idle-level traffic. | 5 |
| MinSpareServers | Normally Apache will kill clients if the number of requests falls back and it cannot justify having them around. This directive sets a lower limit on the number of clients Apache will keep alive. It should not be any lower than StartServers. | 5 |
| MaxSpareServers | This directive sets the point at which Apache will start discarding clients. If it has ten more clients active than the number of concurrent requests it is currently handling, then it will start killing and discarding them until it has reached the MinSpareServers value. Setting this value too low will cause Apache to thrash client processes, so be careful with this setting. | 10 |
| MaxClients | The MaxClients directive sets the maximum number of child processes Apache will spawn, and hence the maximum number of simultaneous or concurrent requests that it can handle. | 150 |
| MaxRequestsPerChild | This directive sets the maximum number of requests that a child process will handle before it is killed and respawned. If set to 0, then the process is permanent and will never die. | 0 |

## Optimizing Memory Use and Preventing Swapping

OK, now you have all the information you need to set up your MPM configuration. From the earlier section, we saw that we can support a maximum of 65 concurrent requests on our 1GB server, with the mix of pages that we saw being used in real life.

The first directive we should change is MaxClients, which should be set to 65, so that we don't overrun our memory.

To ensure that we are not thrashing clients in when the system is running at load, we should probably set the StartServers to half that, i.e., 30, and set MinSpareServers to 30, too. Finally set MaxSpareServers to 40, a good value to prevent client thrashing.

# Other Apache Configuration Tweaks

The Apache web server is replete with configuration options to control every aspect of its behavior. The default delivery configuration of Apache is designed to provide a convenient configuration "out of the box," but many of the defaults delivered in the distribution configuration files may have performance costs that you can avoid if you don't need the particular capability.

It is a good idea to understand how many of these "convenience functions" work at the request level so that you can determine their impact on the performance of your application, and whether you should avoid the use of the functions provided.

## Using .htaccess Files and AllowOverride

In Chapter 3, you saw how the use of the require_once function introduced extra calls to the operating systems "lstat" function, slowing down delivery of pages. A similar overhead exists with enabling the "AllowOverride" directive to allow the use of .htaccess files.

.htaccess files are sort of per request "patches" to the main Apache configuration, which can be placed in any directory of your application to establish custom configurations for the content stored at that location and the directories below it.

"AllowOverride" instructs Apache to check the directory containing the script or file it is intending to serve, and each of its parent directories, for the existence of an ".htaccess" file that contains the additional Apache configuration directives affecting this current request. However, if "AllowOverride" has been enabled, then even if you are not using .htaccess files, this check is still made to determine if the .htaccess file is present, incurring multiple operating system call overheads.

If you are using .htaccess files, then consider moving the configuration directives into the main Apache configuration file, which is loaded once only when the HTTP server is started up, or a new HTTPD client is started, instead of on every request. If you need to maintain different directives for different directories, then consider wrapping them in the <Directory ....> ... </Directory> tags to retain the ability to control specific directories.

The use of .htaccess files may be forced upon you if you are using some limited forms of shared hosting, and don't have access to the full Apache configuration file. But in general to maximize performance, you should avoid use of both the files and the configuration directive; indeed you should strive to ensure that the directive is turned off to ensure the maximum performance gain.

In the following listings, we created a simple static server vhost mapped to www.static.local, and created a three-level-deep path in the docroot of dir1/dir2/dir3. In the deepest directory, we placed a file called pic.jpg, of about 6KB in size. Listing 7–2 shows the performance of the system under siege with the AllowOverride option set to "None," whereas Listing 7–3 shows the results of the same test with AllowOverride set to "All."

*Listing 7–2. Static Object Serving with AllowOverride Directive Disabled*

```
$siege -c 300 -t 30S http://www.static.local/dir1/dir2/dir3/pic.jpg
......
Lifting the server siege...      done.
Transactions:                    15108 hits
Availability:                    100.00 %
Elapsed time:                    29.66 secs
Data transferred:                      100.01 MB
Response time:                         0.00 secs
Transaction rate:                      509.37 trans/sec
Throughput:                            3.37 MB/sec
Concurrency:                           12.99
Successful transactions:         15108
Failed transactions:                   0
Longest transaction:                   0.14
Shortest transaction:                  0.00
```

*Listing 7–3. Static Object Serving with AllowOverride Directive Enabled*

```
$siege -c 300 -t 30S http://www.static.local/dir1/dir2/dir3/pic.jpg
......
Lifting the server siege...            done.
Transactions:                    14440 hits
Availability:                    100.00 %
Elapsed time:                    29.67 secs
Data transferred:                      95.58 MB
Response time:                         0.02 secs
Transaction rate:                      486.69 trans/sec
Throughput:                            3.22 MB/sec
Concurrency:                     11.87
Successful transactions:         14440
Failed transactions:                   0
Longest transaction:                   1.06
Shortest transaction:                  0.00
```

The results show an approximate 5 percent difference in performance by serving static objects with the option turned off, as opposed to it being enabled.

## Using FollowSymlinks

Like the AllowOverride directive just described, the FollowSymlinks option requires extra OS calls to determine if a symlink is present. Turning it off if it is not needed can provide a small benefit in performance.

## Using DirectoryIndex

Another place where it is possible to unintentionally create extra OS system calls on each request is the DirectoryIndex directive. This directive specifies a space-delimited list of default files that are to be used when the request URL refers to a directory instead of a specific file. Apache searches for the default file in the order they are specified in the directive. Make sure that the most relevant name for your particular application is placed first in this list. For example, for a PHP application, this option should be as follows:

```
DirectoryIndex index.php index.html
```

If you have the files in the wrong order, then your web server would be performing an unnecessary search for index.html on each request for a directory. This is particularly important with your home page, which will see the majority of your traffic, and is inevitably an indirect reference to index.php.

## Hostname Lookup Off

We covered DNS lookup earlier in the book. DNS lookup will take a domain name and look up its mapped IP. This process occurs each time the IP is not present, and it increases latency due to this check.

Most Apache distributions have this turned off by default, but if not, it can have a significant detrimental effect. To turn off this feature, we need to make a change to the configuration file's HostnameLookup key. The directive might already be set to "Off," but if it's not, change it to "Off" and restart the server.

## Keep-Alive On

Keep-Alive enables your web server to support persistent connections. By turning on the Keep-Alive directive, Apache can support multiple HTTP requests for each TCP connection. This is an important directive to set because Apache does not use RAM when opening a connection and closing a connection when Keep-Alive is turned on. By removing this overhead, again we speed up our application.

To turn on Keep-Alive, open the configuration file and locate the Keep-Alive directive. In some cases, the directive might already be set to "On." If it's not set, simply set the value to "On," save the changes, and restart Apache.

## Using mod_deflate to Compress Content

The HTTP protocol allows for the use of compressed transfer encodings. As well as speeding up the delivery of compressible files such as html, js or css files, it can also reduce the amount of bandwidth used to deliver your application. If you have a significant amount of traffic and are paying for outbound bandwidth, then this capability can help to reduce costs.

mod_deflate is a standard module shipped with the Apache 2.x server, and it is easy to set up and use. To enable the module, make sure the following line is uncommented in your Apache configuration file. Note the particular path may vary from the one shown here, but the principle is the same.

```
LoadModule deflate_module /usr/lib/apache2/modules/mod_deflate.so
```

For Debian-based distributions such as Ubuntu, there is a mechanism for enabling modules that does not require editing of the configuration file. Use the following command to enable the mod_deflate module.

```
$sudo a2enmod deflate
```

Then restart your Apache server to load the module. To configure the module to compress any text, HTML, or XML sent from your server to browsers that support compression, add the following directives to your vhost configuration.

```
AddOutputFilterByType DEFLATE text/html text/plain text/xml
```

There is, however, one gotcha. Some older browsers declare support for compressed transfers, but have broken support for the standards, so the following directives will prevent mod_deflate from compressing files that are sent to these problematic clients.

```
BrowserMatch ^Mozilla/4 gzip-only-text/html
BrowserMatch ^Mozilla/4\.0[678] no-gzip
BrowserMatch \bMSIE !no-gzip !gzip-only-text/html
```

To test if the compression is working correctly, restart your server, access your home page using Firefox and Firebug, and check using the Net panel that the HTML generated by your home page PHP is being transferred using gzip content encoding.

Figure 7–1 shows the Firebug Net panel after configuring mod_deflate and accessing a URL that returns a text/HTML file. The "Content-Encoding" field in the response header shows that the content is indeed compressed.

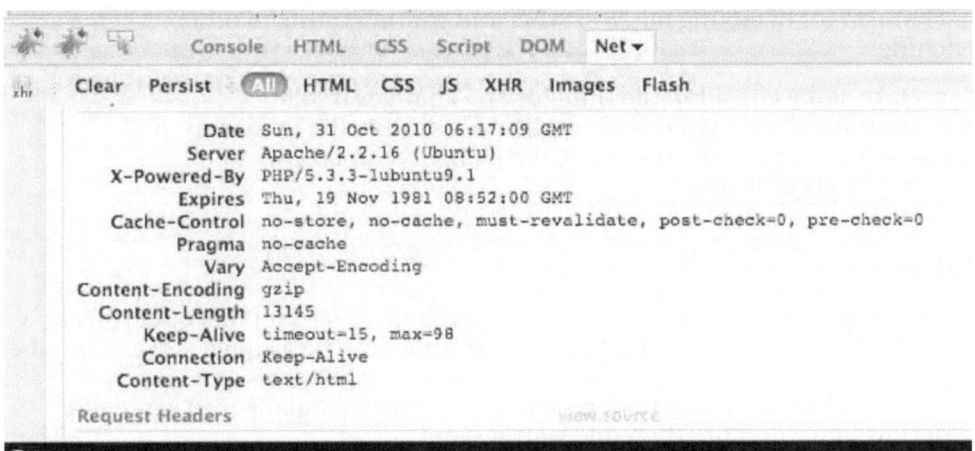

*Figure 7–1. Firebug showing a Content-Encoding value of gzip*

# Scaling Beyond a Single Server

No matter how much optimization you apply to your application or your system configuration, if your application is successful, then you will need to scale beyond the capacity of a single machine. There are a number of "requirements" your application must meet in order to operate in a distributed mode. While the prospect of re-engineering your application for operating in a "farm" of web servers may at first seem a little daunting, fortunately there is a lot of support in PHP and the components in the LAMP stack to support distribution.

In this section, you see some of those requirements and how to achieve them simply and easily.

## Using Round-Robin DNS

The simplest way of distributing traffic between multiple web servers is to use "round-robin DNS." This involves setting multiple "A" records for the hostname associated with your cluster of machines, one for each web server. The DNS service will deliver this list of addresses in a random order to each client, allowing a simple distribution of requests among all of the members of the farm.

The advantages of this mechanism are that it does not require any additional hardware or configuration on your web system. The disadvantages are as follows:

- If one of your web servers fails, traffic will still be sent to it. There is no mechanism for detecting failed servers and routing traffic to other machines.

- It can take some considerable time for any changes in the configuration of your system to "replicate" through the DNS system. If you want to add or remove servers, the changes can take up to three days to be fully effective.

## Using a Load Balancer

A load balancer is a device that distributes requests among a set of servers operating as a cluster or farm. Its role is to make the farm of servers appear to be a single server from the viewpoint of the user's browser.

Figure 7–2 shows the typical layout of a system using a load balancer to aggregate together the performance of more than one web server.

**Typical Distributed Web Application**

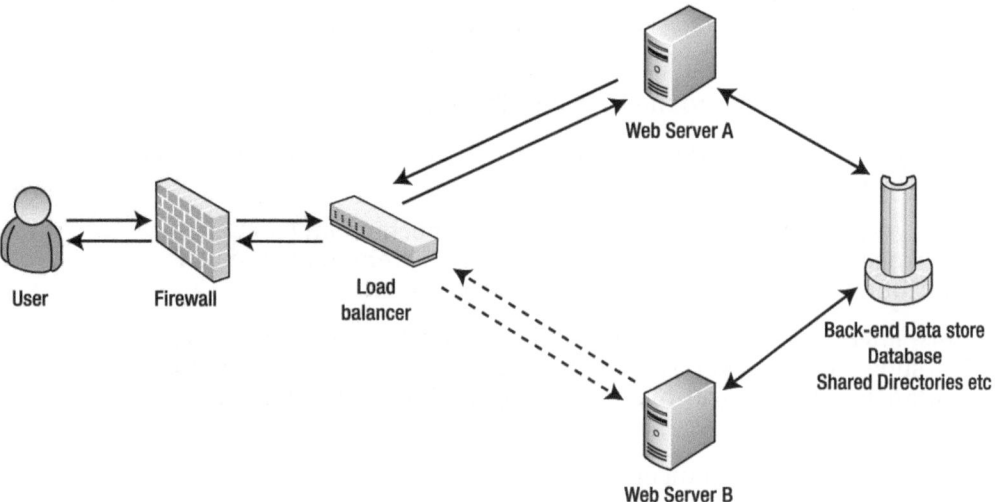

***Figure 7–2.*** *Typical distributed web application*

There are many kinds of load balancers available, both hardware- and software-based. Generally load balancers fall into four categories.

- *Totally software-based solutions*: Solutions such as the Linux Virtual Server project (www.linuxvirtualserver.org) allow you to operate a load balancing service directly on each server of your web farm. One drawback of this solution is that it requires a custom configuration of the network interfaces on each web server, so it will not work with many cloud-based or managed hosting solutions.

- *Software solutions using a separate load balancing server*: You can run a software load balancer on a separate machine that "fronts" your web farm. Products such as HAProxy, Squib, and Apache running with mod_proxy allow you to build your own load balancing appliances.

- *Physical load balancing appliances*: An alternative to rolling your own load balancing appliance is to use a commercial device such as that supplied by F5, Coyote Point, Cisco, and Juniper. These devices often provide many other facilities such as caching, SSL termination, and I/O optimization.

- *Load balancing services*: Many cloud-based solutions provide load balancing services that allow you to map a single IP address to multiple web servers. The Amazon Elastic Load Balancer is a service that is provided to support balancing of requests between instances hosted in the Amazon EC2 cloud.

Load balancers can provide more sophisticated distribution of load than our simple round-robin DNS solution just described. Typically they can provide the following distribution methods.

- *Round-robin*: Similar to the DNS distribution approach

- *Least connections*: Requests are sent to the web server with the least number of active connections.

- *Least load*: Many load balancers provide a mechanism for them to interrogate the web server to determine its current load, and will distribute new requests to the least loaded server.

- *Least latency*: The load balancer will send the request to the server that has shown the fastest response using a moving average monitor of responses. This is a way of determining load without polling the server directly.

- *Random*: The load balancer will route the request to a random server.

In addition the load balancer will monitor the web servers for machines that have not responded to requests, or don't give a suitable response to the status or load monitoring requests directed at them, and will consequently mark those servers as "down" and stop routing requests to them.

Another capability frequently supported by many commercial and open source load balancers is support for "sticky sessions." The load balancer will attempt to keep a particular user on the same server where possible, to reduce the need to swap session state information between machines. However, you should be aware that the use of sticky sessions could result in uneven distribution of load in high-load situations.

Load balancers can also provide help when you get spikes in load that exceed even the capacity of your entire web server farm. Load balancers often provide the ability to define an "overflow" server. Each server in the farm can be set up with a maximum number of connections, and when all the connections to all your servers are in use, additional requests can be routed to a fixed page on an overflow server.

The overflow server can provide an information page that tells the user that the service is at peak load and ask him or her to return later, or if it is a news service, for example, it may contain a simple HTML rendering of the top five news items. This would allow you to deal with situations like 9/11, or the Michael Jackson story, where most news services were knocked offline by the huge demand for information from the public. A static HTML version of your news page can be served to a very large number of connections from a simple static server.

You can also use the overflow server to host a "site maintenance" page, which can be switched in to display to users when you have to take the whole farm offline for updates or maintenance.

# Using Direct Server Return

As your traffic grows and you add more and more servers to your web server farm, another performance issue can surface that limits the rate at which you can deliver pages. In the simple distributed web application just described, both the requests from the user's browser and the responses from your web server have to pass through your load balancing solution. The Linux Virtual Servers solution does not suffer from this limitation by the nature of its design, but most of the other solutions do.

A technique has been developed called direct server return (DSR), which bypasses the load balancing system for web server responses, and writes the response directly from the web server to the user's browser. This sleight of hand is done at the networking level, so your application is not aware of the difference. It means, however, that the load balancer is dealing only with the requests, which tend in the most part to be small compared to the responses.

Figure 7–3 shows the flow of data when the server farm is configured to use direct server return (DSR).

**Distributed Web Application With Direct Server Return**

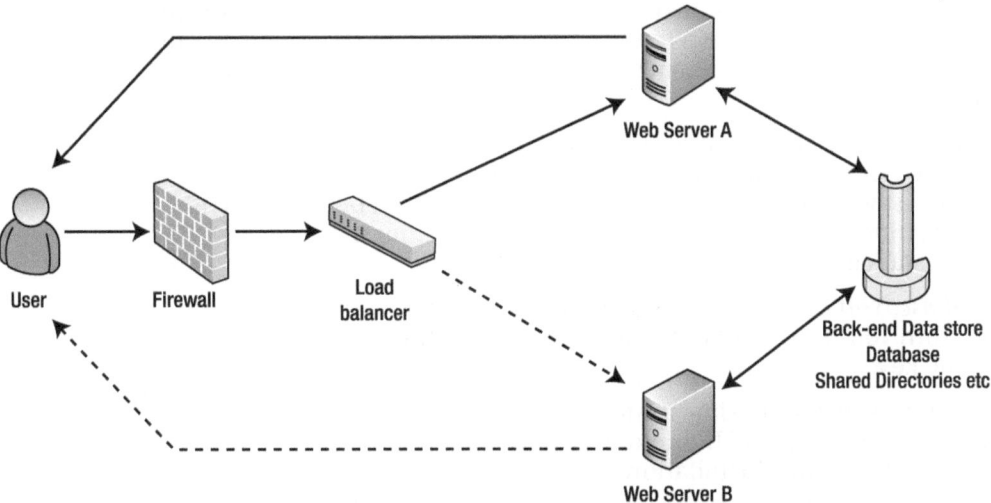

*Figure 7–3. Distributed web application with direct server return*

Again, like the Linux Virtual Server solution, this solution requires a special configuration of your web server's network interface, and specific support from the load balancer to pass across information allowing that direct return connection to be formed. So it is not suitable for cloud-based or virtual hosting solutions, which typically have limited opportunity for changing the way they interface with the hardware.

Because the configuration of DSR is highly specific to each load balancing solution and vendor, it is beyond the scope of this book to describe the setup and configuration.

However, you should discuss it with your hosting provider if you feel it would benefit your circumstances.

## Sharing Sessions Between Members of a Farm

For a simple static web site, sessions are not required, and no special action needs to be taken to ensure they are correctly distributed across all the machines in a farm. However, if your site supports any kind of logged-in behavior, you will need to maintain sessions, and you will need to make sure they are correctly shared.

By default PHP sets up its sessions using file-based session stores. A directory on the local disk of the web server is used to store serialized session data, and a cookie (default is PHPSESSID) is used to maintain an association between the client's browser and the session data in the file.

When you distribute your application, you have to ensure that all web servers can access the same session data for each user. There are three main ways this can be achieved.

1. *Memcache*: Use a shared Memcache instance to store session data. When you install the Memcache extension using PECL, it will prompt you as to whether you wish to install session support. If you do, it will allow you to set your `session.save_handler` to "Memcache" and it will maintain shared state.

2. *Files in a shared directory*: You can use the file-based session state store (`session.save_handler="files"`) so long as you make sure that `session.save_path` is set to a directory that is shared between all of the machines. NFS is typically used to share a folder in these circumstances.

3. *Database*: You can create a user session handler to serialize data to and from your back-end database server using the session ID as a unique key.

Before using a specific sharing strategy, you need to check that support for that method is supported in your PHP build. Use phpinfo to list the details of the session extension available on your installation.

Check to make sure that a suitable "Register Save Handler" is installed for the method you have chosen. Figure 7–4 shows what to expect in your phpinfo page, if your Memcache extension is installed correctly and the Memcache save handler has been correctly registered.

## session

| Session Support | enabled |
|---|---|
| Registered save handlers | files user memcache sqlite |
| Registered serializer handlers | php php_binary wddx |

| Directive | Local Value | Master Value |
|---|---|---|
| session.auto_start | Off | Off |
| session.bug_compat_42 | Off | Off |
| session.bug_compat_warn | Off | Off |
| session.cache_expire | 180 | 180 |
| session.cache_limiter | nocache | nocache |
| session.cookie_domain | no value | no value |
| session.cookie_httponly | Off | Off |
| session.cookie_lifetime | 0 | 0 |
| session.cookie_path | / | / |
| session.cookie_secure | Off | Off |
| session.entropy_file | no value | no value |
| session.entropy_length | 0 | 0 |
| session.gc_divisor | 1000 | 1000 |
| session.gc_maxlifetime | 1440 | 1440 |
| session.gc_probability | 1 | 1 |
| session.hash_bits_per_character | 5 | 5 |
| session.hash_function | 0 | 0 |
| session.name | PHPSESSID | PHPSESSID |
| session.referer_check | no value | no value |
| session.save_handler | files | files |
| session.save_path | no value | no value |
| session.serialize_handler | php | php |
| session.use_cookies | On | On |
| session.use_only_cookies | On | On |
| session.use_trans_sid | 0 | 0 |

*Figure 7–4. Session extension segment in phpinfo*

## Sharing Assets with a Shared File System

Aside from the PHP files that make up your application, you will often need to serve other assets, such as images, videos, .css files, and .js files. While you can deploy any fixed assets to each web server, if you are supporting user-generated content and allowing users to upload videos, images, and other assets, you have to make sure they are available to all your web servers. The easiest way to do this is to maintain a shared directory structure between all your web servers and map the user content storage to that directory. Again, like in the case of shared session files, you can use NFS to share a mount point between machines.

In services like Amazon EC2, you can use an external S3 bucket to store both fixed and user-contributed assets. As S3 supports referencing stored files with a simple URL, the S3 bucket can also be used to serve the files without placing the burden of doing so on your web servers.

## Sharing Assets with a Separate Asset Server

Another strategy for dealing with shared assets is to place them onto a separate system optimized for serving static files. While Apache is a good all-round web serving solution, its flexibility and complexity mean it is often not the best solution for high-performance distribution of static content. Other solutions, such as lighttpd and Nginx, can often deliver static content at a considerably higher rate. We saw how more efficient lighttpd and nginx were when serving static content in chapter 6.

## Sharing Assets with a Content Distribution Network

A content distribution network (CDN) is a hierarchically distributed network of caching proxy servers, with a geographical load balancing capability built in. The main purpose is to cache infrequently changing files in machines that are as close as possible to the user's browser. To that end, each network maintains a vast network of caching servers distributed into key points around the Internet.

The geographical DNS system locates a cache server that is closest to your web site user, and pulls through and caches a copy of the static asset while serving it to the user. Subsequent requests for that asset are serviced from the closest cached copy without the request being sent all the way back to your web server. By serving these requests from the CDN cache server closest to your user, you can gain a considerable boost in the rendering time of your page.

Figure 7–5 shows a simplified diagram of how a CDN caches content close to your users. You have control over which components of your site are cached and which are passed straight through to your system.

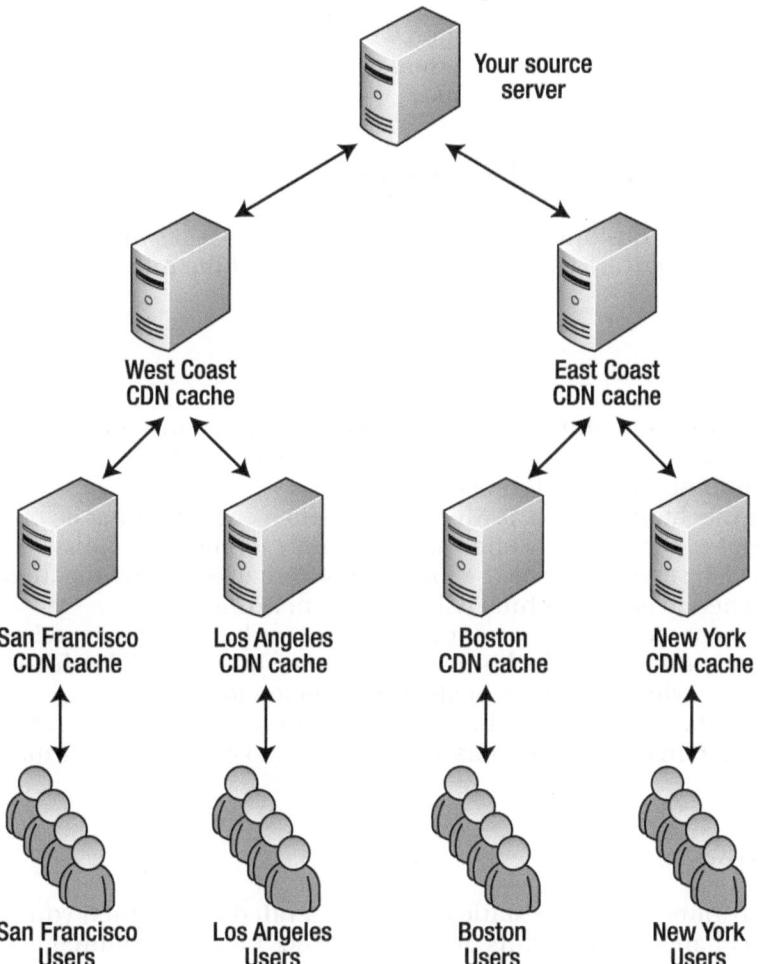

**Figure 7–5.** *Example of geographical distribution via a CDN*

Some typical CDN systems include the following:

- *Akamai*: One of the best-known and most extensive CDN solutions, not really suitable for small to medium sites because of its costs.

- *CD Networks*: Like Akamai, this content distribution network is designed for large-scale deployments.

- *Limelight*: Another well-known CDN system, Limelight also provides remote storage of assets as well as distribution.

- *Amazon CloudFront*: A simple CDN integrated with Amazon EC2/S3, notable for its contract-free pay-as-you-go model; not quite as extensive as previously mentioned solutions

# Pitfalls of Using Distributed Architectures

Distributing your application across multiple servers can lead to some issues that you should be aware of in your planning. Here we will try to define some of the most common problems that can occur.

## Cache Coherence Issues

It is common in many applications to maintain application-level caches—for example, caching RSS feeds. If the caching mechanism is not shared between all members of your web server farm, you may see some cache coherence effects.

If you use a shared cache mechanism such as Memcache, which each member is connected to, then you will not experience any effects. But if your caching mechanism uses local resources on each web server, such as the local file system or APC caching, then it is possible that the data cached in each machine will not be synchronized.

This can result in inconsistent views being presented to a user as he or she is switched from server to server. Somebody refreshing the home page may see the cached RSS feed in a different state depending on which server he or she is connected to.

Wherever possible you should use shared caching mechanisms on web server farms, or ensure that data that is cached in local caches has a long data persistence, to minimize the effects.

## Cache Versioning Issues

If you are using a CDN to distribute and cache static or user-generated assets, then you need to make sure that if you change the contents of any of the files being distributed, you either change the file name or issue any command required to flush the CDN of the old version of the file. If you don't do this, then when you release the new version of your application, you may find that users will see your new page design but with your old images, .js files, or .css files.

Another common way of mitigating these problems is to name assets with a version number—for example, /assets/v5/img/logo.jpg—and increment the version number on each release. You don't need to make separate copies of each version. A simple rewrite rule will make Apache ignore the difference, but will force a CDN to re-cache the asset.

You can make your web server ignore the version element of the URL using the mod_rewrite rule shown below.

```
RewriteEngine    on
RewriteRule      ^/assets/v[.A-Za-z0-9_-]+/(.*) /assets/$1 [PT]
```

Now any request to the following URLs will access the same asset at
/assets/img/logo.jpg.

```
/assets/v1/img/logo.jpg
/assets/vtesting/img/logo.jpg
/assets/v1234/img/logo.jpg
```

To use this in your code, just generate all of your asset URLs using a global version
number that you increment on each release, such as the following:

```
<img src="/assets/v{$global_version}/img/logo.jpg"/>
```

If you are using a version control system like subversion to manage your code, you
could even consider using the version number of your application repository as the
version number.

Another popular method of implementing asset versioning is to use a query string–
based version number, i.e., add a "?nnn" to the end of an asset file reference. However,
this method does not work with all CDN systems; in particular, CloudFront ignores query
strings on URIs.

For example, using the query string method, you would create the versioned logo
reference using the following insert. Using this method, you do not need to use a rewrite
rule, but it is not guaranteed to work with all CDN systems.

```
<img src="/assets/img/logo.jpg?{$global_version}"/>
```

## User IP Address Tracking

One hazard of using a distributed server farm with a load balancer in front of a set of
servers is that the IP addresses that each web server "sees" as the source of the request is
not the client browser IP address, but the address of the load balancing system. This can
have several drawbacks.

It should be noted that many content distribution networks have the same problem,
in that they mask the IP address of the client's browser. Solutions in these cases will be
specific to the network you are using.

The problems you may encounter are:

- If you use a log file analyzer to provide stats for your marketing or
  product management group, the log file analyzer can become
  confused by the lack of the client IP address, and can fail to calculate
  the correct number of unique users and visits to your site. Most load
  balancers and proxies can be configured to insert an "X-Forwarded-
  For" header into the request they pass onto the web server, which
  contains the true IP address of the user's browser. The web server can
  then be configured to use that value instead of the normal IP address
  in its log files, restoring the stats system's ability to discriminate
  unique users.

- If you are using firewall rules or other application-specific mechanisms to block or track IP addresses in each web server, then again they can become confused by the absence of a direct source IP address. While application-based mechanisms can use a similar method as just described to acquire the true IP address, firewall rules such as address blocking generally cannot use the data sent by the CDN or the load balancer, because they operate at the network-layer level, and don't understand HTTP headers. Fortunately most solutions include the ability to define rules outside the web server, in the service or device itself; however, the methods used are specific to the solution and are outside the scope of this book.

For cases where there is an "X-Forwarded-For" header inserted, you can change the format of the standard Apache access log to include it instead of the network IP address by using the following definition inside your vhost description. Place it immediately before the directives that define your log file.

```
LogFormat "%{X-Forwarded-For}i %l %u %t \"%r\" %s %b \"%{Referer}i\" \"%{User-agent}i\""
forwarded
CustomLog "logs/mysite-access_log" forwarded
```

If you want all of your hosts to use this format without having to decleare each one seperately, then add it into your `httpd.conf` file immediately before your vhosts are defined.

```
LogFormat "%{X-Forwarded-For}i %l %u %t \"%r\" %s %b \"%{Referer}i\" \"%{User-agent}i\""
combined
```

## Domino or Cascade Failure Effects

When you use a farm of web servers, you have to pay a lot of attention to the load factors on your servers. There is a condition called "domino failure effect" that can happen if you do not take care in correctly scaling the number of machines you use to match the load you need to support.

Imagine you have a web server farm consisting of two servers, each being loaded to 60 percent of its capacity, based on load average and concurrent requests, etc.

A failure of one of these two machines would result in the transfer of the entire load on that machine to the other server. This would leave the last machine trying to deal with a load of 120 percent of its total capacity, and it is likely to trigger a failure of that machine, too. This is where the domino effect kicks in.

When you design a web farm, you have to make sure that the farm can tolerate the failure of one or a number of machines depending on its size. If you use two machines, then you must monitor the loading factors, and if the load exceeds 50 percent, you should be planning to add an additional machine to the mix. At all times, you must be able to support the capacity being handled by the maximum machines that you plan to support simultaneous failure of being transferred to the rest of the farm, otherwise you are vulnerable to this failure mode.

Remember also that it's not just failure you need to plan for. One of the big advantages of using multiple machines is that you have the opportunity to perform rolling upgrades or maintenance, taking each machine offline in turn.

## Deployment Failures

If you have a single server, then deployment failures are immediately obvious—your site or service does not work. But with a web farm, it's possible to have a machine where, for one reason or another, a deployment or update does not work, and unless you test each and every machine after any change, you may not immediately pick up on it.

You service may appear to function correctly when viewed from the load balancer, especially if your load balancer is attempting to keep connections with Keep-Alive on them routed to the same server. But another user may see random or permanent failures depending on which server he or she is connected to. Make sure that your deployment procedures include a step to check out each server independently. To that end, it is often a good idea to have a DNS entry mapped to each individual server (i.e., `www1.example.com`, `www2.example.com`) so that you can perform this validation step.

# Monitoring Your Application

Once you have your application deployed and operating smoothly, you have to keep it that way. You could just use the procedure we described at the start of this chapter to re-access your application periodically and determine if you need to scale your application hardware up. A better solution is to install a monitoring system.

Having a real-time monitoring system installed allows you to see at a glance how your application is performing. Most monitoring systems are also capable of triggering "alerts" if any parameter of your system moves outside limits that you set. So as well as providing you with confidence that your system is operating well, they can also operate as an early warning system to alert you of trouble.

For example, if one of your web servers drops out, you can have the monitoring system send you an e-mail or SMS message alerting you to the problem.

## Some Monitoring Systems for You to Investigate

We could write a whole book about monitoring systems. Since the subject of installing and setting up a good monitoring solution is beyond the scope of this book, we will confine ourselves to listing some of the more popular open source solutions and allow you to choose between them.

- *Ganglia*: A real-time monitoring system especially suitable for monitoring arrays or farms of servers, as well as providing performance statistics about individual servers, Ganglia is capable of "rolling up" statistics to provide combined statistics for a group of

servers operating in a farm. More information can be found at
http://ganglia.sourceforge.net/.

- *Cacti*: Another well-recommended real-time monitoring tool,
  notable for its very large number of available "probes" for
  monitoring every part of your application stack; more information
  can be found at www.cacti.net/.

- *Nagios*: The grandfather of open source monitoring systems,
  extremely good at system availability monitoring—huge library of
  "probes"; more information can be found at www.nagios.org/.

## Summary

In this chapter, we have learned how to determine the request profile of our application,
and from that determine its memory footprint. We have used that information to limit the
processes on our system to prevent disk swapping.

We have also examined some configuration file tweaks that can improve
performance, especially when serving static objects, a fact often overlooked by engineers
focused on PHP performance.

We have also looked at what we can do when our performance needs overflow the
capacity of a single server, and some of the requirements of operating in a distributed
fashion.

Additionally we have looked at what options exist for offloading the responsibility for
serving static assets such as images, .js files, and .css files.

Finally we have described some of the monitoring tools available from the open
source community, to allow you to keep a close eye on both the health and performance
of your web server, so that you can rest assured that you will have advanced warning of
any developing problems.

# CHAPTER 8

■ ■ ■

# Database Optimization

There have probably been tens of thousands of pages written on the subject of database optimization, a good portion of them relating to MySQL. In one chapter of this book, we will never be able to cover the entire breadth of this subject.

Instead we will focus on what is relevant to you as a PHP programmer, and see if we can provide some tools and rules of thumb that make sure that you can deal with the basics, and not create any problems of performance with your application that may require expensive surgery at a later date to rectify.

In this chapter, we will learn about how MySQL uses memory, and show you a tool that allows you to optimize the configuration of your MySQL server to maximize its performance. We will also look at how you can determine if your CPU or disk system is running out of steam.

Finally, you'll see how to spot bad queries, determine how they are being handled, and optimize your indexes to eliminate unnecessary disk I/O.

As we can see in Figure 8–1, the database layer is one of the last layers of the application before we hit the OS. Because of its foundation position in the application, the whole application's performance will often hinge on the performance of the database server. Hence it is vitally important to shield it from excessive load and ensure it is optimized to run as efficiently as possible.

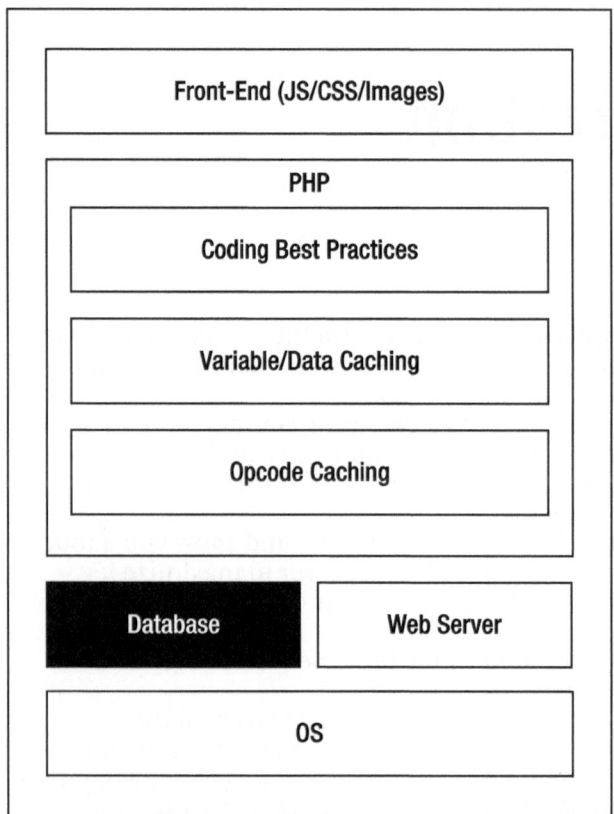

*Figure 8–1. PHP application component stack*

# About MySQL

MySQL is a relational database management system (RDBMS) designed to provide access to data stored in various storage engines using Structured Query Language (SQL).

The MySQL source code is available under the GNU General Public License, but can also be provided under a commercial license, which provides enterprise-level support.

MySQL has inspired many derivative projects that build on various aspects of the project for specialist applications. Alternative projects include MariaDB, OurDelta, Drizzle, and Percona Server (XtraDB).

Specialized distributions or patch-sets are provided by organizations such as Percona, Google, and Facebook, which add extra scalability options to the standard MySQL distribution.

MySQL is available on all mainstream operating systems: Linux, Windows, Mac OS X, Solaris, FreeBSD, etc.

# Understanding MySQL Storage Engines

MySQL is a layered application, with various layers for handling communications, query parsing, optimization, and finally data storage and access (Figure 8–2).

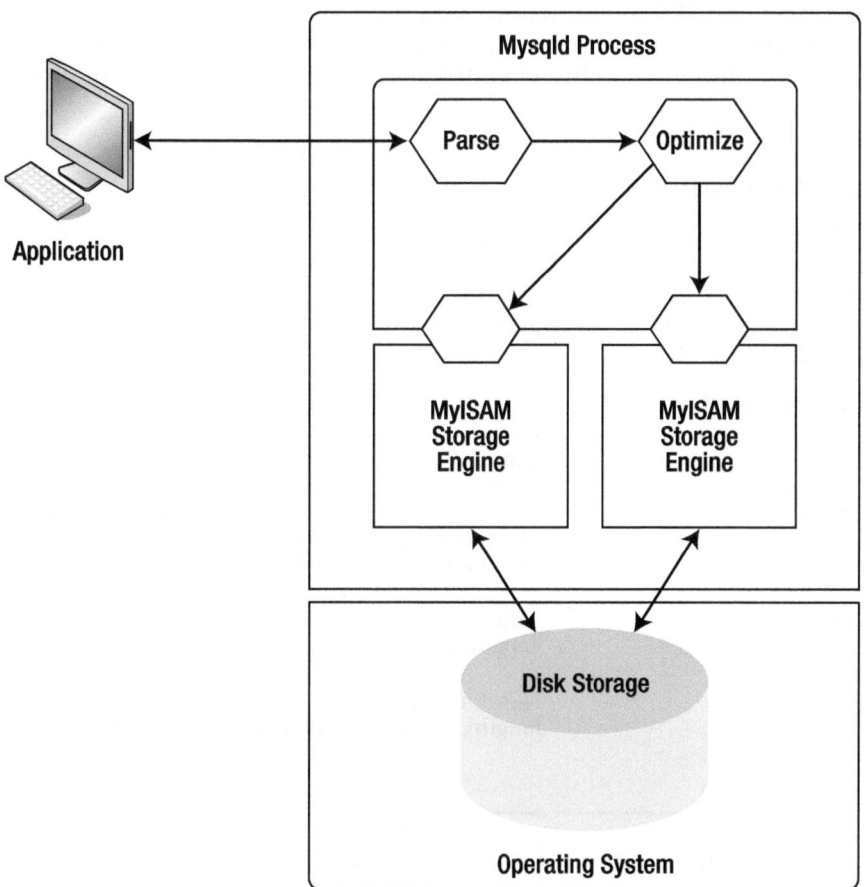

***Figure 8–2.*** *mysqld process and storage engines*

One great MySQL feature is the ability to have multiple data storage and access layers called "storage engines." The default distribution ships with a number of them. The two most well known are the "MyISAM" engine and the "InnoDB" engine.

The other engines are mainly designed for specialist functions and are of little general interest, but MyISAM and InnoDB are heavily used in most installations and merit some further description.

Rather than focusing on the details of each, we will list only some of the main pros and cons of each engine, as a means of helping you understand their strengths and weaknesses, and choose which one you should use.

Unfortunately, it's not just a simple case of saying "xxx" is better than "yyy" and making a simple recommendation; there are multiple attributes of each of these engines that make them more or less suited for certain applications.

You will have to make this decision early on in your development cycle, which may significantly alter the way you not only architect your system, but also set up and deploy it too.

## MyISAM: The Original Engine

MyISAM is the original storage engine that was developed alongside MySQL itself. It was designed for fast retrieval of records in predominantly read-based workloads using a single unique key per record. For sites that are perhaps 95–100 percent read-based, it is without a doubt the best solution. However, it has a few wrinkles that you need to be aware of, which are listed in Table 8–1.

*Table 8–1.* *MyISAM Pros and Cons*

| Pros | Cons |
| --- | --- |
| Fast unique key lookup times | Table-level locking; if your application spends more than 5 percent of its time writing to a table, then table locks are going to slow it down. |
| Supports full-text indexing | Non-transactional, no start => commit/abort capability |
| Select count(*) is fast. | Has durability issues; table crash can require lengthy repair operations to bring it back online. |
| Takes up less space on disk | |

MyISAM is non-transactional, in that it cannot roll back failed transactions or failed queries.

## InnoDB: The Pro's Choice

InnoDB is an ACID-compliant (atomicity, consistency, isolation, durability) storage engine, which includes versioning and log journaling, and has commit, rollback, and crash-recovery features to prevent data corruption. InnoDB also implements row-level locking and consistent non-locking reads, which can significantly increase multi-user concurrency and performance. InnoDB stores user data in clustered indexes to reduce disk I/O for the most popular query type, queries based on primary keys. To maintain data integrity, InnoDB also supports foreign keys, referential integrity constraints.

You can implement InnoDB tables alongside tables from MyISAM, even within the same database. Table 8–2 shows the main pros and cons of the InnoDB storage engine.

*Table 8–2. InnoDB Pros and Cons*

| Pros | Cons |
| --- | --- |
| Transactional; queries can be abandoned and rolled back. Crashes don't result in damaged data. | SELECT count(*) from xxxx queries are considerably slower. |
| Has row-level locking; concurrent writes to different rows of the same table don't end up being serialized. | No full-text indexing |
| Supports versioning for full ACID capability | Auto Increment fields *must* be first field in table; can cause issues with migration |
| Supports several strategies for online backup | Takes up more disk space |
| Improves concurrency in high-load, high-connection applications | Can be slower than MyISAM for some simpler query forms, but excels at complex multi-table queries |

# Choosing a Storage Engine

As stated before, the choice between MyISAM and InnoDB is a complex one; however, we can give you some simple rules of thumb that will help make that choice easier. The following sections provide just some of the reasons.

## When Your Application Is Mostly Read (> 95 Percent)

If when you look at the ratio of reads to writes in your application, you discover that it is predominantly read-only, with infrequent changes to its tables, then MyISAM is definitely the way to go. It is faster in mostly read workloads, and the lack of extensive writes to the tables minimizes performance issues due to MyISAM's lack of row-level locking.

## When You Need Transactions and Consistency Is Important

Again a no-brainer, InnoDB is definitely the right choice here. MyISAM has no support for transactions, and cannot roll back failed updates to maintain consistency.

### When You Have a Complex Schema That Has a Lot of Joined Tables

Again InnoDB is the choice of champions here. InnoDB supports referential integrity checks such as foreign key constraints, an important feature for ensuring large, complex schemas remain intact.

Additionally the transactional capability of InnoDB ensures that if you are updating multiple tables with constrained relationships, any problems with part of an update can trigger a rollback of the entire update—again an important requirement for referential integrity.

### When Non-stop Operation Is Important

The recommendation would be InnoDB if you need to have 24x7 uptime. MyISAM does not have the journaling, versioning, and logging that protect the data from crashes, and almost all MyISAM backup solutions require some form of downtime, even if only momentary.

# Understanding How MySQL Uses Memory

MySQL loves memory—it just drinks it up, and the more you give it, the better its performance will be, up to a point. There is a point where you exceed the "working set" of your data, and beyond that point you will see very little improvement, regardless of how much memory you give it.

The "working set" is that set of data that is in common use, You may have a 15GB database of news articles, but if people are searching back only a maximum of two weeks from the current date in your search interface, then your "working set" would consist of the amount of data represented by all the articles with a publication date less than 14 days old. Once that set of data can comfortably sit in memory, then you probably won't see any major performance gains, especially if you have a good set of indexes.

In order for MySQL to use all the memory you have installed in your system, you have to configure it to use it.

In the next section, we will have a look at some of the directives that are used to control memory usage, and hence directly affect performance.

## InnoDB vs. MyISAM Memory Usage

The MySQL configuration file provides a plethora of directives that can be used to control much of the memory footprint of your server. The information that can be set is broken down into a number of general "classes" of directives.

- Directives that affect the size of buffers and caches that are common to all storage engines

- Directives that affect only the MyISAM storage engine

- Directives that affect only the InnoDB storage engine; generally these directives start with "innodb_".

- Directives that control limits for various resources, such as number of connections, etc.

- Directives that define properties such as character sets, paths, etc.

If you have only one or the other storage engine in play, then you only have to worry about optimizing the memory for that engine. But with MySQL, it is possible to mix storage engines within the same server, even have tables inhabiting different engines within the same database, so you may need to split your memory allocation among two different engines. If you have a mixed storage set, and there are no good reasons to be using the smaller of the two, then it is probably a good idea to convert the database to one single storage engine in order to make things easier to manage. Mixed storage engines also limit some of your options when it comes to performing backups, as we shall see later.

## Per Server vs. per Connection (Thread) Memory Usage

When configuring the size of memory buffers and caches in the configuration file, you have to bear in mind that some memory structures are allocated per connection or thread (see Figure 8–3). MySQL will use more memory as the number of connections made to it rises, so it is vitally important to ensure that you are careful to minimize the number of open connections from your applications to the database server.

Let us look at how MySQL splits memory allocations between dynamic (connection-based) memory use and fixed (instance-based) memory use.

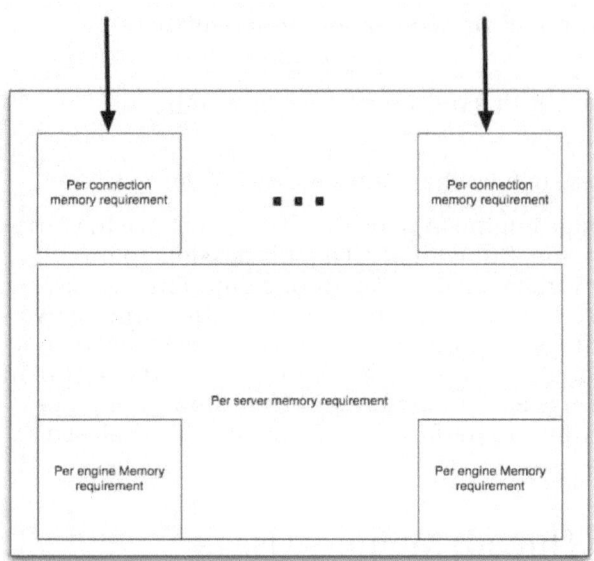

**Figure 8–3.** *Overview of where mysqld allocates memory*

The amount of memory consumed per active connection (dynamic) is as follows:

```
per_connection_memory =
        read_buffer_size                    // memory for sequential table scans
        +read_rnd_buffer_size               // Memory for buffering reads
        +sort_buffer_size                   // Memory for in mem sorts
        +thread_stack                       // Per connection memory
        +join_buffer_size                   // Memory for in mem table joins
```

The amount of memory consumed per server (fixed) is as follows:

```
per_server_memory =
        tmp_table_size                      // memory for all temp tables
        +max_heap_table_size                // max size of single temp table
        +key_buffer_size                    // memory allocated for index blocks
        +innodb_buffer_pool_size            // main cache for InnoDB data
        +innodb_additional_mem_pool_size    // InnoDB record structure cache
        +innodb_log_buffer_size             // log file write buffer
        +query_cache_size                   // compiled statement cache
```

The maximum memory that MySQL can consume is then defined as follows:

```
max_memory = (per_connection_memory * max_connections) + per_server_memory
```

From this you can easily see that if you have a lot of data, then you will need to provide sufficient memory to ensure that as many operations as possible are placed into memory, and don't require expensive disk reads and writes. However, an often overlooked aspect is that MySQL requires memory per connection, so if you have a lot of web servers connected to your MySQL server, each with a lot of active connections, then you may have to provide sufficient memory to support them.

We will now move on to looking at how we can determine the amount of memory that we need to allocate to these memory buffers.

# Locating Your Configuration File

Before we look at optimizing the use of memory, you need to determine where your MySQL configuration file is, so that you can apply any changes that the process outlines. Unfortunately there are many different opinions about where this file should be located.

The standard MySQL daemon looks for its configuration file in the locations listed in Table 8–3. If a file exists in multiple locations, then the files are loaded in top-to-bottom order, with directives in the lower files taking priority over the higher ones.

*Table 8–3. Standard Locations That MySQL Will Search for Configuration Files*

| File Name | Intention |
| --- | --- |
| /etc/my.cnf | Global database options |
| /etc/mysql/my.cnf | Global database options (as of MySQL 5.1.15) |
| [SYSCONFDIR]/my.cnf | Global database options |
| $MYSQL_HOME/my.cnf | Server-specific options |
| [CUSTOM] | The file specified with --defaults-extra-file= |
| ~/.my.cnf | User-specific options |

Each file is laid out as a standard .ini file format, with sections such as "[mysqld]" and directives within each section.

After changing the configuration file, you will need to restart your server for the changes to take effect.

## Mysqltuner.pl: Tuning Your Database Server's Memory

In this section, we are going to work through an assessment of the performance of an existing database server, and show you how, using a few simple techniques and tools, we can determine if the server is correctly configured.

To perform this task, we are going to use a few common or easily available tools to gather some information about the state of our target system.

The first useful bit of information is the first part of the "top" display for this server. It tells us more about how much load is on the server, if it is swapping, and how much of the total memory the mysqld process is using (Figure 8–4).

```
top - 09:38:13 up 235 days,  2:39,  1 user,  load average: 0.62, 0.56, 0.44
Tasks:  69 total,   1 running,  65 sleeping,   0 stopped,   3 zombie
Cpu(s):  4.3%us,  0.0%sy,  0.0%ni, 86.5%id,  9.0%wa,  0.0%hi,  0.2%si,  0.0%st
Mem:  17927580k total, 17851776k used,    75804k free,   185020k buffers
Swap:        0k total,        0k used,        0k free,  4989364k cached


  PID USER      PR  NI  VIRT  RES  SHR S %CPU %MEM    TIME+  COMMAND
16570 mysql     15   0 12.9g  11g 6032 S    9 66.4  3567:29 mysqld
    1 root      15   0 10304  800  672 S    0  0.0  0:07.93 init
```

*Figure 8–4. Top command output for a moderately loaded MySQL server*

From the information just shown, we can see that the server is not particularly loaded. The load factors are only 0.62, 0.56, and 0.44, which is very low for the load on this machine.

The machine is not swapping at all, and the CPU and memory usage for mysqld are 9 percent and 66 percent respectively, again very good. It is not taking up much CPU, and it's using a reasonable amount of the system memory. If the system had been using excessive CPU or memory (swapping), we would focus our attention on reducing the maximum memory footprint of MySQL to prevent the overflow. This particular server is fitted with 17.5GB of RAM.

Now let's look at the I/O performance using the iostat tools. iostat should be installable from your distribution's software repositories, and should be available on all distributions. We will use it with the -d -c and -x options, which enable device, CPU, and extended stats. Figure 8–5 shows the output that is produced when running iostat against our example server.

```
$ iostat -d -c -x 2
Linux 2.6.21.7-2.fc8xen-ec2-v1.0 (db64)         Wednesday, 03 November, 2010

avg-cpu:   %user   %nice %system %iowait   %steal   %idle
            9.83    0.05    2.68    1.29     0.08    86.06

Device:          rrqm/s   wrqm/s     r/s     w/s    ...   await  svctm  %util
sda1               0.00     3.46    0.02    1.33    ...    0.99   0.09   0.01
sdb                0.77     7.26    1.14    2.29    ...   50.77   4.79   1.64

avg-cpu:   %user   %nice %system %iowait   %steal   %idle
            5.84    0.00    0.00   11.68     0.00    82.49

Device:          rrqm/s   wrqm/s     r/s     w/s    ...   await  svctm  %util
sda1               0.00    15.38    0.00    3.08    ...    0.00   0.00   0.00
sdb                0.00     9.74    1.03   17.44    ...  269.78  25.58  47.23
```

*Figure 8–5. iostat -d -c -x 2 output for a moderately loaded MySQL server*

From the iostat report, we can see that the utilization (%util) of the drive that holds the database files (sdb) is varying in the range of 1.64=>47.23 percent. Again this is not particularly of concern. This value (%util) shows how much of the I/O performance of the disk channel is being used during the sample. Our drives are not overloaded—that is also confirmed by the %iowait value, which indicates the amount of time the system is waiting for I/O operations to complete. This is in the range of 1.29=>11.68 percent, which again tells us that all is OK—the system is not particularly I/O bound.

If you see high %util or %iowait values, you should look at the performance of your drives, or look at opening up some of the MySQL memory buffers to reduce the amount of times the MySQL server has to hit the disks. But this system does not exhibit any issues with I/O performance, so we shall move on.

Now you can start to examine the internals of the MySQL server process itself. We will introduce a very cool open source tool called mysqltuner.pl, which takes a lot of the hard work out of configuring and checking a database server. While it is no substitute for having a good in-depth knowledge of the tuning process, it is, however, a great way of getting a fast "sanity" check for your server setup and spotting obvious cases of misconfiguration. The script will also examine the recent usage of the machine and suggest changes that would improve performance based on actual use.

You can run this script against your live server. It is not intrusive and does not impose any significant load in itself, so you can use it to health check your machine on a regular basis.

To install the script, you need to download it to your database server. The author of the script has registered the domain mysqltuner.pl and made the script the equivalent of the home page. So to download and install it, just follow the step here.

```
$wget mysqltuner.pl -O mysqltuner.pl
$chmod +x mysqltuner.pl
```

You should now be able to run the script as shown here. You will be prompted for a username and password that have rights to your database server. Once entered, the script will inspect your server and produce something similar to the output shown in Figure 8–6.

```
$ ./mysqltuner.pl

 >>  MySQLTuner 1.0.1 - Major Hayden <major@mhtx.net>
 >>  Bug reports, feature requests, and downloads at http://mysqltuner.com/
 >>  Run with '--help' for additional options and output filtering
Please enter your MySQL administrative login: root
Please enter your MySQL administrative password:
[!!] Successfully authenticated with no password - SECURITY RISK!

-------- General Statistics -------------------------------------------------
[--] Skipped version check for MySQLTuner script
[OK] Currently running supported MySQL version 5.0.45-log
[OK] Operating on 64-bit architecture

-------- Storage Engine Statistics ------------------------------------------
[--] Status: -Archive -BDB -Federated +InnoDB -ISAM -NDBCluster
[--] Data in MyISAM tables: 589M (Tables: 649)
[--] Data in InnoDB tables: 11G (Tables: 138)
[!!] Total fragmented tables: 32

-------- Performance Metrics ------------------------------------------------
[--] Up for: 19d 21h 25m 22s (237M q [138.423 qps], 13M conn, TX: 688B, RX: 30B)
[--] Reads / Writes: 91% / 9%
[--] Total buffers: 10.1G global + 21.4M per thread (500 max threads)
[!!] Maximum possible memory usage: 20.5G (119% of installed RAM)
[OK] Slow queries: 0% (2K/237M)
[OK] Highest usage of available connections: 7% (39/500)
[OK] Key buffer size / total MyISAM indexes: 512.0M/204.4M
[OK] Key buffer hit rate: 100.0% (45M cached / 6K reads)
[!!] Query cache efficiency: 0.4% (487K cached / 112M selects)
[OK] Query cache prunes per day: 0
[OK] Sorts requiring temporary tables: 2% (133K temp sorts / 6M sorts)
[!!] Temporary tables created on disk: 38% (5M on disk / 14M total)
[OK] Thread cache hit rate: 99% (141 created / 13M connections)
[!!] Table cache hit rate: 1% (512 open / 36K opened)
[OK] Open file limit used: 29% (738/2K)
[OK] Table locks acquired immediately: 99% (4M immediate / 4M locks)
[!!] InnoDB data size / buffer pool: 11.1G/8.0G

-------- Recommendations ----------------------------------------------------
General recommendations:
    Run OPTIMIZE TABLE to defragment tables for better performance
    Reduce your overall MySQL memory footprint for system stability
    Temporary table size is already large - reduce result set size
    Reduce your SELECT DISTINCT queries without LIMIT clauses
    Increase table_cache gradually to avoid file descriptor limits
Variables to adjust:
  *** MySQL's maximum memory usage is dangerously high ***
  *** Add RAM before increasing MySQL buffer variables ***
    query_cache_limit (> 512M, or use smaller result sets)
    table_cache (> 512)
    innodb_buffer_pool_size (>= 11G)
```

*Figure 8–6. Output from mysqltuner.pl on a moderately loaded server*

Under the hood, the tuner script is accessing the database server and running two queries, "SHOW STATUS" and "SHOW VARIABLES." The former returns statistics about the current performance of the server, number of queries, efficiency of the caches, etc. The latter retrieves the size of all the internal data structures. From these two sets of information, the tuner script calculates the results just shown and uses a set of built-in rules to make recommendations.

This server is a medium-sized database server, which is supporting a site with daily user traffic of about 35,000 unique users per day, so it gets a fair number of queries.

While this server is performing fine, it still exhibits a number of issues, which we will examine, and we will determine what can be done about them.

## Possible Issues with Our Example Server

The preceding `mysqltuner.pl` report has highlighted two possible issues—one potentially serious, and the other not so serious.

The first issue is that the system is configured to use too much memory. It claims that it would use 119 percent of system RAM, but our inspection of the server memory usage says we are using only 66 percent. So what gives?

The clues come from the following lines in the report.

```
[--] Total buffers: 10.1G global + 21.4M per thread (500 max threads)
[!!] Maximum possible memory usage: 20.5G (119% of installed RAM)

[OK] Highest usage of available connections: 7% (39/500)
```

Remember the formula we saw earlier for calculating maximum memory usage? Part of that was a per connection value of 21.4MB. And since we have a configured maximum number of connections of 500, that adds up to about 10.7GB. We also have a fixed memory consumption of 10.1GB per server, so the total RAM that MySQL could consume is 20.8GB, which is about 15 percent more than the 17.5GB of RAM that is actually installed in the machine.

What this is saying is that if we allowed the number of connections to grow to its maximum of 500, the machine would be forced to swap. But the maximum amount of used connections is only 7 percent (39). The server has been running for 20 days, and the maximum number of connections has never risen over 39. So the first action that we can take is to reduce the maximum connections from 500 to 100, reducing the per connection pool total to 2.14GB. Now the total of 12.24 GB fits comfortably into the system's RAM of 17.5GB, and the risk of it going into a swap state is removed.

This now leaves us with about 4GB of RAM to spare, so the second improvement we can make is to increase the innodb_buffer_pool from 8GB to 11GB, so that the whole working set now fits into memory. As you can see, that was one of the recommendations that the tuner script made.

```
innodb_buffer_pool_size (>= 11G)
```

Finally the tuner script recommends that we up two other buffers, so we will split the final 1GB between the two, and we are done. Our server is back in tip-top shape.

```
query_cache_limit (> 512M, or use smaller result sets)
table_cache (> 512)
```

It should, however, be noted that this tuning is based on the load and query mix that the server has encountered so far. It would probably be a good idea to run the tuner once a month so you can get early warning of a developing issue that may require a hardware upgrade, such as adding extra RAM.

## Tuning InnoDB

InnoDB in particular is sensitive to being configured with the correct amount of memory. If you starve InnoDB of sufficient memory to buffer a reasonable amount of its data set in memory, then its performance can deteriorate rapidly. Here we provide a couple of simple examples of InnoDB memory settings that work well for a mid-range DB server.

The following settings are based on a 16GB database server, which is a pretty common size.

- *innodb_file_per_table*: By default InnoDB creates a file per database and manages the tables within it. This can mean it is difficult to recover disk space if a table grows and then shrinks in size. Setting this option will make InnoDB use a separate data store file per table. If you want to change this setting on an existing database, then you should back up the database, drop it, change the option, restart the server, and then reload the database from the backup.

- *innodb_buffer_pool_size=*: If you are using only InnoDB tables, then set this to about 70 percent of available memory. If you have a mixed MyISAM/InnoDB setup, then back it up a little to give MyISAM some space.

- *innodb_log_buffer_size=4M*: This size would deal with most record sizes and provide a reasonable performance. If you have large text fields or blobs or have unusually large record sizes, then be prepared to take it up a bit.

- *innodb_log_file_size=256M*: This is recommended and strikes a good balance between the speed of recovering a database and having good runtime performance.

- *innodb_flush_log_at_trx_commit=2*: This controls how often the log file is flushed to disk. If you can tolerate the loss of a few records in the event of a crash, then using a value of 2 eases up the number of disk writes, speeds up performance, and reduces I/O load on the drives.

# Finding Problem Queries

Tuning the server configuration is only one way of improving performance. By far the most common source of performance issues is badly structured queries or missing indexes.

MySQL has a built-in mechanism for logging low performance queries to a log file, so that they can be identified and optimized. To enable the slow query log on MySQL, you have the following two lines to the server configuration file, under the "[mysqld]" section.

```
[mysqld]
log-slow-queries = /var/log/mysql/mysqld-slow.log
long_query_time=1
```

You can substitute your own path as required, but make sure that the MySQL process can write to that folder. The long_query_time directive sets the threshold for execution that categorizes a query as slow. The example given is one second, so any query that takes longer than one second to run is logged to the slow query log file.

Let's look at an example. In my database system, I have a table called "articles," which has an "article_title" field. My application needs to fetch the first ten article titles sorted by title, so it can page through the articles ten at a time. The interface supports sorting by each of the columns displayed in the admin tool, of which the article title is one. The administrator has complained that when he switches to the sort-by-title view, the application becomes slow and moving from page to page is painful.

While we can all probably guess what the issue is with this query, it is useful to walk through the process of determining where the problem lies and correcting it, using tools that would help if it were a more complex problem.

The query that the application issues to get the column view data for the first page is as follows:

```
SELECT article_title from articles order by article_title limit 10;
```

When I run my query in the MySQL query tool, I get the results shown in Figure 8–7.

```
mysql> select article_title from articles order by article_title limit 10;
+-----------------------------------------------------------------------------------------+
| article_title                                                                           |
+-----------------------------------------------------------------------------------------+
| " I want to beat Ferguson's United "                                                    |
| "...one more triumph for the crass stupidity rapidly replacing culture in this country..." |
| "A bad day at the office"...                                                            |
| "A case Metzelder will be no more"                                                      |
| "A Smarter (and Cost-Efficient) Way to Fight Crime"                                     |
| "A Strike Fit To Win Any Game Of Football"                                              |
| "A Win, A Win, My Kingdom For A Win"                                                    |
| "Action" Jackson Asiku will carry the hopes of two nations on Friday night              |
| "Al Arabi Sports" logo unveiled                                                         |
| "All" or Nothing                                                                        |
+-----------------------------------------------------------------------------------------+
10 rows in set (6.92 sec)

mysql>
```

***Figure 8–7.*** *Example of a sorted article title query before optimization*

A time of 6.9 seconds—ouch, that's not very good. It's going to take a long time for our article administrator to page through all the articles if this is the query that is feeding his admin screen. So let's look at our slow query log.

```
# Time: 101103 23:03:00
# User@Host: root[root] @ localhost []
# Query_time: 6.920107  Lock_time: 0.000111 Rows_sent: 10   Rows_examined: 123675
SET timestamp=1288796580;
select article_title from articles order by article_title limit 10;
```

The slow query log is telling me that in order to locate my ten records and send them to me, it had to read 123,675 records from the articles table (the entire contents of the database table), and given that the page size of an article record is quite large because it contains all the article text too, that is clearly a lot of data to read from the disk. In fact, in our particular case, it amounts to almost 400MB of data in that table alone.

Normally you would use the slow query log file to find the queries that were causing problems; in this case, we had already spotted the problem or had the problem reported to us, and used the log to confirm our suspicions.

In the next section, we will use some tools built into MySQL to work out why the query is so slow and determine how we can correct for it.

## Analyzing Problem Queries

Having located our problem query, we can use a facility built into MySQL to show us the steps that the MySQL server would take to retrieve the data. This should give us a good clue about where the problem lies.

MySQL has a query analyzer that examines the query and, using information about the table that it targets, some statistics about the table itself, and its list of indexes. The result of this analysis is what is called an "execution plan," the list of steps it will perform to execute the query.

We can instruct MySQL to display the "execution plan" instead of running the query, so we can see what it would have done. To do this, we use the "Explain" syntax. Adding "Explain" to the front of any query will return a representation of the internal execution plan.

```
mysql> explain select article_title from articles order by article_title limit 10;
+----+-------------+----------+------+---------------+------+---------+------+--------+----------------+
| id | select_type | table    | type | possible_keys | key  | key_len | ref  | rows   | Extra          |
+----+-------------+----------+------+---------------+------+---------+------+--------+----------------+
|  1 | SIMPLE      | articles | ALL  | NULL          | NULL | NULL    | NULL | 123675 | Using filesort |
+----+-------------+----------+------+---------------+------+---------+------+--------+----------------+
```

So what have we learned from this? The important piece of information is the "using filesort" and the reference to 123,675 rows, which basically means take a copy of all the data in the table and sort it using quicksort so we can determine the first 10 records and send those back.

Adding an index on the "article_title" field should improve performance significantly, as the server would not have to create a temporary table and sort the contents. It would be able to determine which records it had to deliver in the correct order, by traversing the first ten items in the index, which is ordered, instead of the data file, which is not. So we added an index to the table with the following:

```
CREATE INDEX title_idx on articles (article_title);
```

And on re-running explain on our query, we can see that the sort is now using our index.

```
mysql> explain select article_title from articles order by article_title limit 10;
+----+-------------+----------+------+---------------+----------+---------+------+------+-------------+
| id | select_type | table    | type | possible_keys | key      | key_len | ref  | rows | Extra       |
+----+-------------+----------+------+---------------+----------+---------+------+------+-------------+
|  1 | SIMPLE      | articles | index| NULL          | title_idx| 767     | NULL | 10   | Using index |
+----+-------------+----------+------+---------------+----------+---------+------+------+-------------+
```

You can see that the number of rows that have been read has reduced down to ten, the same number that our query requests.

Now if we re-execute our query, we can see the effect of applying the index (Figure 8–8).

```
mysql> select article_title from articles order by article_title limit 10;
+-------------------------------------------------------------------------------------------+
| article_title                                                                             |
+-------------------------------------------------------------------------------------------+
| " I want to beat Ferguson's United "                                                       |
| "...one more triumph for the crass stupidity rapidly replacing culture in this country..." |
| "A bad day at the office"...                                                               |
| "A case Metzelder will be no more"                                                         |
| "A Smarter (and Cost-Efficient) Way to Fight Crime"                                        |
| "A Strike Fit To Win Any Game Of Football"                                                 |
| "A Win, A Win, My Kingdom For A Win"                                                        |
| "Action" Jackson Asiku will carry the hopes of two nations on Friday night                 |
| "Al Arabi Sports" logo unveiled                                                            |
| "All" or Nothing                                                                           |
+-------------------------------------------------------------------------------------------+
10 rows in set (0.00 sec)

mysql>
```

***Figure 8–8.*** *Example of our article title query after optimization*

This was a vast improvement in the performance of the query. It's now executing so fast that MySQL is not able to display a value for the duration of the query. So now our admin tool will zip from page to page in sort-by-article-title mode, and my administrator is a happy man again and owes me a big favor.

# Recommendations for PHP Database Applications

There are a couple of design issues that you really should consider before you start coding your application. In many cases, developers tend to go with the defaults that come out of the box on an initial MySQL setup. More often than not, the schema and configuration choices made by the developer inevitably end up becoming the defaults for the production system. Getting these wrong from the start can often mean an expensive process of trying to fix them after your application has gone live, and you hit the problems for the first time.

## Maintaining Separate Read and Write Connections

It is a good idea to initially create two database connections, one for read and one for write, and allow different database servers to be connected to them. If you have only one server, then set them to be the same as each other.

Then as you are coding your application, any query that changes data (UPDATE, INSERT, DELETE, etc.), you make against the write connection, and any query that is a pure SELECT or read, you make against the read connection.

If you have to scale your application, you can separate out the database servers to different machines and connect them via replication. But for that to work, you have to make sure all writes are directed to your master server, and all reads are directed to a suitable slave server.

By using two connections, you make it easy to reconfigure your application to support a number of different scaling options, using one or more slaves to increase query bandwidth. Building this in from the start takes very little effort, but significantly increases your options later on.

## Using "utf8" (Multi-byte Unicode) Character Set by Default

In this day and age, you should be writing all your applications using the "utf8" character set for storage and for page rendering. The overhead in storage density is minimal, and for ordinary ASCII text, there is no overhead at all. But if you have to support storage of any alternative languages to English, or handle foreign names and places in your data set, then you will need to have the capability. Converting a good-sized database from the default ISO-8859-1 format to "utf8" after you have launched your service is a daunting and time-consuming task. Give yourself a break and use "utf8" everywhere from the very start.

You can force all new database, tables, and text fields to be created by default in "utf8" by setting some parameters in the MySQL configuration file.

```
[mysqld]
collation_server=utf8_unicode_ci
character_set_server=utf8
skip-character-set-client-handshake
```

The last directive instructs the server not to perform negotiation for the character set with the clients. By setting this option, you can ensure that all your clients and connections are set to operate in "utf8" without having to specifically configure this on the my.cnf files of each of the servers connecting to this database server. It is a good way of ensuring consistent behavior from all the services interacting with your MySQL server, and to make sure you don't have character set conversion being applied on all data being read from or written to this server, which would impact performance.

Another indirect advantage you get by defaulting the character set, and turning off negotiation, is that you then don't need to send a "set NAMES utf8" statement to the connection to ensure it switched to utf8. While this statement is very small and does not take long to execute, it requires a round trip to and from the server, and many PHP frameworks issue it automatically before every query if you set the database connection to utf8. With the configuration just shown, you can avoid the need to set the connection character set, and avoid the repetitive sending of the statement.

The preceding directives also determine what happens if you create a database or table schema without any specific character-set schema attributes. Any entity created without the "[DEFAULT] CHARACTER SET utf8" attribute will automatically be set to "utf8" regardless. Watch out, however, if you are using a tool to manipulate your schemas, such as phpMyAdmin. Be careful that it does not apply its own defaults and create schema attributes that override the default choices you have just set.

## Using "UTC" Date Format

Likewise it is a good idea to use a common date format to store all date/time values. By doing so, it is easy to compare dates and times without worrying about time zones. Converting dates to and from UTC to a local time zone is easy in PHP.

In order to set MySQL to operating in UTC time zone, you have to make sure that the time zone support is installed in your MySQL instance. This is a database of information about specific time zones that is usually not installed by default.

To install time zone support in MySQL, first you have to find your OS time zone database. On most Linux systems, it can be found in /usr/share/zoneinfo. Once you have located the time zone database, you can use the "mysql_tzinfo_to_sql" utility supplied with MySQL to convert the time zone information into an SQL script suitable for loading into your MySQL system.

```
$ mysql_tzinfo_to_sql /usr/share/zoneinfo | mysql -u root mysql
Warning: Unable to load '/usr/share/zoneinfo/Asia/Riyadh87' as time zone. Skipping it.
Warning: Unable to load '/usr/share/zoneinfo/Asia/Riyadh88' as time zone. Skipping it.
Warning: Unable to load '/usr/share/zoneinfo/Asia/Riyadh89' as time zone. Skipping it.
```

You may see some warnings as just shown, which can safely be ignored.

Having loaded the time zone database into MySQL, you can alter the MySQL configuration file to specify UTC as the default time zone.

Open the configuration file, and add the following directive to the "[mysqld]" section of the file.

```
[mysqld]
default-time-zone=UTC
```

Restart your MySQL server, and it should now default all date/time values to UTC. If, for some reason, your MySQL server does not start, it is likely that the time zone database did not load and it was unable to set the default time zone. Check your mysqld.log file for any evidence that this is the case, and if it is, then double-check the installation of the time zone info database. If you try to set the default time zone without installing the time zone support database, then MySQL will not start.

PHP includes many functions for converting values to and from the UTC date format, many of which are "locale"-sensitive, so it is easy to create user interfaces that allow the user to set a preferred time zone, and have all dates/times displayed in his or her local time zone.

# Summary

In this chapter, we have learned about the overall structure of the MySQL server, and how it supports pluggable storage engines. We have learned about the characteristics of those storage engines, and how to choose one that is relevant to our application. We have examined how MySQL uses memory and learned some techniques for configuring MySQL to make best use of the memory available to it. We have also learned how to detect inefficient queries and learned a process for analyzing them and making corrections.

Throughout this book, we have shown you how to diagnose performance problems at each level of the application stack, from the PHP runtime, to the application code, to the web servers and finally onto the database server itself. In each case, we have shown you how to make changes to eliminate performance bottlenecks, or different coding strategies that minimize the effects.

Writing fast, efficient, scalable code is not about applying a set of rules of thumb. It is more about having a deeper insight into what is happening under the hood at each stage of your app, and coding to avoid the bottlenecks that can choke your application.

We hope that the tools and techniques that we have outlined in this book will help you shine a spotlight on the deeper, darker recesses of your applications, and develop a more complete understanding of how to write great apps.

■■■

# Installing Apache, MySQL, PHP, and PECL on Windows

Throughout the book, we outlined methods of improving different web servers and database configurations but stopped short of outlining a step-by-step guide to installing these tools. This appendix will act as a reference to help you install the main technologies shown here:

- Apache 2.2
- MySQL 5.0
- PHP 5.0
- PECL

## Installing Apache

As of this writing, Apache has released version 2.2.x of its free web server. Using the web site http://httpd.apache.org, click the "Download! from a mirror" link on the left-hand side, as shown in Figure A–1.

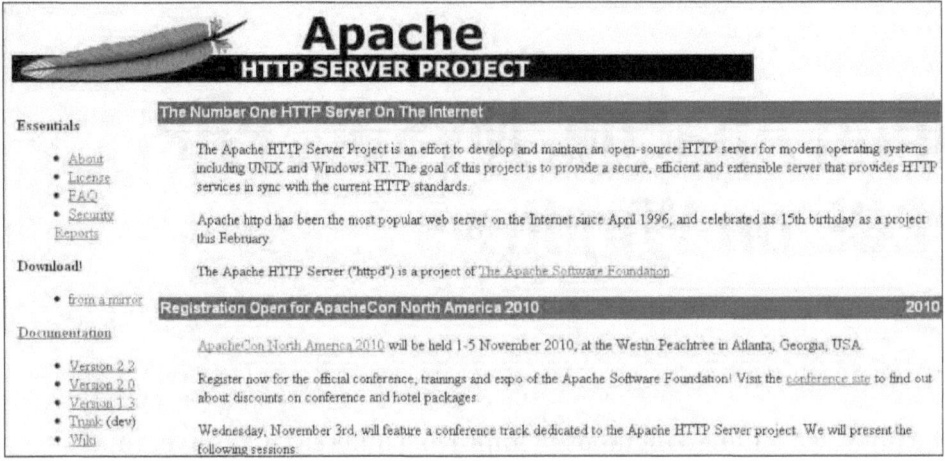

***Figure A–1.*** *Apache HTTP Server Project home page*

Select from one of the mirror sites shown in Figure A–2.

***Figure A–2.*** *Apache Server Windows and Unix download links*

Windows users should download the Windows installer file, `apache_2.2.x-win32-x86-no_ssl-r2.msi`.

Once the file has completely downloaded, open the installer. The initial window will be a security warning, and depending on your version of Windows, ignore it and click the Run button to get into the installation.

The next window is the Apache setup window. For those of you that have a previous version of Apache installed, you might receive another pop-up asking you to remove the previous installation before you begin with the new one. If you do not want to upgrade, skip these steps dealing with Apache. For everyone else, click the Next button in the initial window, shown in Figure A–3.

*Figure A–3. Apache Installation Welcome window*

Now select "I accept the terms in the license agreement," and click Next in the window shown in Figure A–4. Once you reach the next window, click the Next button again.

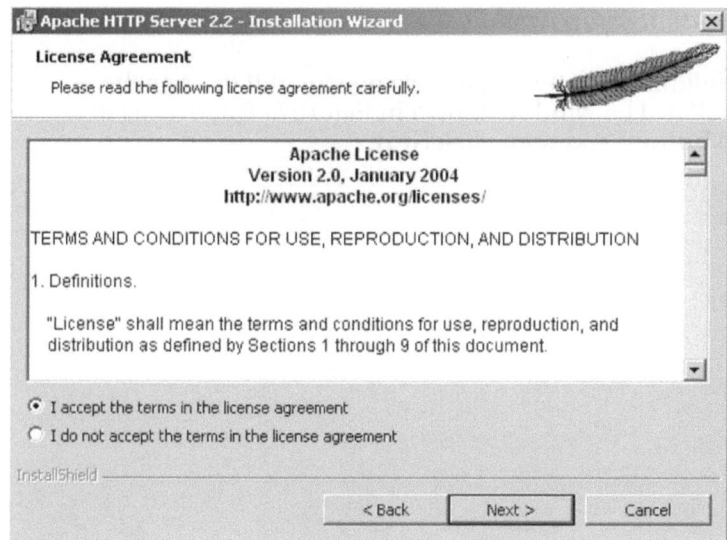

*Figure A–4. Apache Server Terms and Conditions window*

Soon we come to the window shown in Figure A–5. Here, we need to fill in all the fields. Since this will be a web server operating on our desktop, we can add in any network domain and server names into the "Network Domain" and "Server Name" fields respectively. I chose to enter "localhost" for both of those fields. For the "Administrator's Email Address" field, enter your e-mail address, and click Next.

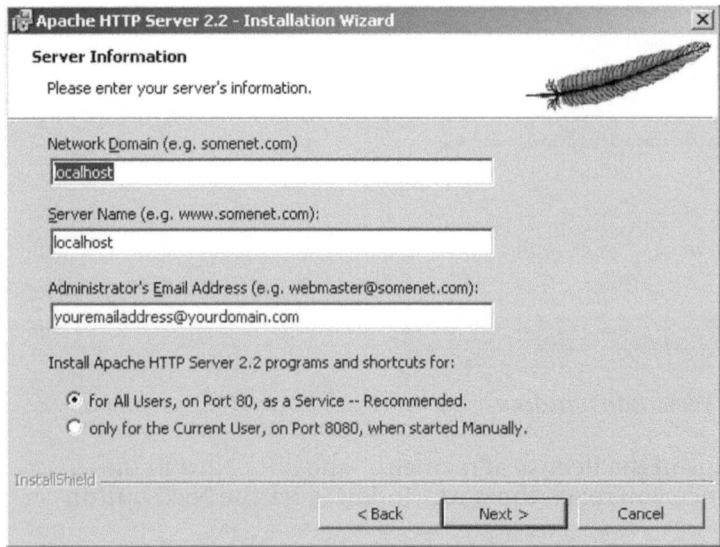

*Figure A–5. Apache Server Information Setup window*

Next we're going to start installing the software, but we need to tell the Apache installation wizard where to install it. The window shown in Figure A–6 allows us to do just that. Click the Custom radio button, and then click Next.

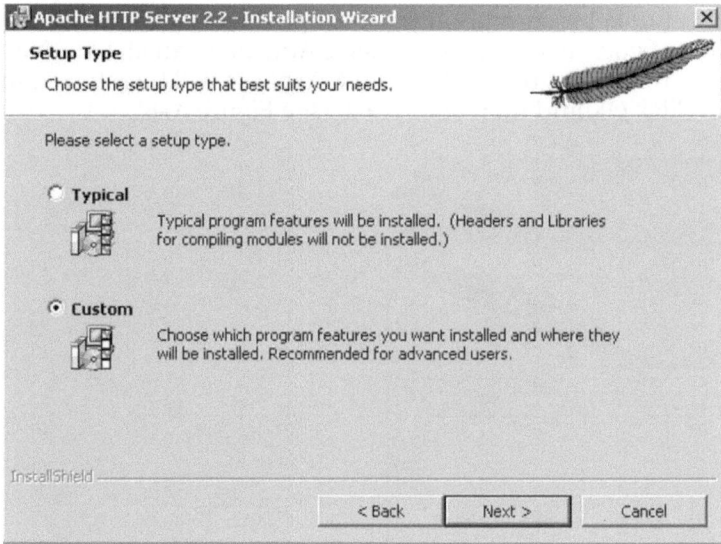

**Figure A–6.** *Apache Setup Type window*

In this screen, shown in Figure A–7, we click the Change button.

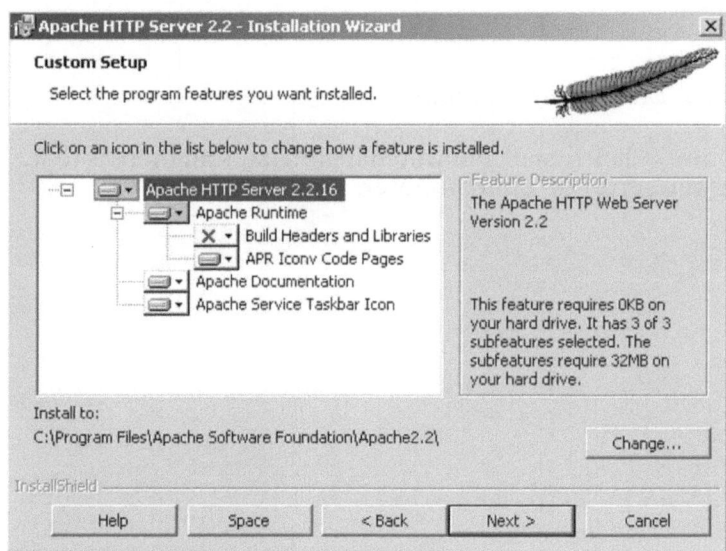

**Figure A–7.** *Apache Custom Setup window*

For ease of use throughout this book, I recommend you change the location of the installation directory to C:\Apache; of course, if you wish to save Apache in an alternative location, that's fine, too. For future reference, remember that C:\Apache will be referred to as APACHE_HOME from here on out. Click OK and then click Next (see Figure A–8).

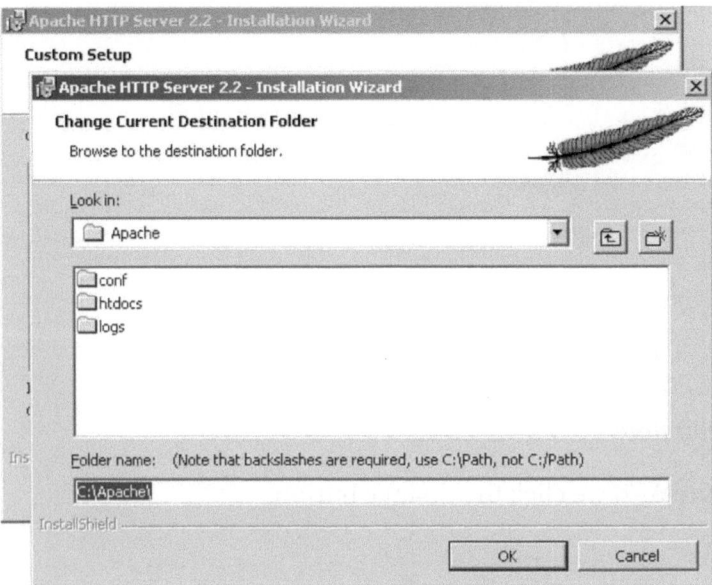

**Figure A–8.** *Apache Change Current Destination window*

Finally you're at the last window. Click Install and watch it go. That's all there is to it. We have successfully installed a web server on our computer.

## Post–Apache Installation

If there were no errors during the installation of Apache, you should now see the Apache Monitor icon in your task bar, as shown in Figure A–9. Right-click it and click "Open Apache Monitor". This is the tool that allows us to start and stop our web server.

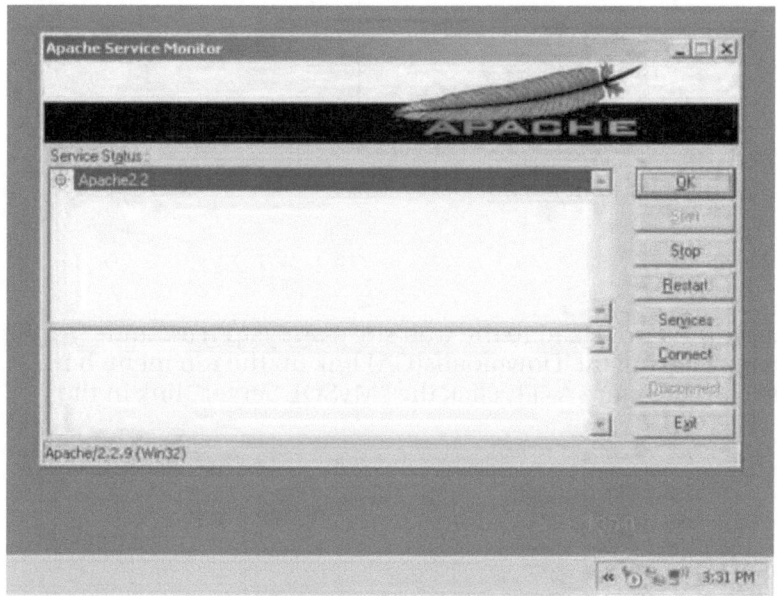

*Figure A–9. Windows task icon for the Apache Monitor*

Let's now make sure Apache is running on our computer. In order to do this, we need to call Apache from our web browser, so pull up your favorite web browser and type in the URL http://localhost. You should now see the Apache welcome home page, as shown in Figure A–10. If you have any issues and can't see the page, look in the Apache error logs, located at APACHE_HOME/logs/error.log. Many times the problem can be found here and be easily taken care of by simply reading the errors saved to these files

*Figure A–10. Apache Server welcome web page*

## Installing MySQL

Installing MySQL is also straightforward. Head to the web site www.mysql.com, and download the latest software by clicking the Downloads(GA) link on the top menu bar. Once you reach the screen shown in Figure A–11, click the "MySQL Server" link in the left-hand menu bar.

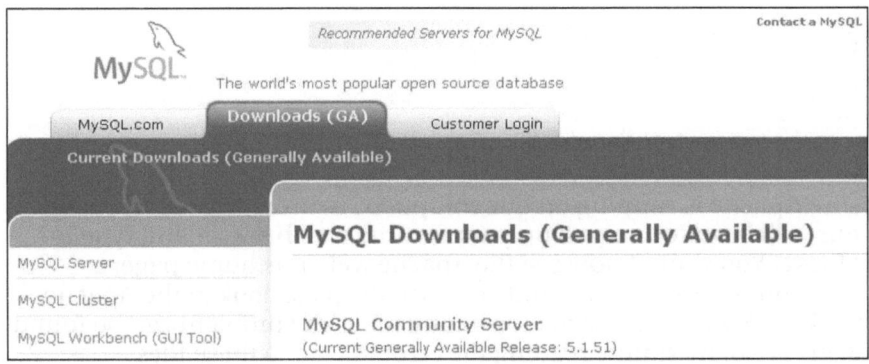

*Figure A–11. MySQL Downloads home page*

You should be taken further down the page and should now scroll down until you reach a portion of the page that looks like Figure A–12.

| | | | |
|---|---|---|---|
| Windows (x86, 32-bit), MSI Installer | 5.1.51 | 105.9M | Download |
| (mysql-5.1.51-win32.msi) | | MD5: 1acc454da2caa07db29463e3012c29d3 | |
| Windows (x86, 32-bit), MSI Installer Essentials - Recommended | 5.1.51 | 38.9M | Download |
| (mysql-essential-5.1.51-win32.msi) | | MD5: 1e2552aea2fb460f107b7803e8aab64c | |
| Windows (x86, 64-bit), MSI Installer Essentials - Recommended | 5.1.51 | 31.5M | Download |
| (mysql-essential-5.1.51-winx64.msi) | | MD5: 9a9e4ea15746b6d592ee723a30130404 | |
| Windows (x86, 64-bit), MSI Installer | 5.1.51 | 99.0M | Download |
| (mysql-5.1.51-winx64.msi) | | MD5: 8156af479173149e40c8042bcda31c9e | |

***Figure A–12.*** *Mysql Windows download links*

MySQL, like Apache, has given us the option to install the software in either Windows or Unix. Windows users should download the Windows installer, Windows ZIP/Setup.EXE (x86), and Unix users should download the appropriate installer for their Unix flavor by selecting "UNIX OS" from the drop-down menu. Once you select a package, you will be asked to log into your account. Click "No thanks, just take me to the downloads!" shown in Figure A–13, and a list of mirror links will be displayed. Select one of the mirror links, and start downloading.

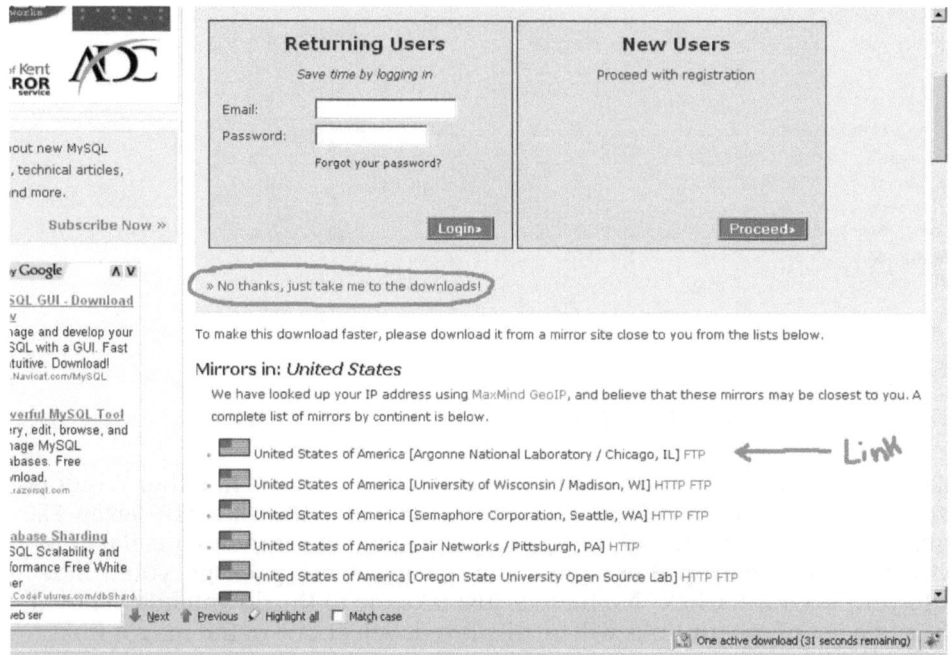

**Figure A–13.** *Mysql Download Installer login window*

As soon as the download has completed, open the `.zip` file and run the setup file to start installing MySQL. On the initial welcome window, simply click Next.

In the Setup Type window, we're presented with the option of setting up a typical installation or a custom installation. Click the Custom radio button, and then click Next. This will allow us to install MySQL in a directory of our choice.

As soon as the Custom Setup window is displayed, click Change and type in your `MYSQL_HOME` directory. For simplicity we will install our MySQL files under the location `C:\mysql`. Going forward in subsequent chapters, we will refer to this path as `MYSQL_HOME`.

Click OK and then click Next. Once you reach the "Ready to Install the Program" window (Figure A–14), click Install and watch MySQL install. If you are prompted with additional screens, click Next.

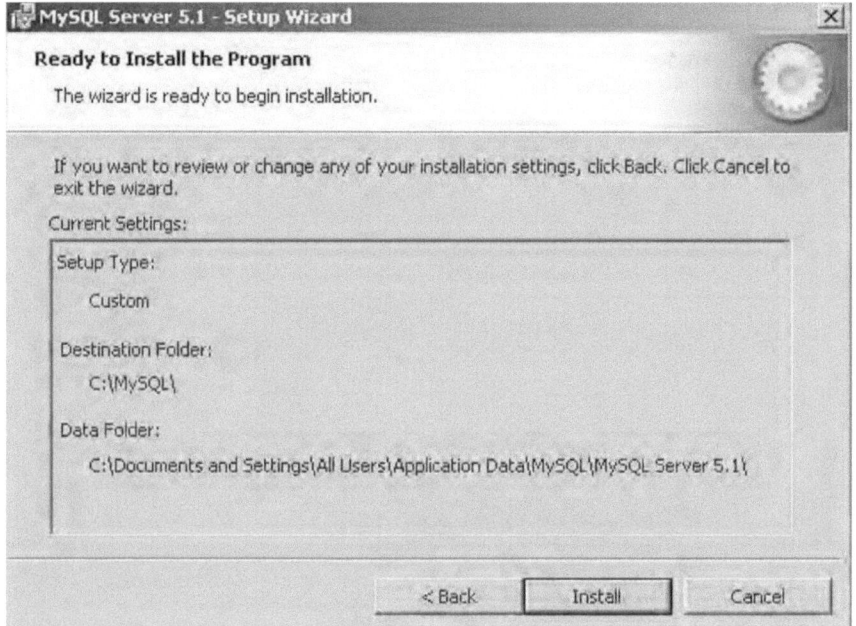

***Figure A–14.*** *MySQL Ready to Install window*

If there were no errors during the MySQL installation process, MySQL has been installed on our computer and a configuration window will pop up. Let's go through the steps of configuring our instance of MySQL now.

## Configuring MySQL

Configuring MySQL will only take a minute. On the initial first window, we click Next to start the configuration process (Figure A–15).

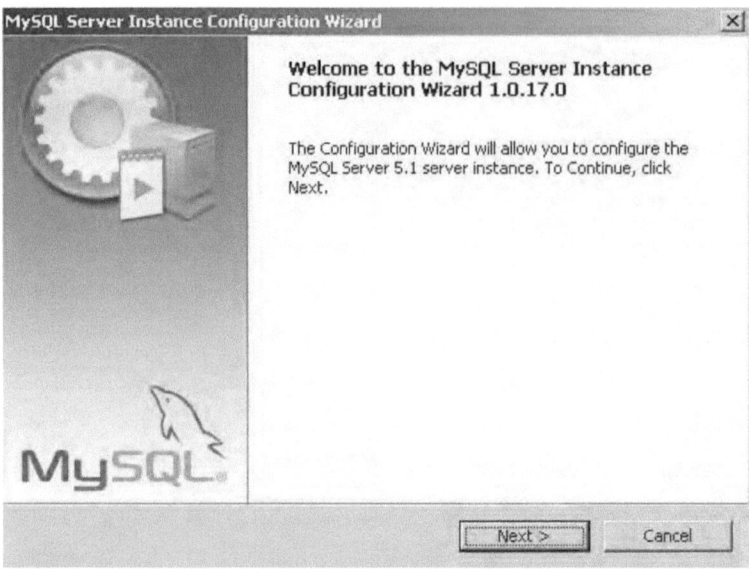

*Figure A–15. MySQL Config Welcome window*

In the window shown in Figure A–16, we will click the "Standard Configuration" button to speed up the process of configuration and then click Next.

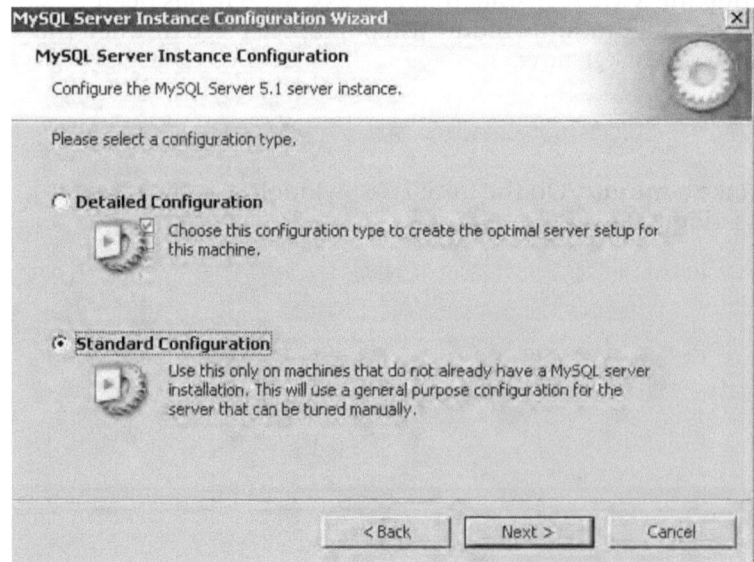

*Figure A–16. MySQL Config Type window*

In the next screen, we need to accept the default setting, "Install as Windows Service," which is already selected for us (shown in Figure A–17), and click Next.

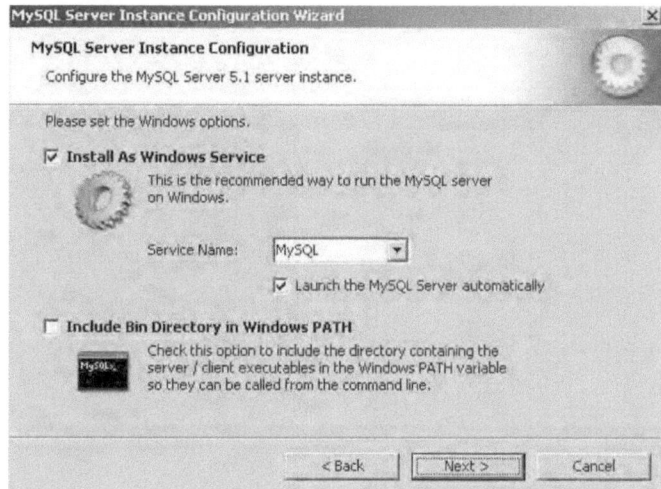

**Figure A–17.** *MySQL Config Windows Options window*

In one of the last windows we need to go through before completing the MySQL configuration process, we set up a password for our setup. Enter a password for all two of the fields, leaving "Modify Security Settings" checked, and then click Next (Figure A–18).

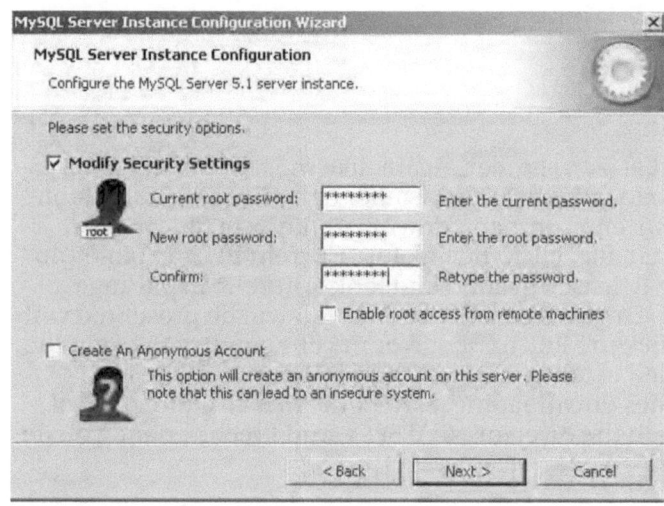

**Figure A–18.** *MySQL Config Security Options window*

Finally, click the Execute button, and watch the check marks come up. If the installation and configuration completed successfully, you will see a MySQL window with four check marks in the small bubbles, indicating there were no errors, as shown in Figure A–19. Congratulations—we're done with the setup. Click Finish and relax.

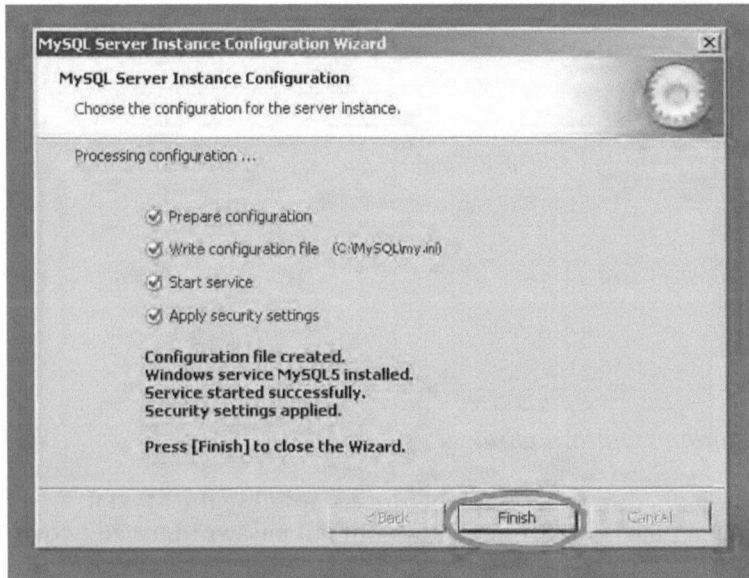

*Figure A–19. MySQL Processing Config window*

## Installing PHP

The PHP installer can be downloaded at www.php.net. Again, like most of the downloads thus far, we have an option to download either a Unix installer or a Windows executable. In this case, if you are using a Windows environment, download the .zip file, not the Windows .exe installer. To find the .zip file, click the link for "Current PHP 5 Stable" on the right of the page under the Stable Releases header, and look for the .zip package under the Windows Binaries heading. Once you click that link, you will be presented with a list of mirrors to download from. Click the link for a mirror in your country to begin the download. The .zip file contains added extensions and libraries that we will need.

As soon as the PHP installer finishes downloading, extract the files to a directory of your choosing. I'm installing the files in the directory C:\PHP5\, and I recommend you do the same for ease of use throughout this book.

## Getting PHP5 and MySQL to Talk

When all the files have been extracted, we need to modify the httpd.conf file that was installed by Apache. Go to the directory APACHE_HOME/conf and open the file.

This file allows Apache to be manually configured. Since Apache by default does not know how to interpret PHP files, we need to tell Apache what translator it needs to use when a request for a .php file by our users is made. If we miss this step this far in the process of installing our environment, any time we try to load a .php file on any browser, the browser will either prompt us to download the file or in some cases simply display the PHP code on the page. So let's tell Apache what translator to use. In this case, the translator is the PHP engine we finished installing. Toward the end of the file, type in this text:

```
AddType application/x-httpd-php .php
PHPIniDir "C:/PHP/"
LoadModule php5_module "C:/PHP/php5apache2_2.dll"
```

---

■ **Note** By issuing the commands apachectl start, apachectl stop, or apachectl restart in the Windows shell (Run cmd) or the Unix shell, we can start, stop, or restart Apache. Of course, you can also click the Apache Monitor icon in the system tray and select Apache2 Stop or Apache2 Restart.

---

Save the file and restart Apache. This is done by using the Apache Service Monitor. Bring up the Apache Service Monitor window, and click the Restart button on the right-hand side. You will see a success message if everything went well.

To test out PHP installation, create a phpinfo PHP script by referring to the next section, "Creating a phpinfo() Script." If all went well, you should now see Apache translating PHP into a web page that looks like Figure A–20.

# Creating a phpinfo() Script

Throughout the book, we referred to a phpinfo() script that allows you to check if a PHP extension was properly installed and if PHP configuration settings were set correctly. This PHP script contains no more than three lines of code, shown in Listing A–1.

*Listing A–1. phpinfo() Script Code*

```
<?php
echo phpinfo();
?>
```

To create the phpinfo() script, open a text file and copy the code shown in Listing A–1. Save the file as info.php and place it within your web server. If you have been following the installation instructions of Apache within the appendix, place the file within the `APACHE_HOME/htdocs` location.

Load the `.php` file using a browser by loading the URL `http://localhost/info.php` to view the PHP settings your current installed PHP installation is using. You will see an HTML page with the information shown in Figure A–20.

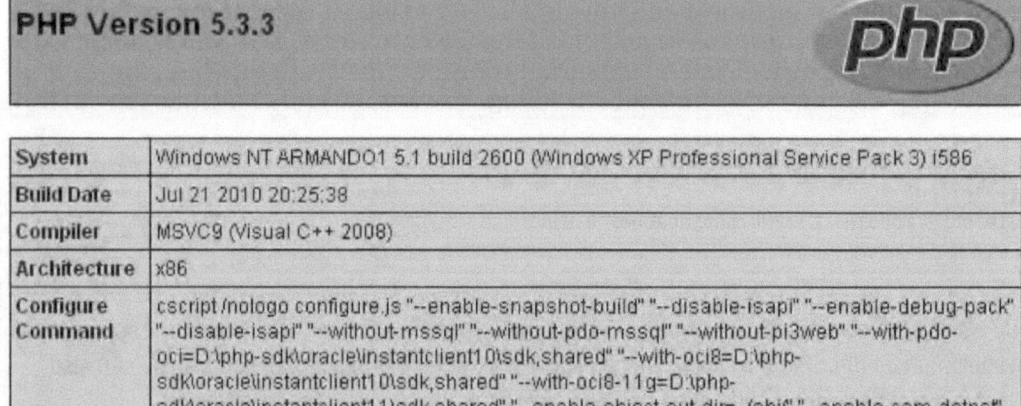

*Figure A–20. PHP info page*

Scroll down the page, and review the different configuration settings and modules your current PHP installation is using. You can find a list of modules installed and server settings, as well as the location to the `php.ini` file loaded within this page.

# Installing PECL

PECL is a PHP extension repository containing some of the best PHP extensions available for PHP developers. They range from encryption to XML parsing, with the complete list of extensions located on its official web site, `http://pecl.php.net`.

The majority of the extensions outlined in this book can be quickly and effortlessly installed using PECL and its command-line tool. Here, we will install PECL on Windows by initially installing PEAR, a package repository for PHP.

The initial step to installing PECL is to install PEAR. PEAR, as mentioned before, is a package repository for PHP. To begin installing PEAR, you are required to have PHP installed on your system. By now you should have PHP installed in your `PHP_HOME` directory.

Open a command-line window by typing `cmd` into the `Start->Run…` window. Once the window is open, navigate into the directory where you have PHP installed, and type in `php go-pear.bat`. This will install PEAR as well as PECL for you. If there were no errors during installation, PECL should now be installed. To verify the installation, type pecl into the command-line window. You should see the help menu, as shown in Figure A–21.

```
Commands:
build                   Build an Extension From C Source
bundle                  Unpacks a Pecl Package
channel-add             Add a Channel
channel-alias           Specify an alias to a channel name
channel-delete          Remove a Channel From the List
channel-discover        Initialize a Channel from its server
channel-info            Retrieve Information on a Channel
channel-login           Connects and authenticates to remote channel server
channel-logout          Logs out from the remote channel server
channel-update          Update an Existing Channel
clear-cache             Clear Web Services Cache
config-create           Create a Default configuration file
config-get              Show One Setting
config-help             Show Information About Setting
config-set              Change Setting
config-show             Show All Settings
convert                 Convert a package.xml 1.0 to package.xml 2.0 format
cvsdiff                 Run a "cvs diff" for all files in a package
cvstag                  Set CVS Release Tag
download                Download Package
download-all            Downloads each available package from the default channel
info                    Display information about a package
install                 Install Package
list                    List Installed Packages In The Default Channel
```

***Figure A–21.*** *PECL help menu*

# APPENDIX B

■■■

# Installing Apache, MySQL, PHP, and PECL on Linux

In Appendix A, we saw how to install a full WAMP stack on Windows. In this appendix, we will show you how to install the equivalent LAMP stack on Linux.

Because there are many flavors and variations of Linux, we will focus on the two largest distributions:

- RPM/yum–based in the form of Fedora 14, which is representative of Red Hat–, CentOS-, and Fedora-based distributions

- Debian-based (Ubuntu 10.10)

By focusing on these two major platforms, we hope to cover the majority of Linux-based development workstation setups, as the focus of the book is on the developer.

## Fedora 14

Fedora is an RPM/yum–based Linux distribution, developed by the Fedora Project and supported by Red Hat. Fedora shares a common packaging methodology and file system layout with Red Hat RHEL and CentOS distributions, commonly used in high-reliability web serving solutions.

Fedora 14, the latest incarnation, code-named "Laughlin," was released on November 2, 2010.

The sequence of terminal commands shown in Listing B–1 can be used to create a LAMP stack on Fedora 14, which has all of the components discussed in the book and also includes all of the tools that have been described.

***Listing B–1.*** *Installation Instructions for Fedora 14*

```
$su -
# Install Apache
$yum -y install httpd

# Install Mysql
$yum -y install mysql-server
$yum -y install mysql

# Install PHP
$yum -y install php
$yum -y install php-mysql
$yum -y install php-pecl-apc
$yum -y install php-gd
$yum -y install php-pecl-xdebug

# Install phpinfo page on http://localhost/phpinfo.php
$echo "<?php phpinfo(); ?>" > /var/www/html/phpinfo.php

# Install Memcache and php extension
$yum -y install memcached
$yum -y install php-pecl-memcache

# Install Benchmarking and monitoring tools. Note: iostat is in systat package
$yum -y install apachetop
$yum -y install siege
$yum -y install systat

# Set services to start at boot time
$chkconfig mysqld
$chkconfig memcachd
$chkconfig httpd

# Start the services.
$service httpd start
$service mysqld start
$service memcached start
$exit
```

# Component Versions and Locations

The versions of the application components installed using the foregoing procedure on Fedora 14 are shown in Table B–1. These versions were correct at the time of publication. Later updates to the packages may result in versions that are greater than shown.

***Table B–1.*** *Fedora 14 Component Versions and Configuration File Locations*

| Component | Property | Value |
| --- | --- | --- |
| Apache | version | Apache/2.2.17 (Fedora) |
| | Configuration directory | /etc/httpd/conf |
| | Default Access Log | /var/log/httpd/access_log |
| | Default Error Log | /var/log/httpd/error_log |
| | Default document root | /var/www/html |
| Mysql | Version | 5.1.52 |
| | Configuration file | /etc/my.cnf |
| | Default Socket | /var/lib/mysql/mysql.sock |
| | Data Dir | /var/lib/mysql |
| | Log File | /var/log/mysqld.log |
| PHP | Version | 5.3.3 |
| | Default PHP.ini file | /etc/php.ini |
| | Configuration directory | /etc/php.d |

# Ubuntu 10.10

Ubuntu is a Linux distribution based on the Debian GNU/Linux distribution format. The name Ubuntu means "humanity toward others" in the Bantu-based languages, originating from South Africa.

Ubuntu is mainly intended as a desktop distribution, although server versions exist. This focus on being a desktop distribution makes it an ideal developer's workstation OS, often integrating the latest development tools and IDEs. Many commercial tools are also distributed specifically for Ubuntu.

Ubuntu version 10.10, code-named "Maverick Meerkat," was released on October 10, 2010.

The sequence of terminal commands shown in Listing B–2 can be used to create a LAMP stack on Ubuntu 10.10 that has all of the components discussed in the book and also includes all of the tools that have been described.

*Listing B–2. Installation Instructions for Ubuntu 10.10*

```
# Install Configuration manager
$ sudo apt-get install tasksel

# Install basic LAMP stack
$ sudo tasksel install lamp-server

# Install additional PHP extensions
$sudo apt-get install php-apc
$sudo apt-get install php5-xdebug

# Install Benchmarking and monitoring tools. Note: iostat is in sysstat package
$sudo apt-get install apachetop
$sudo apt-get install systat
$sudo apt-get install siege

# Install memcache and php extension
$sudo apt-get install memcached
$sudo apt-get install php5-memcache

# Install Pear/Pecl
$sudo apt-get install php-pear

# Create phpinfo page at http://localhost/phpinfo.php
$sudo bash -c "echo \"<?php phpinfo(); ?>\" > /var/www/phpinfo.php"

# Restart web server to ensure all modules are loaded.
$sudo service apache2 restart
```

## Component Versions and Locations

The versions of the application components installed using the foregoing procedure on Ubuntu 10.10 are shown in Table B–2. These versions were correct at the time of publication. Later updates to the packages may result in versions that are greater than shown.

*Table B–2. Component Versions and Configuration File Locations for Ubuntu 10.10*

| Component | Property | Value |
|---|---|---|
| Apache | version | Apache/2.2.16 (Ubuntu) |
| | Configuration directory | /etc/apache2 |
| | Default Access Log | /var/log/apache2/access_log |
| | Default Error Log | /var/log/apache2/error_log |
| | Default document root | /var/www |
| Mysql | Version | 5.1.49-1ubuntu8.1 |
| | Configuration file | /etc/mysql/my.cnf |
| | Default Socket | /var/run/mysqld/mysqld.sock |
| | Data Dir | /var/lib/mysql |
| | Log File | /var/log/mysql/mysql.log |
| PHP | Version | 5.3.3-1ubuntu9.1 |
| | Default PHP.ini file | /etc/php5/apache2/php.ini |
| | Configuration directory | /etc/php5/apache2/conf.d |

## Tasksel

The installation script in Listing B–2 makes use of a tool called "tasksel," which is a tool unique to Ubuntu. tasksel allows the installation of predefined sets of packages making up particular configurations, one of which is a "LAMP server." If you want to see the exact list of packages installed in this configuration, then execute the following:

```
$ tasksel --task-packages lamp-server
```

# PECL

As mentioned in Appendix A, PECL is a PHP extension repository containing some of the best PHP extensions available for PHP developers. They range from encryption to XML parsing, with the complete list of extensions located on its official web site, http://pecl.php.net.

Unix users, you're in luck. As mentioned before, PEAR is required to be installed to use PECL, and for Unix users, this is automatically installed when installing PHP version 4.3.0 or above. If you are certain that you have not installed PEAR, download the go-pear.php file from http://pear.php.net/go-pear as go-pear.php and run the script within a shell by running the command php go-pear.php. Once the installation is complete, verify that PEAR and PECL were installed by running the commands pear and pecl within a shell.

# Index

■ ■ ■